D1084943

Fads, Fallacies
and Foolishness in
Medical Care
Management and Policy

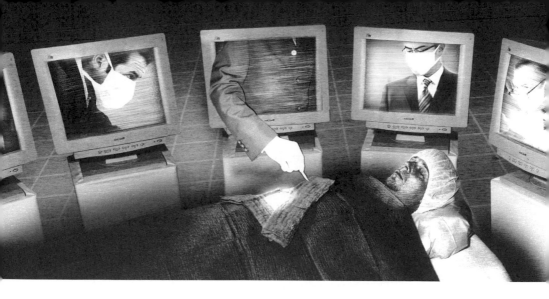

Fads, Fallacies
and Foolishness in
Medical Care
Management and Policy

T. R. Marmor

Yale University, USA

World Scientific

NEW JERSEY · LONDON · SINGAPORE · BEIJING · SHANGHAI · HONG KONG · TAIPEI · CHENNAI

Published by

World Scientific Publishing Co. Pte. Ltd.

5 Toh Tuck Link, Singapore 596224

USA office: 27 Warren Street, Suite 401-402, Hackensack, NJ 07601

UK office: 57 Shelton Street, Covent Garden, London WC2H 9HE

Library of Congress Cataloging-in-Publication Data
Marmor, T. R.
    Fads, fallacies and foolishness in medical care management and policy /
by T. R. Marmor.
        p. cm.
    Includes bibliographical references and index.
    ISBN 978-981-256-678-2
        1. Managed care plans (Medical care). 2. Medical policy. 3. Medical economics. I. Title.

    R729.5.H43M37 2007
    362.1'04258--dc22

                                            2006050980

British Library Cataloguing-in-Publication Data
A catalogue record for this book is available from the British Library.

Typeset by Stallion Press
Email: enquiries@stallionpress.com

Printed in Singapore by World Scientific Printers (S) Pte Ltd

Preface

This book of essays reflects my interest in exposing both fads, fallacies and foolishness in the health policy and management literature. No one in medical care can miss the onslaught of claims about reforming modern medicine. How doctors should be paid, how hospitals should be governed, organized, and financed, how much patients should pay when sick in co-payments, how the quality of care could be improved, and how governments and other buyers could better control the costs of care — all find expression in the explosion of medical care conference proceedings, op-ends, news bulletins, journal articles, and books. This collection of articles takes up a key set of what I regard as particularly misleading fads and fashions. In selecting them for book publication, I used as a criterion how much an idea contributed to misunderstandings in contemporary discussions of how to organize, deliver, finance, pay for, and regulate medical care services in modern industrial democracies.

Each of the essays in the book takes up major examples of fads in the management and policy literature. In the case of management, the fads dissected include the faith in marketing nostrums, the celebration of integrated delivery systems, and enthusiasm for simpleminded clichés like management by objective. The topic of "managed care" justified a chapter, given just how confused and confusing this faddish notion was in the 1990s.

The policy chapters addressed four fads: the celebration of explicit rationing as a major cost control instrument, the belief in a "basic package" of health insurance benefits to constrain costs, the faith that contemporary cross-national research can deliver a large number of transferable models, and the belief that broadening the definition of what is meant by health will constitute some sort of useful advance in practice.

Each of these chapters, separately published, critically reviews ideas that health care managers, policy makers, and students will have read about in the literature of the past decade or more.

T. R. Marmor

Acknowledgments

I want to thank two members of my Yale staff for help in putting this book together: Nicholas Gerry-Bullard, the research assistant in the summer of 2006 who handled the tasks with gusto and competence, and Camille Costelli, my aide for many years in every professional task I take on.

Contents

Fads in Medical Care Policy and Politics: The Rhetoric and Reality of Managerialism

T. R. Marmor

I. Introduction

I am honored to be asked to give the annual Rock Carling lecture. I am grateful to the stewards of this fellowship — especially John Wyn Owen and Sir Maurice Shock — for the opportunity. I am also grateful as an American who has had a 40-year history of education, friendship, and professional stimulation in Great Britain. This lecture provides me the chance to acknowledge my debt to these friends and colleagues — and most especially my Wadham College tutor of 1961, Pat Thompson.

My topic tonight is *Fads in Medical Care Policy and Politics: The Rhetoric and Reality of Managerialism*, or "managerialism in medical care." I will introduce the broader topic of fads and then turn to how fads management commentary has shaped (and mis-shaped) understandings of medical care on both sides of the Atlantic.

By fads I simply mean enthusiasms for particular ideas or practices. In clothing, we have no difficulty in identifying what is faddish. Either our adolescents or the press tell us what constitutes the current fad. In the world of ideas, there are similar rushes of enthusiasm, though the character and the pace of change of these fads differ greatly over time and space. There is a considerable sociological literature on the subject of fads in social practices.[1] There are fads in names for children, items of home decoration, television soap operas, and the like. But the fads that interest me in this lecture concern fashionable managerial ideas, particularly ideas that in their dissemination are presented as panaceas for longstanding policy and organizational problems.

II. The Problem of Managerial Fads, or Managerialism

My fundamental contention is that the discussion of modern medicine's most prominent topics — cost, quality, access, and organization — is marked by linguistic muddle and conceptual confusion. I want to distinguish two sorts of jargon within the broader category of business talk. Bottom lines, entrepreneurship, free competitive markets, M&A, which is now the Lingua Franca of globalism — the first jargon is the management jargon that comes out of B-schools and consultancies, and makes its way into the discourse via popular "business books." The second is marketing jargon, or hype as I call it — a very different thing. My coinage, "managerialism," covers both. It, to my mind, is a threat to clear thought or reasoned argument.

One sees this vividly as the managerial fads of one period give way to the enthusiasms of the next. As John Hunt of the London Business School put it, there is a "product cycle" in managerial fads.[2] New enthusiasms are promoted by author consultants and their publishers — with high hopes and inflated rhetoric. The fads are also abandoned even by their authors, when their consultant firms without much regret. Indeed, managerial gurus like Tom Peters shed failed models quite easily and embrace the newest fashions promiscuously. Declarations of failure follow cycles of enthusiasm, as the managerial journals and scholarly literature document.[3] Both permit fame (and fortune) to be first made out of distributing the managerial equivalent of snake oil and then scholarly reputations out of discovering the pattern.[4] I might mention in passing the corruption that goes on with consultancies buying up thousands of copies to get their author's book on the bestseller lists. The list makers are wise to this ploy now, but maybe you have never heard of it. I had not before investigating this copy.

Many of you in the audience will be familiar with some of the shifting fads in management — both for private and for public organizations. Let me briefly remind us of the shifts themselves. Twenty

Best Selling Books
Business
(Source: *The Wall Street Journal* Friday, October 26, 2001)

Rank	Title (*Author*)
1	Who Moved My Cheese? (*Spencer Johnson*)
2	Jack: Straight From the Gut (*Jack Welch*)
3	Good to Great (*Jim Collins*)
4	Fish! (*S. Lundin, H. Paul, J. Christensen*)
5	Rich Dad Poor Dad (*R. Kiyosaki, S. Lechter*)
6	7 Habits of Highly Effective People (*Stephen Covey*)
7	Side by Side Leadership (*Dennis A. Romig*)
8	Now, Discover Your Strengths (*M. Buckingham, D. Clifton*)
9	First, Break All the Rules (*M. Buckingham, C. Coffman*)
10	Gung Ho (*K. Blanchard, S. Bowles*)

2

Theodore R. Marmor Yale School of Management

years ago or more, Management by Objective (MBO) and Zero Based Budgeting (ZBO) were the rage in boardrooms and bureaus. In recent years, the language of corporate seminars shifted to such expressions as "re-engineering" and "core competencies." "Quality circles" were popular for a time, soon to be displaced by an emphasis on synergy, mergers and acquisitions, and the like. At one point, big was better. Politicians as well as managers embraced larger scale operations, called "conglomerates" in the private sector and "super-agencies" in the public sector. Within a few years, small became beautiful. Divestiture, devolution, decentralization, and specialization became the watchwords of managerial correctness. One need not remind an audience in the United Kingdom about the cycles and recycling of managerial models. But, for visual clarity, take note of the list an Australian management consultant provided me this summer:

Managerial Fads

1. Flatten the Structure – Eliminate Hierarchy
2. Empowerment – Leaderless Teams
3. TQ C/M/? – V A/B M/?
4. Vision, Mission, Values
5. Customer Focused / Service Organization
6. Trait Leadership
7. Continuous Improvement – Learning Organization
8. Process Re-engineering
9. Cultural Transformation

"Strongly held but largely unfounded beliefs and formulas about how to manage"
(Source: F. Hilmer and L. Donaldson. (1996) *Management Redeemed*, The Free Press)

3

Theodore R. Marmor Yale School of Management

There is already a great deal of contemporary discomfort with managerial fads; so I risk being accused of beating a dead horse.

Let me use a visual aid to get us to "Bull... Bingo," and a more analytical discussion of fads and what they produce.

More seriously, realism about what management can and cannot do might guard against swallowing the more dangerous panaceas offered by managerial gurus. Dissecting the linguistic modes of managerial fads highlights fallacies that are more serious in their effects than simple exaggeration. But let me elaborate the counter-argument that some have made about the effort this lecture represents.

My cautious warnings about the rhetoric of managerial thoughts are misplaced, I am told, because sophisticated audiences ignore the sloganeering. They simply get on with the job. On this view, no one needs to worry about large numbers of misled and subsequently disappointed audiences. In short,

Bull**** Bingo

Do you keep falling asleep in meeting and seminars? What about those long and boring conference calls? Here is a way to change all of that!

How to play: Check off each block when you hear these words during a meeting, seminar or phone call. When you get five blocks horizontally, vertically or diagonally, stand up and shout **BULL****!!**

Synergy	Strategic Fit	Gap Analysis	Best Practice	Bottom Line
Revisit	Bandwidth	Hardball	Out of the Loop	Benchmark
Value-Added	Proactive	Win-Win	Think Outside the Box	Fast Track
Result-Driven	Empower [or] Empowerment	Knowledge Base	Total Quality [or] Quality Driven	Touch Base
Mindset	Client Focus[ed]	Ball Park	Game Plan	Leverage

Testimonials from satisfied players:

"I had only been in the meeting for five minutes when I won." – Jack W. – Boston

"My attention span at meetings has improved dramatically." – David D. – Florida

"What a gas. Meetings will never be the same for me after my first win." – Bill R. – New York City

"The atmosphere was tense in the last process meeting as 14 of us waited for the 5ᵗʰ box." – Ben G. – Denver

"The speaker was stunned as eight of us screamed 'Bull****' for the third time in 2 hours." – Kathleen L. – Atlanta

4

Theodore R. Marmor Yale School of Management

my topic could be thought of as an indulgence, a wasteful deflection of your time and mine.

My response: Whether managerial gurus convince audiences or not, they take up time and energy — if only because their notions bewilder. I am reminded of a conversation in the waiting room at the Department of Health in Whitehall this past spring. A group of four from a regional health authority were, to use the jargon itself, "debriefing." I listened as they tried to decipher the meaning of the bewildering terms used in the meeting from which they had just emerged. I could not help but hear their plaintive remarks and told them I was a student of managerial jargon and thought they would be much better off if they regarded the jargon much more skeptically. This appeared to give them some symptomatic relief.

All too many audiences find themselves either fooled or furious about what turns out to be misleading, needlessly obscure, or downright fraudulent language. At the very least, managerial obscurity directs discussion away from topics more worthy of the attention of those who provide medical care, receive care, pay for it, or manage those services. At worst. . .

III. Why Managerialism (and Market Enthusiasm) in Medical Care

So, I want now to turn to the context that proved to be such a fertile setting for the transfer of business models of management to medical care. The decade of the 1970s — marked by stagflation and intense fiscal pressure in all the industrial democracies — provided just such a context. In that decade medical care policy leapt to the forefront of public agendas. First, paying for/medical care became a major burden on the budgets of mature welfare states precisely when public finances fell sharply from prior forecasts.[5] When there is a fiscal strain, policy scrutiny is the predictable result. Accordingly, welfare states, as my friend, Rudolf Klein argued in the late 1980s, had less capacity for bold fiscal expansion in new areas.[6] This meant managing existing programs necessarily assumed a larger share of the public agenda. Tight welfare budgets foreclosed expansive reform? Lastly, there was what might be termed the wearing down — some people would say, "wearing out" — of the post-war consensus about the welfare state.[7]

Having begun in earnest during the 1973–1974 oil shock, sustained by stagflation, and bolstered by electoral victories (at least or advance) of parties opposed to welfare state expansion, these critics assumed a bolder posture. Mass public came increasingly to hear challenges to social programs that had for decades seemed sacrosanct.[8] From Mulroney to Thatcher, from New Zealand to the Netherlands, the message was one of necessary change. The incentives to explore transformative but not fiscally burdensome options became stronger. That context, I suggest, helps to explain the international pattern of welfare state review — including healthcare policy — over the past two decades. And it also helps to explain why the appeal to market mechanisms and business-like management became so much more compelling: they were more sellable to more business-minded constituencies.

IV. Market Talk, Management, and Medical Care: The Impact in America on the Medical World and the Public

Here is where you pick up on the "business discourse" distinction you made at the outset.

There was a perceptible increase during the 1970s in proposals to make medicine better managed and subject to market-like competition. Simultaneously, a dramatic shift took place in the language of medical commentary, a case study of, following Orwell, "the politics of language." To change thinking, one manipulates language. The traditional doctor–patient relationship becomes, in the language of competitive markets, provider–consumer, buyer–seller, or supplier–demander relationship. Medicine in this way becomes just another business. The fallout from this refashioned language came to be a threat to the professional ethos of medicine, most obviously in America, but elsewhere as well.

Traditionally, much of the "income" doctors, nurses, and other medical practitioners earn has been non-economic: self-esteem, respect from the community, indeed idealization as selfless professionals. In casting medical care as no different from other industries, medical professionals are reconceptualized. They no longer deserve (and increasingly no longer receive) as much of the non-economic benefits of public esteem and gratitude. The stereotype of the medical professional as a self-interested (selfish) agent of business feeds on itself. And, over the quarter century we are surveying, the American public's esteem for medical practitioners indeed fell sharply. Public confidence in medicine and health institutions dropped from 73 to 33 percent between the mid-1960s and the mid-1980s. While all major American institutions experienced a loss of public support, the medical profession lost support faster than any other professional group.[9]

Part of the decreased satisfaction with American medicine undoubtedly arose from worries over our very high and rapidly rising costs. Although it is impossible to establish a clear causal connection between the demystification of the medical profession and the increased incomes of doctors, the phenomena went hand in hand. Despite sharp increases in the number of new physicians, doctors' incomes grew by 30 percent in the 5 years from 1984 to 1989 — twice that of the increase of full-time workers over the same period.[10] It should not be surprising that, to the extent professional medical work was increasingly regarded as ordinary commercial activity, higher physician incomes were increasingly understood as the result of market power or greed rather than a professional's just desserts.

External criticism and constraints on professional autonomy begot doctor dissatisfaction. Doctors complained bitterly about the losses of discretion. Elaborate, intrusive, and administratively expensive procedures proliferated, including utilization reviews, requirements for pre-admission certification, and other forms of second-guessing. In an often-quoted 1991 article in *The Atlantic*, Regina Herzlinger reported that despite increased incomes more than a third of physicians in their 50s said they would not have attended medical school had they known what their futures had in store.[11]

The language of business management — and competitive markets — did not just affect doctors. Hospitals and hospital administrators recast themselves as businesses and began speaking the language of business in new terms. The hospital administrator increasingly became the chief executive officer (CEO). Assistant administrators were refashioned as vice-presidents for their respective functions. These changes were not merely semantic exercises. Rather, they represented a fateful shift in the way Americans were encouraged to think of medical care. The vision of a hospital as primarily a business — and the concomitant shift in administrative power away from medical staff and toward professional managers — inevitably affected how Americans regarded medical care. It would be wrong to assume unanimity on this and equally wrong to presume that American physicians and nurses think of themselves as business figures. The point here is narrower. Over time, the managerial attack on the dominance of medical professionalism helped to deflate public confidence and to increase the probability of proposals threatening professional autonomy.

As hospital administrators gave way to CEOs, so too did their incomes increase. By 1990, hospital CEOs earned an average base salary of over $103,000: those receiving incentive pay averaged $125,000. The year 1990 was in the midst of a supposed "crisis" in health spending. And, by 2000, those figures had increased sharply.

There are, of course, advantages to treating hospitals more like a typical business firm. Improved capital budgeting, financial monitoring, and accounting systems are all vital in getting better value for health expenditures. Nor can one pretend that medical practitioners are all selfless workers concerned only for the welfare of their patients. Clearly, economic motives are important, as they are for professors too. Indeed, many of the concerns of those who subscribe to pro-competitive strategies are identical to that of mine. Asymmetries of information and bargaining strength between doctors and patients do require attention.

But the rhetoric of the competitive market — and the rhetoric of managerialism — helped to disguise what sets medicine apart from other industries. It was that broader development that made it possible for a Democratic president like Bill Clinton to marry ideas of universal health insurance to "pro-market" managerialism. No one can make sense of the Clinton embrace of his reform plan of "managed competition" without appreciating just how much the celebrations of markets and management had depleted faith in ordinary public administration. It is worth noting that the very term managed competition is itself an example of an oxymoron. A managed system is one whose parties control operations by various managerial techniques — for good or for ill. By contrast, the results of a competitive market are largely up for grabs. Individual actors pursue their own interests without central direction. No single actor can determine the outcome. The occurrence of coordination is not by managerial design, but a consequence of individual adaptation to market conditions. The results are not planned and may not be desirable. We regulate competition, well or poorly. And we manage resources, well or poorly. What no one does is manage competition.

In arguing against governmental provision of medical care (or the financing of it), traditional business advocates predictably argue that governments are not competent as managers. The inevitable concessions of the political process, they claim, deplete resolve and hamper efficiency so that programs over time bear less and less resemblance to their initial design and purpose.

Ironically, from the 1970s to the present, advocates of competition have proposed a variety of detailed government programs, laws, and regulations designed to address and to eliminate the market failures that occur in unregulated medical markets. The dilemma hardly addressed in public discussion of competition in medical care arises precisely here. What happens to the logic of competitive proposals when government incompetence contaminates the efforts to reform medical markets?

The answer is that most competitive plans are not and were not robust precisely in this crucial respect. They would not perform well unless conditions were just right. By the very detailing of the government actions required to eliminate market failures, backers of competitive market reform implicitly acknowledged that without these remedies, a competitive system does not work very well in medical care.

The characterization of medical care as just another business also had implications for the way in which the potential for improvement from government intervention came to be judged. The dichotomy drawn between private competition and public regulation invoked choice and well-functioning free markets on the one hand, and failed government programs on the other. But the dichotomy was, and is, artificial and misleading. The properties of the medical sector are such that substantial regulation is inevitable, as every serious writer on the subject has noted. Ironically, the most widely disseminated schemes of market competition in medicine have all entailed a myriad of regulatory restrictions on practitioners, patients, and program managers alike.

V. So, How Can We Move from Idealized Markets to Misleading Managerialism: The Case of Managed Care

Now I want to return to the connection between market enthusiasm and managerial fads, including language fads like persuasive definitions. Consider, for example, medical expressions like "managed care" or more general public management labels like "joined up" government or "integrated delivery systems." All of these are slogans, persuasively defined terms that imply success by their very use. Also consider this feature. In every case of such slogan, the opposite has no appeal. So, for example, the appeal to integrated systems has no defenders of "disintegrated" ones. Disease management is set against the non-management of disease, a null category. Even that familiar slogan in research circles — evidence-based medicine, policy, or whatever — has no credible antonym.

Precisely because so much of the language used to describe medical care today is meant to convince rather than to describe or to explain, even

Slogans / Antonyms

- Managed Care
- Integrated Delivery System
- Joined Up Government
- Empowerment of Employees
- Evidence-Based Medicine

- Customer Focused
- Learning Organization

- NON-Managed Care
- DIS-Integrated Delivery System
- DIS-Jointed Government
- DIS-Empowerment of Employees
- NON-Evidence-Based Medicine

- NON-Customer Focused
- NON-Learning Organization

5

Theodore R. Marmor **Yale School of Management**

thoughtful observers often end up endorsing claims instead of assessing their validity. I cannot think of a better illustration of this process than the widespread appeal to "managed care" in medical reform circles.[12] (And here I want to warn you... United States)

The expression "managed care" is actually a product of marketing sloganeering, and managerial jargon. Insofar as it is an incoherent notion, most claims about managed care suffer from incoherence as well. The term came into widespread usage only in the 1990s. The expression does not appear once, for example, in Paul Starr's exhaustive 1982 history *The Social Transformation of American Medicine*. The phrase first appeared in *The New York Times* in 1985 but surfaced in only a handful of articles during the decade. In the 1990s, however, *Times* articles mentioning the phrase exploded, increasing from 27 in 1990 to 287 in 1994 to 587 in 1998. Because "managed care" has become something of a household term, it is difficult to recognize how recently it entered medical discourse.

10

Theodore R. Marmor Yale School of Management

What exactly managed care is, however, has never been entirely clear, even among its strongest proponents. To some, the crucial distinguishing feature is a (i) shift in financing from indemnity-style fee-for-service, in which the insurer is little more than a bill-payer, to per capita payment methods. Yet there is nothing intrinsic to fee-for-service payment that requires reimbursement to be open-ended or insurers passive. Many, if not most, American health insurance plans that are labeled "managed care," in fact, do not rely primarily on capitation. (ii) To others, the distinctive characteristic is the creation of administrative protocols for reviewing and sometimes denying care demanded by patients or preferred by medical professionals. But such microlevel managerial controls are not universal among so-called managed care health plans either. In fact micromanagement may be obviated by payment methods, like capitation or regulated fee-for-service reimbursement, that create more diffuse constraints on medical practice instead of their means. Finally, to some, what distinguishes managed care is the establishment of integrated networks of health professionals from whom patients are required to obtain care. Yet some so-called managed care plans have no such networks. And what is called a network by many plans is little more than a list of providers willing to accept discounted fee-for-service payments. In short, what constitutes the subject matter of managed care is utterly obscure. Even thoughtful critics of managed care face confusion. Donald Light's essay, "Managed Care: False and Real Solutions," in *The Lancet*, Vol. 344, October 29, 1994, described managed care as "the hot new export from the United States, promoted by major consultants as the most efficient way to integrate primary care, sub-specialization, and everything in between."[13] He goes on to suggest that "these days (1994), the term managed care means any of several institutional arrangements," but then goes on to employ the expression even though it is not clear which of the "several" arrangements constitutes the relevant noun. It reminds one of the joke that if you do not know where you are going, any road will get you there; so with managed care. If it has no settled meaning, conversations about it are certain to be misleading.

Conflating organization, technique, and incentives leads to serious confusion. When we contrast health plans we often compare them across incommensurable dimensions (assuming, for example, that an HMO is somehow more "managed" than a well-controlled fee-for-service plan). It means, too, that we are tempted to presume necessary relationships between particular features of health plans (such as their payment method) and specific outcomes that are alleged to follow from these features (such as the degree of integration of medical finance and delivery) — even when not true. And finally, it encourages a wild goose chase of efforts to come up with black-and-white standards for identifying plan types. As health organizations employ increasingly diverse payment methods and organizational forms, the search for the "essence" of a particular plan will become all the more futile.

The "managed care revolution" is really a set of related trends, few of which are accurately captured by the blanket term. When these trends are distinguished from one another, evidence suggests that American health insurance has moved simultaneously in several different, perhaps even contradictory, directions in recent years and that many of the changes are longer standing than the rhetoric of managed care celebrants implies.

Labels and categories are indispensable, but they clarify, not simply amplify hyperbole. "Managed care" fails that test. And I wish I could get it — and its cousins — banished.

From this extended American example of linguistic and conceptual muddle, let me turn to the use of managerial jargon in the UK context. But first, let me contrast the cross-Atlantic contexts. In the United States, the language of medical manageralism — and managerial practices more generally — has produced a backlash, a sense of outrage. The recent disputes about the patient's bill of rights, for example, reveal this.[14] The critics of the managers of health insurance plans portray them as greedy profiteers who extracted funds from the health insurance pools to line their pockets and obscured what they were doing under misleading labels like managed care, integrated delivery systems, and the like.

To turn to the NHS, the complaint is much more likely to be dismayed at managerial changes that are recurrently imposed in the name of slogans, but with the force of budgetary authority. In the United States, where no one is in charge of a national system of medical care financing, obscurantism more easily leads to disperse rage and a search for scapegoats in the face of distress whose sources are not simple to identify. In the NHS context, where somebody is indeed in charge of policy, perhaps excessively so, sullen resentment appears a more common response to managerial excess.

VI. NHS Management: Styles and Responses

Visitors from abroad should, in my view, adopt a posture of hesitant certitude in commenting on the complexities of policy and management in another country. So, what might this outsider say prudently about the reactions not only to the newly announced policy of dispersing managerial authority,[15] but also to the style of policy making and management in the NHS more generally? Here the outsider has considerable help from a number of scholars who have written about what can be called the new public management in the United Kingdom. I have relied on that literature in understanding the type of managerial rhetoric that is now dominant and in making sense of why reactions to managerial fads here are often so hostile.

My guides to what is called the new public management in Britain are the writings of Michael Barzelay, Christopher Hood, and Michael Power — and Rudolf Klein.[16] Power has brilliantly summarized the central ideas, suggesting that the new public management "consists of a cluster of ideas borrowed from the conceptual framework of private sector management." Among the ideas most emphasized are

(i) cost control, financial transparency, and decentralization of management authority,

(ii) the creation of market and quasi-market mechanisms separating purchasing and providing functions and their linkage via contracts, and

(iii) the enhancement of accountability to customers for the quality of service via the creation of performance indicators.[17]

It does not take exhaustive research to see just how widely these ideas have spread in the world of the NHS. So, for example, consider this brief survey of faddish presentation of managerial ideas in recent years. In December 1997, the white paper announcing the "New NHS" promised dramatic changes in the way Labour would manage things.[18] "Integrated care" would replace the internal market of the Thatcher reforms, building on "what has worked, but discarding what has failed." This, we were told, would save huge amounts of red tape and put "money into frontline patient care." Here, we have the familiar appeal to a persuasively defined slogan, integration (also, the promise that clinical audits would produce wondrous improvement in patient care. But that aim has hardly experienced embrace from those whose professional performance is the object of improvement). Performance targets, quantitative measures, monitoring, and evaluating became watchwords of NHS reforms.

But the reality appears to contain more variability than what these expressions suggest. As Christopher Hood has argued, the new public management is more a story of successive shifts in approach over the last 20 years than steady reinforcement of a single trend. Indeed, Hood suggests over the 1980s a shift in emphasis "from efforts to… equip ministers to be effective managers of their departments… to the effort to take management away from ministers… by the creation of executive agencies at arm's length from the departments." The drumbeat of changing fads is evident in Hood's depiction of the themes of managerial innovation. So one notes the "move from the stress on 'results' or 'outputs' that were the catchwords of public management reformers in the early 1980s to the stress on 'governance' (a euphemism for 'process') as the hot topic of the mid-1990s." Rather than a coherent doctrine, these persistent adjustments in doctrine might be regarded, Hood notes, as a "ceaseless activity to grapple with the unacknowledged consequences of yesterday's mistakes."[19]

It is to the "ceaseless activity" that I want to call attention. It is striking to the visitor how unanimous NHS commentators are in both their criticism of and their cynicism about proposed NHS shifts in policy and management. Rudolf Klein, in discussing the "much advertised" speech about devolution by the Secretary of State for Health Alan Milburn in 2001,[20] predicted that "the first reaction to Mr. Millburn's speech is... likely to be cynicism."[21] In published reactions to the Milburn policy during the summer of 2001, both analytical rage and policy skepticism were wide spread. This seemed true from observers as different as Nicholas Bosanquet and Charles Webster, and across a wide spectrum of general political views. To this observer, it seems plain that Bosanquet and Webster are not ideological cousins, but they both find nothing to recommend in the NHS's mode of policy making. Bosanquet's claim that "there never has been a greater gap between the view of solutions at the center and the realities as they appear day to day at the local level" should, if true, worry the government greatly. And that critical stance is common to David Hunter (emphasizing the dismay of managers) to Charles Webster (emphasizing the secret and detached quality of the Blair government's policy making in healthcare) to Bob Sang's invocation of high managerial doctrine in lamenting what the NHS debate lacks. Only Jennifer Dixon saw a "chink of light," itself a qualifying metaphor for Dixon's effort to explain the "gripes" about what she describes as New Labor's "tendency toward hierarchy and centralism." Hierarchy and centralism is the common theme of the criticism here and the explanation of why these analysts were so cynical about the NHS plan to shift the balance of power.[22]

What the outsider wonders about is whether there is any reason to think this 2001 plan was any more than another centralist move in decentralist clothing.[23] The NHS appears to have been on a centralizing mission for decades now, masking that for a time with one or another reorganization. And the reorganizations themselves have sapped morale and disturbed lives enough to make managers more likely candidates for psychotherapy than corporatist cooperators with central office. None of these commentators find much to say about announced aims of Shifting the Balance. Since paying more attention to "local level" actors — providers, patients, and payers — is what most of the commentators applaud, this inattention to the stated policy goals is a striking testimony to the distrust of the NHS and its policy making modes.

There have been good grounds for that distrust in the reviews of NHS history since the 1970s. First, as Webster notes incisively, the rhetoric of local level decision making goes back to 1979, but the reality of both the Thatcher and Blair policies have not been "conducive to such decentalization of power."[24] David Hunter emphasizes, as do others, what he calls "control freakery" and concludes that managers at the local level have been "unwilling to say what they think" about proposals like Mr. Millburn's on shifting the balance.[25] And most of the comments converge on disbelieving the commitment to devolution, whatever the rhetoric. They believe the history, the Blair (and Thatcher) style of policymaking, and the structure of the British government support their cynical reaction.

While appreciating the grounds of these critiques, I want to offer two somewhat different perspectives on this evaluation. First, I want to call attention to the more general trends in national health decision-making that are not at all the topic in this NHS debate. From Australia to New Zealand, from the United States to Canada, and from Holland to Germany, dismay about modern medical care financing, quality, and management is apparent. The attack on medical errors and the distrust of physician self-government are trends that are cross-national in the OECD world. Moreover, the claim that good science, proper information, and appropriate monitoring can raise the quality of health care among industrial democracies is an article of faith among the devotees of what could be called the "new public management" in medical care.

These views are neither new nor restricted to public management. They inform not only the development in the United States of new agencies of government devoted to the improvement of quality standards but also the rise of private firms advertising their capacity to separate good from bad hospitals, competent from incompetent physicians, and worthy from worthless drugs. A United Kingdom audience will think of NICE, a Canadian audience will think of the Canadian Institute for Health Information, CIHI, and others will find their own acronyms. But the common element is the distrust of collegial authority and celebration of either market means or government hierarchies as the right measure for a lamentable state of "local self-government" of clinical matters.

What distinguishes the NHS is the degree of centralism in the day-to-day mode of policymaking. As David Hunter rightly notes, a non-political NHS is a fantasy, a goal that will not (and could not) be entertained in a democratic society.[26] But the extent of the political control has varied across time in the United Kingdom. There were decades when central budgetary control combined with considerable medical and managerial discretion about how to live within budgets, not so for more than the last decade.

This brings us back to the question of whether this new turn of policy is to be taken seriously. The only grounds for doing so is to see the connection, as Rudolf Klein did, between the "corset of control" that the Blair government has already established and a new freedom justified by the conviction that it will not be a "license for poor standards or inadequate performance."[27] This interpretation rests on the premise that no British government could ignore inappropriate variation in care standards. But, if the new Modernization Agency could count on prior constraints, then its posture could be one of promoting good practice without missionary zeal.

This is the most generous interpretation one could make of the logic of the Blair government's newest policy. But it also suggests a way of discussing such policy initiatives: namely, to add to justified criticism and cynicism a set of indicators of what would count as evidence that the new policy was being carried out. Without that, commentary stays girdled by past disappointments and leaves little opportunity for those within government to show they mean what they say.

VII. A Return to Realism: Why Sensible Management Requires Modesty, Not Zeal[28]

The review of these cynical responses to the most recent shifts in NHS managerial directives does not mean I endorse all the criticism (or cynicism).

But it does remind one of both the persistence of organizational changes and the weariness of those whose lives are thereby affected. At the same time, the prominence of cynical commentary reminds one of the costs of massive gaps between what is claimed and what is true. And that in turn leads me to comment on the incantation throughout contemporary management talk about the importance of having clear, measurable, and limited organizational objectives. An unfortunate consequence of the injection of managerial fads into medical care is the suggestion that there is some right way, some panacea, for rationalizing the delivery of decent, affordable medical care.

The objectives of any institution are multiple, shifting, and often contradictory. It would be quite surprising if any single managerial approach could cope effectively with differing objectives, let alone with changes in priority among different objectives over time. To make this point clear, consider for a moment just how one might answer the following question: "What is a hospital's purpose?" At different periods, and often during the

What is the Purpose of a Hospital?

1. A hospital is designed to contain the spread of contagious diseases.
2. A hospital is a place that provides hygienic surroundings for otherwise dangerous interventions.
3. A hospital is designed to economize on the cost of access to expensive technology.
4. A hospital provides respite from normal social roles that are producing physical or mental breakdown (strain) in patients.
5. Hospitals are intended to economize on the transmission of information and the process of learning among professionals who have clinical responsibilities and require multiple clinical encounters to validate their procedures.
6. Hospitals are designed to centralize medical activities sufficiently to achieve economies of scale in different healthcare tasks.
7. Hospitals provide symbolic reassurance that social effort is being devoted to the health of citizens in a culture with considerable faith in technological remedies.
8. Hospitals are institutions designed to improve the health of the population.

7

Theodore R. Marmor **Yale School of Management**

19

same period, one might answer that hospitals serve various purposes such as:

1. contain the spread of contagious diseases,
2. provide hygienic surroundings for otherwise dangerous interventions,
3. economize on the cost of access to expensive technology,
4. provide respite from normal social roles that are producing physical or mental breakdown in patients,
5. economize on the transmission of information and the processes of learning among professionals who have clinical responsibilities and require multiple clinical encounters to validate their procedures,
6. centralize medical activities sufficiently to achieve economies of scale in different healthcare tasks,
7. provide symbolic reassurance that social effort is being devoted to the health of citizens in cultures with considerable faith in technological remedies, and
8. improve the health of the population,

Hospitals, in short, serve quite varied purposes, all of which cannot be pursued through the same internal authority structure, with the same information technology, or on the same scales. They give rise to starkly different images of what counts as a well-managed hospital. For example, emphasizing purposes 1 or 4 implies a relaxed approach to length of stay; stressing purposes 3 or 6 might mean treating longer hospital stays as evidence of managerial failure. Purpose 5 suggests a team approach to management, with authority centralized among the professionals; purpose 3 bolsters hierarchical forms of bureaucratic authority. Purposes 1 through 7 suggest allocations of authority within the hospital as a separate institution; purpose 8 suggests a much broader structure of authority, one including outside stakeholders with the power to define and redefine the institution's primary mission.

What should one make of this? The first lesson here is a simple one. Institutions such as hospitals have multiple tasks, which imply different managerial approaches. Good management is not what slogan the administrator has emblazoned on the tee shirts of employees but how well the manager's particular approach balances the different demands of the multiple purposes of the institution. I would not belabor this simple point but for the overwhelming evidence that it is often, if not usually, forgotten. Indeed, when some clone of managerial guru Tom Peters next says to health care managers that to have multiple objectives, or even two objectives, is to have no objectives at all, he or she should be condemned to spend the rest of their life in the ER.

A second observation about managerial technique is the truism that every upside has a downside. For instance, when moving into a world of managerial cost containment, we should reflect on what can be lost as well as gained. Cost containment in practice stresses the reduction of questionable doctor–patient encounters, diagnostic procedures, and treatments. The bureaucratic routines required to implement these actions may or may not contain costs. But they may very seriously reduce the choices, morale, and satisfaction of both patient and health care professionals. Different managerial techniques and different organizational configurations will be required if old values are not to be unduly sacrificed to mindless cost control. Moreover, the managerial techniques imposed in the name of reducing costs do little to encourage innovation, patient control, or professional autonomy. Repeating the mantra of TGM or "integrated systems management" every day will not eliminate the stress built into serving different purposes and clienteles with multiple objectives. Good management requires multiple approaches to balance the "goods" and the "bads" of each approach. In other words, there are no managerial panaceas available — now or ever.

Finally, there is a deep ambivalence in managerial theorizing about the effectiveness of, very broadly speaking, technological as opposed to cultural solutions to managerial problems. On the one hand, there are technological recommendations based on improved structures, processes, and technologies and, on the other, cultural ones based on learning, motivation, and culture. One cannot decide which managerial strategy to believe in because both work some of the time, but neither works all of the time.

The same is true in the reorganization of health care systems. It is hard to believe that a cultural approach will be appealing from the cost containment standpoint. Managing costs is mostly about information systems, the determination of what is cost-effective, and the delivery of incentives or coercion to act on those judgments. On the other hand, if there is cultural vision of the caring medical professional, there will be a need for internal structures that emphasize professional autonomy, team effort, group responsibility, and patient involvement in an overall culture of humane care. Under such circumstances, managerial arrangements will to some degree work at cross-purposes. The technology of cost containment confronts the professional culture of patient care. Good managers balance these perspectives in ways that cope with our conflicting purposes and necessarily inconsistent desires.

Management is not a solution to seemingly intractable stresses. Rather it is a means of coping with and sometimes improving only marginally tractable situations. This more modest vision of management has much to teach those in the reform business about the appropriate level of aspiration for anyone engaged in re-forming complex systems. But management thinkers cannot teach others that lesson until they give up the quasi-religious adoption of one management slogan after another as the solution to getting management right. There is no best management theory, technique, or slogan. In particular contexts, some are better than others. But that must be shown, not glibly claimed by persuasive definitions that presume saying so makes something so.

"High-minded theory yields to the basics of running a good company"

"Something funny happened on the way to the future of business. It turned out to be hard work. Technology is not magical. There is no single catch phrase, whether "re-engineering" or "business-to-business software," that can automatically transform the nuts and bolts of how companies operate. And chief executives with "visions" cannot necessarily ride in on their white horses to save organizations single-handedly.

If the latest offerings from management gurus are any indication, the whole focus of business is shifting from theory to practice, and it has nothing to do with terrorism or recession. It appears that the euphoric days of "revolutionary" and "radical" change in business are giving way to the painstaking and detailed work of reshaping companies, department by department and division by division."

(Source: *The New York Times*, Sunday, November 25, 2001)

8

Theodore R. Marmor Yale School of Management

Endnotes

*Theodore R. Marmor, Professor of Public Policy & Management, Professor of Political Science, Yale School of Management, New Haven, Connecticut, USA.

[1]To understand the "emergence, diffusion, and decline" of fads, see Carson, P. P., P. A. Lanier, K. D. Carson, and B. N. Guidry, "Clearing a Path through the Management Fashion Jungle: Some Preliminary Trailblazing," *American Academy of Management Journal,* 43.6 (2000): 1143–1158.

The diffusion or rejection of technologically inefficient fads is discussed in Abrahamson, E., "Managerial Fads and Fashions: The Diffusion and Rejection of Innovations," *Academy of Management Review,* 35.3 (1991): 596–612.

The stages in the life of a fad are discussed in Meyerson, R., and E. Katz, "Notes on a Natural History of Fads," *American Journal of Sociology,* 62.6 (1957): 594–601.

The psychology behind fads is examined in Krugman, H. E. and E. L. Hartley, "The Learning of Tastes," *Public Opinion Quarterly,* 24.4 (1960): 621–631. For a more specific case study of what counts as a fad and why people participate, see Aguirre, B. E., E. L. Quarantelli, and J. L. Mendoza, "The Collective Behavior of Fads: The Characteristics, Effects, and Career of Streaking," *American Sociological Review,* 53.4 (1988): 569–584.

For an examination of how language helped create and sustain the dot-com boom, see Shister, N., "South Park: New-Economy Drivel Leaves a San Francisco Neighborhood High and Dry," *Boston Review,* February/March 2002.

[2]Hunt, J. W. "An Appetite for Ideas: US Research Shows That the Life Cycle of Management Fashions are Getting Shorter," *The Financial Times,* 16 May 2001. Hunt's analysis is very similar to my own. He reviews the research that identifies the "path" of managerial ideas "from invention through acceptance to disenchantment and decline." And he emphasizes the speeding up of the product cycle of fads, with chief executives "exploiting and rejecting fashions within three or four years."

[3]As Richard Freeman has pointed out in Letters to the Editor in the *British Journal of Health Care Management,* 8.2 (February 2002): 69–70, one of the intriguing aspects of fads is that they are not just rhetorically superficial, but also — by definition — short-lived. Still, the very process by which they are created helps ensure their danger later on. Fads arise, he postulates, through competition between management consultants and business schools, and then later, political competition (government officials looking to be viewed as "change makers"). Sadly enough, the very managerialism of medical care exacerbates this problem, since, as Freeman aptly puts it, managerialism serves as "an institutionalised cadre dedicated to the consumption and reproduction of the fad," thus allowing fads to feed off of and perpetuate themselves. See also Carson, *supra* note 1.

[4]Two scholarly works were very helpful in identifying and documenting these developments. Staffan Furusten's *Popular Management Books* (London: Routledge, 1999) is a sociological study of the origins and dissemination of managerial ideas in the United States and Western Europe; Andrzej Huczynski's *Management Gurus* (London: Routledge, 1996) is more concerned with how particular marketers of management ideas promote the dissemination of their nostrums.

[5]Technically, this is not strictly true of course, as is evident in the sickness fund financing of care in Germany, the Netherlands, and elsewhere. But since mandatory contributions are close cousins of "taxes," budget officials must obviously treat these outlays as constraints on direct tax increases.

[6]See Klein, R. and M. O'Higgins, "Defusing the Crisis of the Welfare State: A New Interpretation," in Marmor, T. and J. Mashaw (eds.), *Social Security: Beyond the Rhetoric of Crisis* (Princeton, New Jersey: Princeton University Press, 1988) esp. pp. 219–224.

[7]The bulk of this ideological struggle took place, of course, within national borders, free from the spread of "foreign" ideas. To the extent similar arguments arose cross-nationally mostly that represented "parallel development." But, there are striking contemporary examples of the explicit international transfer and highlighting of welfare state commentary. Some of this takes place through think-tank networks; some takes place through media campaigns on behalf of particular figures; and of course, some takes place through academic exchanges and official meetings. Charles Murray — the controversial author of *Losing Ground* (Basic Books, 1984) and coauthor of *The Bell Curve* (Free Press, 1994) — illustrates all three of these phenomena. The medium of transfer seems to have changed in the postwar period. Where the Beveridge Report would have been known to social policy elites very broadly, however much they used it, the modern form seems to be the long newspaper or magazine article and the media interview.

[8]This is the argument developed in Marmor, T., J. Mashaw, and P. Harvey, *America's Misunderstood Welfare State: Persistent Myths, Continuing Realities*. (New York: Basic Books, 1992) esp. ch. 3. The wider scholarly literature on the subject is the focus of a review essay, "Understanding the Welfare State: Crisis, Critics, and Counter-critics," *Critical Review*, 7.4 (1993): 461–477.

[9]Insofar as high levels of public trust are associated with altruistic behavior and sense of social mission of a profession, at least some of the lost support was no doubt due to the increasing commercialization in the medical profession. In his analysis of survey data, Robert Blendon found that while most (64 percent of those polled) supported advertising by physicians, 58 percent did not expect it to be truthful. Blendon R., "The Public's View of the Future of Medical Care," *Journal of the American Medical Association*, 259 (1988): 3587–3593.

[10]Fuchs, V. R., "The Health Sector's Share of the Gross National Product," *Science*, 247 (1990): 534–537.

[11]Herzlinger, R., "Healthy Competition," *The Atlantic*, 268 (1991): 71.

[12]The following section draws on an article written with Hacker, J. S., "How Not to Think About Managed Care," *Michigan University Journal of Law Reform*, 32.4 (Summer 1999): 661.

[13]*The Lancet*, 344 (29 October 1994).

[14]See news reports from around the US, for example, Hotakainen, R. and G. Gordon, "Patients Testimony Helped Bill in Senate," *Minneapolis-St. Paul Star Tribune* (2 July 2001): A1; or Kurtz, H., "Some GOP Hopefuls Echo Democrats on Health Care," *The Washington Post*, (29 July 2000): A7.

[15]Milburn, A., "Shifting the Balance of Power in the NHS," Speech delivered on 25 April 2001. http://tap.ccta.gov.uk/doh/intpress.nsf/page/2001-0200. For a critique of the Milburn Plan, see Klein, R., "Milburn's Version of a New NHS: Adopting the Missionary Position," *British Medical Journal*, 322 (5 May 2001): 1078–1079.

[16]See Power, M., *The Audit Society: Rituals of Verification* (Oxford: Oxford University Press, 1997); Barzelay, M., *The New Public Management* (Berkeley: University of California Press, 2001); Hood, C., *The Art of the State* (Oxford: Oxford University Press, 1998).

[17]Power, *Id.* at 43.

[18]*The New NHS: Modern. Dependable: Beyond the Internal Market*. Department of Health 1997. Published by the Stationary Office.

[19]Hood, *supra* note 16 at 201.

[20]Milburn, *supra* note 15.

[21]Klein, *supra* note 15.

[22]Bosanquet, N., J. Dixon, T. Harvey, D. Hunter, A. Pollock, B. Sang, A. Wall, and C. Webster, "Across the Great Divide: Discussing the Undiscussable," *British Journal of Health Care Management* 7.10 (2001): 395–400; Hunter, D. J. "Policy-Making in the NHS," "Across the Great Divide: Discussing the Undiscussable," *British Journal of Health Care Management*, 7.10 (2001): 397; Webster, C., "Brave New NHS," "Across the Great Divide: Discussing the Undiscussable," *British Journal of Health Care Management*, 7.10 (2001): 399–400. Sang, B., "Confronting Machiavelli's Dilemma: Are Managers Part of the Solution, or Part of the Problem," "Across the Great Divide: Discussing the Undiscussable," *British Journal of Health Care Management*, 7.10 (2001): 398–399; Dixon, J., "Why the Gripes," "Across the Great Divide: Discussing the Undiscussable," *British Journal of Health Care Management*, 7.10 (2001): 396.

[23]Milburn, *supra* note 15.

[24]Webster, *supra* note 22.

[25]Hunter, *supra* note 22.

[26]Hunter, *Id.*

[27]Klein, *supra* note 15.

[28]This section of the chapter has appeared in different forms in two other articles: Marmor, T. and J. Mashaw "Rhetoric and Reality," *Health Management Quarterly*, 15.4 (Oct.–Dec. 1993); Marmor, T. R., "Hope and Hyperbole: The Rhetoric and Reality of Managerial Reform in Health Care," *Journal of Health Service Research & Policy*, 3.1 (January 1998).

How Not To Think about "Managed Care"†

J. S. Hacker* and T. R. Marmor**

The state of American health insurance has been a leading topic on the national policy agenda for much of the past decade. In the early 1990s, the political debate focused on two contentious goals: the expansion of health insurance and the control of medical costs.[1] The critical question for health policy analysts — and the nation — was whether President Clinton's ambitious proposal for universal coverage through "managed competition" would be enacted.[2] As the decade wore on without much progress toward universal coverage, the debate turned to the quality of health insurance for those who have it.[3] The rhetorical centerpiece shifted from "managed competition" to "managed care," a blanket expression denoting a mix of changes in private insurance that many Americans appear to view with anxiety and even hostility.[4] And the critical question that came to preoccupy health policy analysts was how to make sense of the "managed care revolution" and its future prospects.[5]

The premise of our argument is that this question cannot be answered as currently formulated. The very term "managed care" — much like that ubiquitous reform phrase of the early 1990s, "managed competition"[6] — is a confused assemblage of sloganeering, aspirational rhetoric, and business-school jargon that sadly reflects the general state of discourse about American medical institutions. Because managed care is an incoherent subject, most claims about it will suffer from incoherence as well. Moreover, to incorporate "managed care" and other similar marketing terms into health policy research is to presuppose answers to some of the most crucial questions about the recent evolution of medical care in the United States and its political effects.

Our reflections on this topic fall under four headings. The first section briefly discusses the context in which contemporary marketing slogans about medical care have emerged. The second turns to analysis of the term "managed care," in particular, and illustrates the quite diverse trends to which the category is regularly and confusingly applied. In attempting to clarify the different developments in health insurance that "managed care" seems intended to capture, we suggest in the third part what we hope is a constructive route for further discussion of the topic. The fourth part completes the circle by returning to the original topic of the politics of health insurance and posing some final questions in light of our discussion of the language of medical insurance and management. Our overarching argument is that analysts should shun industry-promoted slogans and instead develop more precise and neutral conceptual tools with which to evaluate changes in modern medicine's reimbursement methods, managerial techniques, and organizational forms. Not only would analytic discussions be improved by greater clarity of this sort, but we also believe that any policy response to recent developments would also benefit from a more precise examination of the specific changes in American health insurance that have fostered public concern and professional resistance.

I. Medical Care and the Rise of Corporate-Speak

The discussion of many of the major topics in modern medical care is marked by fads, sloppiness, and confusion. Marketing hyperbole and managerial jargon, rather than careful consideration of alternative claims, dominate contemporary reflections on the management, cost, quality, and organization of medical care.[7]

Management commentary resembles a perpetual motion machine more than a stable source of carefully considered ideas. The popular innovations of one period give way to the enthusiasms of the next with hardly a pause. Each managerial fad is launched with high hopes and inflated rhetoric and then abandoned even while many of the promoters escape criticism for their hyperbolic rhetoric. Cycles of enthusiasm are regularly followed by declarations of failure, and both allow fortunes to be made out of the selling of the managerial equivalent of snake oil.

Health policy audiences will be familiar with some of the shifting fashions in general managerial commentary over the past two decades. In the 1970s, Management by Objective (MBO) and Zero Based Budgeting

(ZBO) were the rage in corporate boardrooms, non-profit offices, and government bureaus.[8] In recent years, corporate-speak has shifted to expressions like Total Quality Management, Integrated Delivery Systems (IDS), and, in the case of this symposium's focus, "managed care."[9]

In the 1970s, big was regarded as better. Politicians as well as managers embraced larger scale operations. Good managers were those who horizontally and vertically integrated firms, bureaus, and organizations into ever larger conglomerations of functions and product lines. The emphasis was on synergy, economies of scale, coordination, and the unification of functions.[10] Then, within a few years, one was encouraged to think that small was beautiful. Divestiture, devolution, decentralization, and specialization became the watch words of managerial correctness, both public and private.[11]

Indeed, the sheer number of internal management models has increased considerably over the past two decades — from simple hierarchies with a strict division of labor to cooperative teams.[12] The favored models among managers and employees have ranged from those emphasizing adversarial combat to those featuring bonding mechanisms.[13] Within these broader notions of organizational design emerged a dizzying array of techniques from "just in time" inventory management to statistical quality assurance.[14] In contemporary discussions of quality in medical care there are the much heralded technical panaceas of "outcomes measurement," "integrated delivery systems" and "evidence-based medicine."[15]

Expressions like "managed care," "integrated delivery systems," and "evidence-based medicine" are in some respects all slogans, persuasively defined terms that imply success by their very use. We do not, for example, routinely speak of "unmanaged care," "disintegrated delivery systems," or "non-evidence based medicine." The relative absence of such categories suggests that the purpose of terms like "managed care" is less to clarify than to convince, and less to illuminate what an organization does or how it is structured than to bolster empirical claims and normative connotations that are neither self-evident nor, in most cases, subject to critical scrutiny.

Of course, the claims and connotations are not always positive. With the emergence of a backlash against recent developments in private health insurance, "managed care" has in many quarters mutated from a term of approval into one of opprobrium.[16] The danger to coherent thought, however, is the same in either case. The categories we use to understand and explain organizational change should not prejudge its desirability, nor should they reflect uncritically the aspirations or allegations of its critics or defenders. Such categories should tell us about the structure, behavior, and evolution of an organization, not whether it is good or bad, successful or unsuccessful, and benevolent or sinister. Precisely because much of the language used to describe American medical care today is meant to persuade rather than explain, even thoughtful observers often end up endorsing claims instead of assessing their validity.[17]

II. Managed Care: Further Discussion, Additional Confusion

Our argument is straightforward. By adopting the marketing jargon of corporate medical care, analysts risk adding credence to the claims and associations that come with it. Yet we also wish to emphasize an additional, and in many ways more serious, risk posed by unreflective reliance on persuasive definitions like "managed care" — namely, that analysts will fail to understand the very organizational developments that they seek to explain. For contemporary medical jargon not only embodies often questionable claims; it also prevents us from identifying or understanding what is distinctive about recent organizational changes. Nothing illustrates this better than the ubiquitous term "managed care."

The expression "managed care" came into widespread usage only in the past decade.[18] A revealing sign of its ascendance was the decision of the American Medical Care and Review Association, an insurance industry group founded in 1971, to rename itself the American Managed Care and Review Association in 1989.[19] The term "managed care" does not appear once in Paul Starr's exhaustive 1982 history of American medical care, *The Social Transformation of American Medicine*.[20] Nor can it be found in other books on American health policy written before the early 1980s, including Lawrence Brown's classic 1983 work on the Health Maintenance Organization Act of 1973.[21] As recently as 1989, in fact, newspapers were publishing stories that introduced and explained the new development called "managed care."[22] In *The New York Times*, the phrase first appeared in 1985, but it surfaced in only a handful of articles during the late 1980s. In the 1990s, however, articles mentioning the phrase exploded, increasing from 27 in 1990 to 287 in 1994 to 587 in 1998.[23] Because "managed care" has become such a commonly used and widely recognized expression, it is difficult to recognize just how recently it entered the mainstream of American discourse.

From the beginning, "managed care" was a category with a strong ideological edge, employed to imply competence, concern, and, above all, control over a dangerously unfettered health insurance structure. "Managed care," as the executive vice president of the American Managed Care and Review Association put it in 1989, was an alternative "to the unbridled fee-for-service non-system" that sent "blank checks to hospitals, doctors, dentists, etc." and led to "referrals of dubious necessity" and "unmanaged and uncoordinated care... of poor or dubious quality."[24] As these words indicate, managed care was portrayed less as a means to control patient behavior than as a way to bring doctors and hospitals in line with perceived economic realities. Moreover, managed care promised not just cost-control but also coordination and cooperation, not just better management but also better care.[25] By imposing managerial authority on an anarchic "non-system," managed care would simultaneously restrain costs and rationalize an allegedly archaic structure of medical care finance and delivery.

What exactly constitutes "managed care," however, has never been made clear, even by its strongest proponents.[26] To some, the crucial distinguishing feature is a shift in financing from indemnity-style fee-for-service, in which the insurer is little more than a bill-payer, to capitated payment, in which medical providers are paid a fixed amount to treat an individual patient regardless of the volume of services delivered.[27] However, there is nothing intrinsic in fee-for-service payment that requires open-ended reimbursement or passive insurance behavior.[28] Conversely, many, if not most, health insurance plans labeled "managed care" do not rely primarily on capitation.[29] To others, the distinctive characteristic is the creation of administrative protocols for reviewing and sometimes denying care demanded by patients or medical professionals.[30] Such micro-level managerial controls are likewise not universal among so-called managed care health plans.[31] In fact, such controls may be obviated by particular payment methods, like capitation or regulated fee-for-service reimbursement, that create more diffuse constraints on medical practice. Finally, to some what distinguishes managed care is its reliance on "integrated" networks of health professionals from which patients are required to obtain care.[32] Yet some self-styled managed care plans have no such networks, and what is called a network by many plans is little more than a list of providers willing to accept discounted fee-for-service payments — hardly the dense coordination and integration that industry insiders routinely celebrate.[33]

Perhaps the most defensible interpretation of "managed care" is that it represents a fusion of two functions that were once regarded as largely separate entities: the financing of medical care and the delivery of medical services.[34] This, at least, provides a reasonably accurate description of the most familiar organizational entity that marched under the managed care banner until the late 1980s: the health maintenance organization (HMO), a successor to the pre-paid group practices of the immediate post-World War II era.[35] When the vast majority of American health insurers used fee-for-service payment and placed few restrictions on patient or provider discretion, it was at least possible to identify a small subset of renegade health plans that existed outside this insurance mainstream, however poorly the expression "managed care" described the organization of such plans or what they did.

Today, however, that is no longer the case. In 1997, according to estimates of the Health Insurance Association of America, only 2 percent of private health plans conformed to the traditional model of fee-for-service indemnity insurance.[36] Another 16 percent used fee-for-service payment but employed some form of utilization review.[37] Thus, between 80–98 percent of today's private health insurers appear to fall into the broad category of managed care. "Managed care" therefore does not offer any guidance as to how to distinguish among the vast majority of contemporary health plans.[38]

The standard response to this problem has been to subdivide the managed care universe into a collage of competing acronyms, most coined by industry executives and marketers: HMOs, Preferred Provider Organizations (PPOs), Exclusive Provider Organizations (EPOs), to name a few.[39] This is the approach taken by Jonathan Weiner and Gregory de Lissovoy in their frequently cited 1993 article "Razing a Tower of Babel: A Taxonomy for Managed Care and Health Insurance Plans."[40]

Weiner and de Lissovoy argue that "what usually distinguishes… managed care plans from [plans] that are more traditional is that there is a party that takes responsibility for integrating and coordinating the financing and delivery of services across what previously were fragmented provider and payer entities."[41] They then proceed to divide managed care into five mutually exclusive types of plans: fee-for-service plans with utilization review (what they call "managed indemnity plans" or MIPs), PPOs, EPOs, open-ended HMOs (O/HMOs), and regular HMOs.[42] Weiner and de Lissovoy propose a fairly complicated scheme for distinguishing among these five plan types (reproduced in Table 1).[43] A closer examination of their scheme indicates, however, that there are actually just two crucial distinguishing features: (i) whether plans require that patients see only certain specified medical providers (EPOs and regular HMOs do, MIPs do not, and PPOs and O/HMOs do but penalize patients who receive care from providers outside the network) and (ii) whether physicians bear financial risk.[44] Thus, as Table 1 shows, an MIP is a plan that uses utilization controls but does not have a network of providers. A PPO is a plan that has a network but allows patients to opt out of it for a price. An EPO is a PPO that does not allow opt-outs. An O/HMO is a network plan that allows opt-outs but, unlike a PPO, uses capitation. Finally, a regular HMO is a capitated network plan that does not allow opt-outs. With the exception of MIPs, Weiner and de Lissovoy dub all these plans "integrated delivery systems."[45]

This taxonomy, if nothing else, conforms to popular usage. It introduces a new and more comprehensible plan moniker — open-ended HMOs — to substitute for the commonly used yet confusing label point-of-service plan (or POS).[46] Otherwise, however, it merely offers extended definitions of the most common labels already used by industry actors and observers. Weiner and de Lissovoy deserve credit for trying to simplify the jumble of marketing slogans and acronyms that surround American health insurance, but the complicated scheme they come up with does not so much "raze a tower of Babel" as rehabilitate it.

Table 1. A taxonomy for categorizing health insurance plans.

Dimension	Type of plan					
	FFS	MIP	PPO	EPO	O/HMO	HMO
Weiner and de Lissovoy's taxonomy						
Sponsor assumes financial risk[a]	−/+	−/+	−/+	−/+	−	−
Intermediary assumes financial risk[a]	+/−	+/−	+/−	+/−	+	+
Physicians assume financial risk[b]	−	−	−	−	+	+
Restriction on consumer's selection of provider[c]	−	−	+/−	+	+/−	+
Significant utilization controls placed on provider's practice[d]	−	+	+	+	+	+
Plan obliged to arrange for care provision	−	−	+/−	+	+	+

Key: FFS: "traditional" fee-for-service indemnity plan; MIP: managed indemnity plan; PPO: preferred provider organization; EPO: exclusive provider organization; O/HMO: open-ended health maintenance organization; HMO: health maintenance organization (including independent practice association).

−: absent; +: present.

[a]The left side of the slash reflects a plan where an employer purchases a full-premium benefit from the insurer. The right side reflects a self-insured (or minimally insured) private plan or a government plan where risk resides with the sponsor.

[b]Primary care physicians at a minimum, but may also involve other providers.

[c]In PPOs and O/HMOs, consumer's choice is limited through incentives and disincentives rather than mandatory restrictions. They have the option to seek covered care from outside the plan. The right side of the slash reflects care when this "out-of-plan" option is exercised.

[d]Usually defined as mandated "prior-authorization" for non-emergency hospitalization.

To begin with, Weiner and Lissovoy's scheme actually tells us relatively little about each type of health plan. If a plan places financial risk on sponsors, it may be an MIP, PPO, EPO, or even a traditional fee-for-service plan.[47] If it puts intermediaries at financial risk, it may be any of the plan types.[48] If a plan is a "managed care" plan, we know that it places "significant utilization controls" on medical practice.[49] However, what these controls constitute (besides hospital precertification, which Weiner and de Lissovoy say is the threshold consideration), or how they might differ across plan types (if they in fact do) is left unspecified.[50] We are told that if a plan has a network of providers, it is an "integrated medical system,"[51] but what integration means in this context is unclear, especially since it is a characteristic apparently shared by all but one of the managed care plan types.[52] Why MIPs are not considered integrated medical systems is also unclear. After all, they are counted as managed care plans,[53] and, according to Weiner and de Lissovoy's definition, the essence of managed care is the "integration" and "coordination" of the financing and delivery of medical care.[54] Virtually the scheme's only clear criterion is that if medical providers bear risk, then the plan is an HMO of some sort.[55]

Even this distinction is problematic, however. Many different types of health plans are experimenting with ways to shift risk onto medical providers through payment methods, withholding arrangements, and bonus schemes, as Weiner and de Lissovoy themselves note.[56] Virtually all health financing methods, even tax-financed national health insurance, place some risk on providers. The real questions are, first, how concentrated is the risk, and, second, is it immediate or long-term? Salaried doctors working for HMOs may face much less concentrated and immediate financial risks than those physicians who, despite arms-length relationships to health plans, face financial penalties if they provide too costly care to individual patients. Over time, the salaried doctor's income will depend on the performance of the HMO, but his individual treatment decisions may be relatively unencumbered by financial concerns. Rather than classifying risk-bearing as present or absent, it is far more instructive to identify the locus of risk. This might range from all providers within a geographic area (as in a national health insurance scheme with a global budget) to a specific group of providers (such as an HMO's medical group) to an individual professional (as in many of the most recently developed incentive schemes).[57]

The central problem with Weiner and de Lissovoy's taxonomy and with most contemporary American commentary about health insurance is the tendency to confuse reimbursement methods, managerial techniques, and organizational forms. For example, fee-for-service, a payment method, is regularly contrasted with "managed care," presumably an organizational form.[58] In this taxonomy, MIPs are distinguished from traditional fee-for-service plans by their reliance on a particular managerial technique, namely utilization review.[59] In contrast, PPOs and EPOs are distinguished from

MIPs by their particular organizational form, namely their reliance on a network of participating providers.[60] HMOs are distinguished from all these plans by their particular payment method, namely capitation.[61]

The practice of conflating organization, technique, and incentives leads to worrisome and unnecessary confusion. It means that when we contrast health plans we are often comparing them across incommensurable dimensions. So, for instance, an HMO becomes by definition more "managed" than a fee-for-service plan with utilization review even when the latter uses much stricter controls on individual treatment decisions. Similarly, by conflating distinct characteristics, we are tempted to presume necessary relationships between particular features of health plans (such as their payment method) and specific outcomes that are claimed to follow from these features (such as the degree of integration of medical finance and delivery). Finally, the desire to describe an assortment of disparate plan features with a few broad labels encourages a wild goose chase of efforts to come up with black-and-white standards for identifying plan types. If a plan relies on capitation (a payment method), it is an HMO, if it has a network (an organizational form), it is an integrated medical system, and so on. As health plans employ increasingly diverse payment methods and organizational forms, the search for the "essence" of a particular plan will become all the more futile.

Another hallmark of the way we talk about health insurance today is the conspicuous failure to distinguish among the perspectives of different actors. The answers to such questions as whether a health plan is integrated or coordinated, whether it manages treatment decisions, and whether it imposes risk all depend crucially on whose perspective (patient, provider, or purchaser) we are assuming in making such assessments. A plan that appears "integrated" to outside observers, combining the delivery and financing of care in a seamless package, may rightly seem fragmented to patients who discover they have to endure complex authorization procedures and pick from a list of certified providers scattered across a region. To an employer, "management" of care may mean an administrator handling self-insured claims; to a doctor, it may signify outside control over medical decisions; and to a patient, it may be restrictions on the providers and services covered by a plan. This is not to suggest, of course, that our judgments about health plans are entirely subjective, but rather, to indicate that blanket terms like "management" or "coordination" are empty abstractions without specifying who is managing or coordinating what, for whom, and why.

Given the overlap among Weiner and de Lissovoy's categories and the lack of clear distinctions between them, it is hard to know what these plan types represent, except perhaps some elusive Platonic ideal never actually realized in practice. If these are simply abstract ideal types, however, then there is no reason why they should conform to the messy categories that industry actors and their promoters employ. For these categories, as we have seen, manifestly fail to clarify the differences among plans. Instead, they identify a hodge-podge of features that are rarely exclusive to any one plan and vary nearly as much within plan types as across them. We think there is a better alternative.

III. A Revised Conception of Health Insurance Organization

In understanding the structure of health insurance, the crucial relationship is between those who deliver medical care and those who pay for it. Even a passive indemnity insurer stands between the patient and the medical provider as a financial intermediary and an underwriter of risk. Today, with risk shifting from insurers to employers, and with financial intermediaries playing more of an administrative role than in the past, the trilateral relationship is more complex.[62] Nonetheless, it still remains the locus of the insurance contract. To characterize this trilateral relationship, we focus on three of its essential features: first, the degree of risk-sharing between providers and the primary bearer of risk (whether an insurer or a self-insured employer), second, the degree to which administrative oversight constrains clinical decisions, and, third, the degree to which enrollees in a plan are required to receive their care from a specified roster of providers. As Figure 1 shows, these three criteria create a three-dimensional space within which alternative health plans can be arrayed. We have placed a few illustrative descriptions of health plans in this space, as well as indicated where we think the federal Medicare program and most other nations' universal health programs should be located.

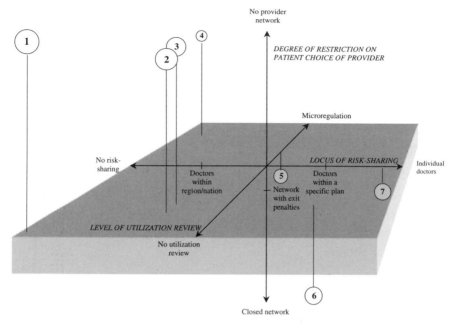

Figure 1. The three dimensions of health plan organization. Key: 1. Traditional Blue Cross/ Blue Shield indemnity insurance; 2. National health insurance in most other advanced industrial democracies; 3. Medicare; 4. Indemnity insurance with utilization review; 5. Typical PPO; 6. Staff-model HMO; 7. Future direction of private health plans? Note: The circles indicate the placement of the health plans. The dotted lines are included to aid in the location of the plans on the utilization review axis.

Our aim here is not to construct an exhaustive typology of health plans, if that were even possible given the rapid pace of change in American medical care. Rather, we wish to challenge the common way of thinking about how to classify health plans. Our argument is that health plans differ across at least three principal dimensions: risk-sharing between plan and provider, managerial control of clinical decision-making, and limits on patient choice of medical professional. Each dimension crucially affects the trilateral connections among provider, patient, and plan. We also wish to emphasize that there is no simple relationship between plan label and the placement of a plan along these axes. Staff-model HMOs may seem like the quintessence of "managed care," yet because they place financial constraints at the group level they do not necessarily concentrate as much risk on physicians as do other network-based health plans. Moreover, they do not necessarily entail as much clinical regulation at the micro-level. Microregulation may go hand in hand with restrictions on patient choice of provider, but it may not, either. Indeed, management of individual clinical decisions and the creation of broad incentives for conservative practice patterns may very well be alternative mechanisms for lowering the cost of medical care. Finally, as recent developments in the health insurance market suggest, greater risk-sharing can co-exist with almost any set of arrangements. It does not require a closed network, much less strict utilization review. Risk sharing is a product of the payment methods and incentive structures that connect risk-bearing agents and medical providers. It does not exclusively occur in HMOs, nor does it require capitation.[63]

Notice, too, that Figure 1 makes no mention of those popular buzzwords "integration" and "coordination." Movement toward a closed network, toward greater utilization control, or toward increased risk-sharing can create the conditions under which integration or coordination may occur.[64] They do not imply, however, that such integrative activities actually take place. Getting the right care to the right patient at the right time is a managerial accomplishment, not a product of labels.

Finally, the conventional fee-for-service versus capitation dichotomy does not remain a very useful means of distinguishing among different health plans. Instead, the crucial issue is what incentives medical providers actually face. The particular mix of payment methods that create those incentives is less important and will undoubtedly change as health plans experiment with new reimbursement modalities in the future.

Disaggregating health insurance into its constituent features not only helps to clarify what health plans do and how they are structured; but also makes it easier to identify the specific trends in medical finance and delivery that are carelessly jumbled together when we speak of such grand events as the "managed care revolution."[65] Although we cannot provide a comprehensive empirical survey in this context, our reading of the evidence leads us to believe that the developments of the past decade have not pushed American health insurance in a consistent direction, much less toward any single organized entity that might be labeled "managed care."

Indeed, movement along these axes has been halting and inconsistent. Through roughly the late 1980s, an increasing number of health plans moved toward closed networks.[66] In the 1990s, on the other hand, the trend has been toward intermediate levels of compulsion, with formerly closed plans offering opportunities for patients to opt out with a penalty and with new plans shying away from closed-network structures.[67] Utilization review was also fashionable during the 1980s,[68] yet it too has fallen somewhat into disfavor as plans have moved toward greater reliance on plan-provider risk-sharing, which in turn has become more focused at the level of the individual provider and individual service category over time.[69] If there has been any general movement in the past two decades — and surely there has been — it has been from the front-left-top portion of the figure toward the back-right-bottom portion. Even this development, however, has been neither consistent nor evenly paced. In fact, the most clear and unmistakable trend has been in the direction of straightforward price-discounting, as plans have used their market clout to selectively contract with physicians willing to accept negotiated rates. This is an important development, but in both international and historical perspective, it is hardly as unprecedented as such grand phrases as "the managed care revolution" imply.

IV. The Politics of a Contested Category

If recent trends in the organization of American medicine remain elusive, the political responses to these changes are in some ways fairly simple to describe. Driven in part by heart-wrenching stories about the denial of care to sick and dying patients, scores of states have enacted new health insurance regulations. Although the motives for these laws have varied, most seem to reflect generalized public fears about a perceived loss of control over medical decision-making, as well as the specific complaints of both medical professionals and patients about managerial and financial policies that are alleged to encourage providers to deliver inadequate or substandard care.[70]

In response to these trends, scores of states have introduced new legislation to regulate health plans and protect "consumer rights."[71] Nearly all states have enacted at least one or two reforms, and many have implemented several different reform packages.[72] These include protections for emergency room patients,[73] requirements of access to out-of-network providers,[74] granting of direct access to specialists for the seriously ill and to obstetricians/gynecologists for women,[75] the creation of independent appeals processes for those denied care,[76] the establishment of consumer assistance programs,[77] the banning of gag clauses and "inappropriate" financial incentives,[78] and, at the extreme, legislation permitting subscribers to sue health plans.[79] By June 1998, the majority of states had passed more than one but fewer than five such protections.[80] Not surprisingly, the regulatory policies differ significantly from state to state (although some changes, like emergency room protections, are almost universal in states that have passed reforms).[81] As of June 1998, South Dakota was the only state not to have passed any of these regulatory reforms.[82] On the other hand, only Missouri and Texas had allowed enrollees to sue their health plans.[83]

The ability of the states to regulate private health insurance is constrained, however, by the Employee Retirement Income Security Act of 1974,[84] which preempts most state regulations of self-insured health plans (those in which employers pay medical claims themselves) and also precludes lawsuits seeking punitive or compensatory damages against all employer-sponsored health plans. Only federal regulations will thus reach the roughly 51 million Americans covered by self-insured plans, and only federal laws can establish an expanded right to sue for the more than 124 million Americans covered by employment-based health plans. At the federal level, however, the debate over regulatory protections stalled during 1998. The Clinton impeachment struggle dominated Washington and distracted attention from health insurance reforms. Moreover, Democrats and Republicans were far apart on the appropriate legislative responses to the problems many states had already addressed. In 1999, however, a faction of House Republicans that included several Republican physicians endorsed a limited right to sue, paving the way for compromise legislation in the House.[85] Although the House proposal remains much broader than the narrowly passed counterpart bill in the Senate,[86] it is nonetheless striking that any legislation survived in the acrimonious partisan climate in Congress. This suggests the degree to which members of both parties interpret public dissatisfaction with contemporary health insurance developments as a potent political topic that Democrats in particular can use on the campaign trail.

Although the broad contours of that debate are clear, the underlying issues are not in our view deeply understood, even by defenders of particular legislative solutions. As political scientists, we wonder, for example, from where the pressure for federal reform is coming. One recent article attempts to measure the depth of the managed care backlash.[87] Its conclusion is hardly startling: The backlash is real but not extremely deep, and dissatisfaction is with the medical system as a whole rather than with personal experiences with managed care health plans.[88] Many have argued that managed care regulations are being promulgated by doctors and nurses angry about challenges to their income and autonomy.[89] It is not clear, though, that there is much evidence for that claim at the national level. One wonders about how exactly "the backlash" emerged, and how it changed; about how reformers decided on specific strategies and how they got so many states to pass laws. The ground-level politics of the issue are simply not well understood.[90]

Furthermore, as students of health policy, we have serious questions about the desirability and presumptions of some of the proposed regulations. Two divergent tendencies appear to be at work. On the one hand, between 1993 and 1998, many commentators celebrated the health insurance industry's apparent achievements in controlling costs.[91] On the other, few seemed to like how the industry controlled costs.[92] The two positions appear, if not to contradict one another, at least to call into serious question the sustainability of a lowered rate of medical inflation into the next century. Similarly, the push to regulate health plans appears at odds with the popular goal of increasing coverage. Almost every analyst acknowledges that new restrictions will increase costs, thus reducing rates of coverage.[93] The push for regulation does seem to be a distinctly American response — a juridical-regulatory style of policy intervention that brings in government through the back door and deals in the language of rights rather than broader issues of social allocation.[94]

Although aggressive regulation of private institutions is a recurrent strain in American politics, it runs sharply against the grain of recent national policy developments. After the failure of the Clinton health plan in 1994 and the subsequent election of a Republican Congress, congressional leaders sought to ease regulations on a wide range of industries, including the private medical sector. Along with maverick Democrats like Senator John Breaux, they also attempted to incorporate a greater role for private health insurance within Medicare, with the ultimate goal of replacing America's federal health insurance program for the aged with a system of competing private health plans.

The rise of "managed care regulation" as a leading political issue indicates that the unbridled enthusiasm for private cost-containment that motivated these efforts has waned considerably. At the same time, it highlights many of the unresolved contradictions inherent in recent public policy. Private health plans have perhaps never been more celebrated by American policy makers as the appropriate means for providing health coverage. Yet dissatisfaction with the specific practices of private health plans has probably never been greater either. For example, even as state and federal politicians have actively shifted beneficiaries of government health insurance programs into private health plans, they have loudly criticized such plans for overriding patient and provider preferences or delivering substandard care.

Although policymakers have directed much of their regulatory ire at the broad (and hazily defined) target of "managed care," much of the legislative momentum thus far has been toward the passage of specific, piecemeal responses to particularly salient complaints. The regulatory reaction reflects undeniable dissatisfaction, to be sure, but this dissatisfaction seems to be with selected features of the changing health insurance market, not with a clearly understood world of "managed care." Indeed, what ultimately seems to underlie recent state and federal activity is a more fundamental tension in the United States. health policy — between a national health insurance strategy that relies heavily on nongovernmental institutions, on the one hand, and the understandable desire to alter the behavior of these putatively private institutions when they fail to meet public expectations, on the other.

V. Conclusion

We have argued that a striking feature of the discussion of American managed care is its linguistic confusion. Both political actors and medical commentators regularly trade in persuasive definitions and stylized facts, the truth or falsehood of which remain unproven. The use of the term "managed care" exemplifies this practice and illustrates how many unanswered questions it leaves. What are the essential features of managed care, if any? How does it differ from indemnity-style fee-for-service health insurance? How does it differ from insurance plans that just rely on utilization review? Are plans we label "managed care" more different from traditional fee-for-service insurance than they are from one another? Simply put, a sensible discussion of managed care — much less of the appropriate means by which to regulate it — requires that we know what is being discussed.

The starting point for improved discussion and analysis, we have argued, is the acknowledgment that many of the categories we are accustomed to employing are essentially slogans that are used for self-promotion by various actors in contemporary American medicine. In that respect, they are appropriate objects of study in their own right, but they are not analytical terms that can frame our investigations, at least not without considerable further specification.

Once we address specific features of health insurance, moreover, the category "managed care" itself becomes ambiguous. The "managed care revolution" is really a set of related trends, few of which are accurately captured by the blanket term. When these trends are distinguished from one another, the evidence suggests that American health insurance has moved simultaneously in several different, perhaps even contradictory, directions in recent years and that many of the changes are longer standing than the rhetoric of managed care implies. This does not mean that the recent interest in regulating private health insurance is misguided or unfounded. It is only to emphasize that demands for regulation are motivated by a constellation of related but distinct changes in American health insurance that are not accurately described by the generalized expression "managed care." Moreover, to date, state and federal policymakers have largely advocated targeted and piecemeal regulatory measures designed to alter particular features of private health plans — features that are deemed undesirable quite apart from their association with the broader label of "managed care."

The rapid changes taking place in American medical care impose a special burden on analysts to be precise about the criteria and considerations that underlie their empirical evaluations and, ultimately, their judgments and assessments. Labels and categories are indispensable, but they should be designed to elucidate the techniques, organizational forms, and incentives that characterize alternative health plans, rather than to confirm or deny the claims of industry friends or foes. The term "managed care" fails that test, and although we hardly expect our words to be heeded (especially since both of us have reluctantly used the term in our own writings), we think that it and other terms like it should be banished from the health care lexicon for good.

Endnotes

[†]Originally published in the *University of Michigan Journal of Law Reform*, Volume 32, Issue 4, Summer 1999, © University of Michigan. We wish to thank Mark Peterson and Bill Sage for their thoughtful comments (without, of course, implying that they endorse the argument presented here) and Camille Costelli for here tireless assistance, Lauren Dame deserves special mention. A lawyer and public health expert, she signed on to help us with a handful of footnotes, but ended up contributing to nearly every aspect of this project. That she was able to guide two political scientists through the unfamiliar world of legal citation is the ultimate measure of her professionalism, precision, and, above all, patience.

[*]Jacob S. Hacker, B.A., Harvard University, 1993; Ph.D. candidate in Political Science, Yale University; Society of Fellows, Harvard University, 1999–2002; author of *The Road to Nowhere: The Genesis of President Clinton's Plan for Health Security* (Princeton: Princeton University Press, 1997).

[**]Theodore R. Marmor, B.A., Harvard University, 1960; Ph.D. Politics & History, Harvard University, 1966; Professor of Public Policy and Management, School of Management, Yale University and Professor of Political Science, Yale University, 1983 to present; author of numerous books and articles on health care policy, including *The Politics of Medicare*, 2nd Ed. (Aldine de Gruyter, 2000).

[1]See, e.g., Eckholm, E., "Introduction to the President's Health Security Plan" (The White House Domestic Policy Council, 1993): vii, asserting that President Clinton took office determined to solve two related crises in health care: the first being "the growing number of Americans who lacked the basic security of health insurance," and the second, "the spiral in health spending that threatened to bankrupt the government and cripple American industry."

[2]See generally Hacker, J. S., *The Road to Nowhere: The Genesis of President Clinton's Plan for Health Security* (Princton: Princeton University Press, 1997).

[3]See, e.g., Chassin, M. R., "Quality of Care — Part 3: Improving the Quality of Care," *New Eng. J. Med.*, 335 (1996): 1060, stating that in the 1960s, improving quality was discussed in terms of increasing access to care for certain populations, while in the 1990s, quality seems to mean marketplace competition and "report cards" on health plans; see also Schroeder, S. A., "The Medically Uninsured — Will They Always Be With Us?," *New Eng. J. Med.*, 334 (1996): 1130, 1133, lamenting that the issue of expanded medical insurance coverage "erupts onto the national scene" only periodically, such as in 1993, and then disappears "back underground."

[4]See, e.g., Blendon, R. J., *et al.*, "Understanding the Managed Care Backlash," *Health Affairs*, 17 (Jul.–Aug. 1998): 80, 90–91, reporting on survey findings that Americans who were satisfied with their current health plan were still fearful that their managed care plans would not provide care or pay for care in the future when they got sick; Kassirer, J. P., "Managing Managed Care's Tarnished Image," *New Eng. J. Med.*, 337 (1997): 338, criticizing the superficial public relations efforts by the American Association of Health Plans to improve the public's opinion of "managed care," and suggesting that there is good reason for the American public to be critical of managed care.

[5]See, e.g., Thorpe, K. E., "The Health System in Transition: Care, Cost, and Coverage," *J. Health Pol., Pol'y & L.*, 22 (1997): 339, noting that the growth in market-based contracting and the "ascendancy of managed care" have generated substantial change in American medical care, and arguing that "[u]nanswered in the managed care revolution is the means for financing care for the 41 million uninsured Americans;" see also Cain II, H. P., "Privatizing Medicare: A Battle of Values," in J. K. Iglehart, ed., *Medicare and Managed Care: A Primer from Health Affairs and the California Health Care Foundation* (Millwood, VA: Project Hope, 1999): 41–47, arguing that "[m]ost of us would agree that a full-scale revolution is underway."

[6]"Managed Competition" is a phrase originally coined by economist Alain Enthoven in the early 1980s, and as a theory was expounded and debated in the academic literature over the next decade. See, e.g., Enthoven, A. C., "The History and Principles of Managed Competition," *Health Affairs,* 12 (Supp. 1993): 24, 44–46. The term came to be used in such a variety of ways over the years, however, that in this 1993 article, Enthoven not only retraced the development of his ideas, but also explained in some detail what managed competition was "not," stating that "[m]anaged competition is not just the latest buzzword that anybody should feel free to appropriate. . . Managed competition is not just a grab bag of ideas that sound good. It is an integrated framework that combines rational principles of microeconomics with careful observation and analysis of what works." *Id.* at 45. In spite of Enthoven's efforts to reclaim the phrase "managed competition," however, the term still suffers from multiple warring definitions and inherent contradictions. See Marmor, T. R., *Understanding Health Care Reform* (New Haven: Yale University Press, 1994): 170.

[7]These arguments have been made elsewhere, see Marmor, T. R., "Forecasting American Health Care," *J. Health Pol., Pol'y & L.*, 23 (1998): 551. The fuller statement of this critique can be found in Marmor, T. R., "Hope and Hyperbole: the Rhetoric and Reality of Managerial Reform in Health Care," *J. Health Serv. Res. & Pol.*, 3 (Jan. 1998): 62.

[8]Marmor, "Hope and Hyperbole," *supra* note 7 at 62–63.

[9]*Id.* at 63.

[10]*Id.*

[11]*Id.*

[12]Huczynski, A. A., *Management Gurus: What Makes Them and How to Become One* (Routledge, 1996): 11–58.

[13]*Id.*

[14]Marmor, "Hope and Hyperbole", *supra* note 7.

[15]*Id.*

[16]See, e.g., Kuttner, R., "Must Good HMOs Go Bad? First of Two Parts: The Commercialization of Prepaid Group Health Care," *New Eng. J. Med.*, 338 (May 21, 1998): 1558; Kuttner, R., "Must Good HMOs Go Bad? Second of Two Parts: The Search for Checks and Balances," *New Eng. J. Med.*, 338 (May 28, 1998): 1635; Anders, G., *Health Against Wealth: HMOs and the Breakdown of Medical Trust* (Mariner Books, 1996); Makover, M. E., *Mismanaged Care: How Corporate Medicine Jeopardizes Your Health* (Prometheus Books, 1998).

[17]Consider, for example, a recent article written by two Georgetown law professors, Gostin, L. and Bowser, R., "Managed Care and the Health of the Nation." *S. Cal L. Rev.*, 2 (Summer 1999), drawn from *Health Law and Policy Abstracts*, 1.2 (Dec. 16, 1998), Legal Scholarship Network: http://papers.ssrn.com/paper.taf?ABSTRACT_ID=139927 (visited 9/1/99). The article's abstract explains that the "trend toward managed care presents promising opportunities for improving the health of large populations. Capitated financing arrangements and performance-based reimbursements, in theory, create imperatives for these plans to promote behavior that reduces health risks and to emphasize preventive services that may forestall costly future medical treatments." We shall leave aside for the moment the vast indeterminacy of the phrase "trend toward managed care" or the blithe equation of the organizational form "managed care" with capitation, a payment method in which medical providers are paid a fixed amount to treat an individual patient regardless of the volume of services delivered. For now, we simply wish to note the staggering number of unexamined assumptions that these two sentences, in their deployment of medical industry jargon, invoke.

Gostin and Bowser state, for example, that there is a trend toward managed care. Managed care means capitation and — that magical phrase — "performance-based reimbursements." These payment methods create incentives for plans to "promote behavior that reduces health risks and to emphasize preventive services," two other favorite industry claims. Thus the trend toward managed care should improve the "health of the nation." Surely all these are common assertions made by proponents of prepaid capitated health plans. Surely, too, if every step of this familiar syllogism were true, the final claim might well be true. The point is that we do not know if the steps of the argument are true. Gostin and Bowser simply assume that they are.

[18]See *infra* text accompanying notes 19–23.

[19]The Association, known before 1983 as the American Association of Foundations for Medical Care, was later to merge with the Group Health Association of America to form

the American Association of Health Plans. American Association of Health Plans Press Release, "New Association Announces Name and Philosophy of Care: 'American Association of Health Plans' Created From the Merger of GHAA and AMCRA," (Feb. 26, 1996), http://www.aahp.org/services/communications/media/1996/name.htm (visited 9/1/99).

[20]Starr, P., *The Social Transformation of American Medicine* (Basic Books, 1982).

[21]Brown, L. D., *Politics and Health Care Organizations: HMOs as Federal Policy* (The Brookings Institution, 1983).

[22]See, e.g., Cohn, V., "Someone Besides You and the Doctor May Be Deciding How You Get Treated," *Wash. Post,* (Nov. 21, 1989): z12.

[23] Based on a search of *The New York Times* file in LEXIS-NEXIS, using the keywords "managed care." The file goes back to the 1970s.

[24]Cohn, *supra* note 22.

[25]See, e.g., Ignagni, K., "Covering a Breaking Revolution: The Media and Managed Care," *Health Affairs*, 17 (Jan.–Feb. 1998): 26, 27, describing managed care as a "system of care whose goal is to offer superior coverage, state-of-the-art care, unprecedented accountability, and an unparalleled commitment to continuous quality improvement — all at affordable cost."

[26]For an introduction to the multiple, confusing, and invariably normative definitions of "managed care," see Rhea, J. C., S. Ott, and J. M. Shafritz, *The Facts on File Dictionary of Health Care* (Facts on File Publications, 1988): 376–377, "health insurance plans that reduce unnecessary health care costs by way of increased beneficiary cost sharing, controls on inpatient admissions and lengths of stay, the establishment of cost-sharing incentives for outpatient surgery, selective contracting with health care providers, and the direct management of high-cost health care cases;" Freudenheim, E., *Healthspeak: A Complete Dictionary of America's Health Care System* (Facts on File Publications, 1996): 155, "a comprehensive approach to health care delivery that encompasses planning and coordination of care, patient and provider education, monitoring of care quality, and cost control;" and *The American Heritage Stedman's Medical Dictionary* (Houghton Miflin Co., 1995): 487, "Any arrangement for health care in which an organization. . . acts as an intermediate between the person seeking care and the physician."

[27]See, e.g., Morrissey, M. A., "Introduction," in *Managed Care and Changing Health Care Markets*, ed. M. A. Morrissey (American Enterprise Institute Press, 1998): 1–23, at 3, "The term [managed care] has taken on a variety of meanings. To some it means capitation; providers are paid a fixed amount per subscribers for all or some well-defined component of their care."

[28]"Fee-for-service" is a system of reimbursement in which a medical provider charges a patient (or third-party payer) a specific price for a specific service. See Marmor, *supra* note 6 at 260. An insurer may pay a provider on a fee-for-service basis while still requiring a patient to obtain approval before seeing the physician, limiting the number of times the patient may see the provider, or otherwise imposing restrictions on the provider and patient behavior. Moreover, most advanced industrial democracies, as well as the US Medicare and Medicaid programs, pay providers on a fee-for-service basis but according

to an agreed-upon fee schedule that has been established by the government (often in consultation with providers) and which is designed to account for the intensity, characteristics, and volume of the specific medical services provided. This is also the practice in many private health plans that contract with specific providers who agree to accept discounted fee-for-service payments.

[29]See Gold, M., R. Hurley, T. Lake, T. Ensor, and R. Berenson, "A National Survey of the Arrangements Managed Care Plans Make With Physicians," in M. Gold, ed., *Contemporary Managed Care: Readings in Structure, Operations, and Public Policy* (Health Administration Press, 1998): 101–113. This study, which examined 108 health maintenance organizations and preferred provider organizations, found that capitation was the predominant method of payment for primary care physicians in only 37 percent of plans and the predominant method of payment for specialists in just 18 percent of plans. See also Haugh, R., "Son of Capitation," *Hospitals and Health Networks*, 73.1 (Jan. 1999): 38–39, at 38, pointing out that "only 5 percent of hospitals are paid capitated rates... About a third [of doctors] have capitated contracts... and they account for less than one fourth of doctors' revenue." For a definition of "capitation," see *supra* text accompanying note 27.

[30]See, e.g., Schlesinger, M. J., *et al.,* "Medical Professionalism Under Managed Care: The Pros and Cons of Utilization Review," *Health Affairs*, 16 (Jan.–Feb. 1997): 106, 109, "[T]hird-party authorization of medical decisions perhaps most clearly embodies what many physicians fear about managed care: its intrusiveness into clinical settings and its potential for inappropriately standardizing treatment practices."

[31]*Id.* "Review practices vary considerably. A number of review organizations do little to threaten physician autonomy."

[32]See Field, M. J. and H. T. Shapiro, eds., *Employment and Health Benefits: A Connection at Risk* (National Academies Press, 1993): 339, defining managed care as a term "used more narrowly to identify group or network-based health plans that have explicit criteria for selecting providers and financial incentives for members to use network providers." See also Morissey, *supra* note 27 at 3; Weiner, J. P. and G. de Lissovoy, "Razing a Tower of Babel: A Taxonomy for Managed Care and Health Insurance Plans," *J. Health Pol., Pol'y & L.*, 18 (1993): 75.

[33]"According to the Health Insurance Association of American (HIAA), preferred provider organizations (PPOs) made up roughly half of all health insurance plans in the United States in 1995, up from 28 percent in 1992," *Source Book of Health Insurance Data* (HIAA, 1998): 59. By the Association's definition, "PPOs contract with networks of providers to offer medical services according to a negotiated, discounted, fee schedule." *Id.* at 54.

[34]See, e.g., Jacobson, P. D., "Legal Challenges to Managed Care Cost Containment Programs: An Initial Assessment," *Health Affairs*, 18 (Jul.–Aug. 1999): 69, 72, pointing out that in health insurance litigation under managed care, the context of the case is different from traditional health insurance litigation because "with the integration of financing and care delivery under managed care, refusing coverage means denying care altogether;" see also Robinson, J. C., "The Future of Managed Care Organization," *Health Affairs*,

18 (Mar.–Apr. 1999): 7, from the Prologue: "For the past fifteen years the words 'managed care' have been the shorthand label for a wide variety of health plans that . . . have combined the functions of delivering and financing medical care."

[35]See Starr, *supra* note 20 at 320–327, describing the growth of prepaid group practice after 1945. Traditional HMOs such as Kaiser-Permanente of California and the Group Health Cooperative of Puget Sound employed their own salaried doctors, operated their own medical facilities, and charged subscribers a fixed fee per month regardless of the volume of services delivered. Not only did they operate quite differently from most other insurers, they were not run by conventional commercial insurance companies. Most "managed care" plans today, however, are operated by commercial insurers such as Blue Cross/Blue Shield. And very few are "staff-model" plans like Kaiser-Permanente and Group Health Cooperative. Only 15 such plans existed in 1997. See American Association of Health Plans, *Managed Care Facts* (AAHP, 1998): 2.

[36]HIAA, *supra* note 33 at 58.

[37]*Id.* at 58.

[38]This is one reason why it makes little sense to claim, as does a 1997 *Health Affairs* article, that "managed care isn't coming; it has arrived." Jensen, G. A., *et al.*, "The New Dominance of Managed Care: Insurance Trends in the 1990s," *Health Affairs*, 16 (Jan.–Feb. 1997): 125. Perhaps it has, but one might reasonably ask what precisely "it" is, or whether it makes sense to lump together recent developments in American health insurance within a single general category — especially because the article ignores any conceptual discussion of what is meant by the term "managed care" itself.

[39]See, e.g., the website of the American Association of Health Plans, where under the category of "Information for Consumers—Definitions," it lists and defines the following terms as being "Network-Based Health Plans": Exclusive Provider Organizations (EPOs), Foundations for Medical Care (FMCs), Health Maintenance Organizations (HMOs), [further divided into Staff Model, Group Model, Network Model and Independent Practice Association (IPA)], Medicare Health Care Prepayment Plan (HCPP), Point-of-Service (POS) options, Preferred Provider Organization (PPO), Specialty HMOs, and Specialty PPOs. http://www.aahp.org/services/consumer_information/definitions/definit.htm (visited 9/01/99).

[40]Weiner and Lissovoy, *supra* note 32.

[41]*Id.* at 78.

[42]*Id.* at 87 (Table 1).

[43]*Id.*

[44]They do only in HMOs, Weiner and de Lissovoy argue, because HMOs rely on capitation. *Id.* at 88.

[45]*Id.* at 90.

[46]In a "point-of-service" health insurance plan, patients are financially rewarded for using a limited group of providers, but are permitted to seek out-of-network care at higher cost. See Marmor, *supra* note 6 at 265.

[47]See Table 1, *supra*.

[48]*Id.*

[49]Weiner and de Lissovoy, *supra* note 32 at 89.

[50]*Id.*

[51]*Id.* at 90.

[52]*Id.*

[53]*Id.*

[54]*Id.*

[55]*Id.* at 88.

[56]*Id.*

[57]*Id.*

[58]*Id.* at 75–80.

[59]See Table 1, *supra.*

[60]*Id.*

[61]*Id.*

[62]See *supra* note 34.

[63]For a general discussion of financial risk sharing in health insurance, see Gold, M., L. Nelson, T. Lake, R. Hurley, and R. Berenson, "Behind the Curve: A Critical Assessment of How Little Is Known About Arrangements between Managed Care Plans and Physicians," in Gold, *supra* note 29 at 67–100, esp. 86–89.

[64]See generally Miller, R., "Health System Integration: A Means to an End," *Health Affairs,* 15 (Summer 1996): 92, describing the variety of ways in which integration can occur in healthcare systems; explaining that integration is only a means to an end; and concluding that the results of integration — positive or negative — depend upon the subsequent behavior of managers, physicians, and other actors.

[65]See Thorpe, *supra* note 5; see also Ignagni, *supra* note 25 at 27, "A revolution is taking place in the organization and delivery of health care in the United States. Practically overnight, managed care has replaced fee-for-service as the nation's health care system of choice."

[66]HMO enrollment grew at an annual rate of more than 20 percent in the mid-1980s, but growth slowed to single digits in the late 1980s and early 1990s. HIAA, *supra* note 33 at 51.

[67]Between 1993 and 1995, enrollment in fully closed plans grew by 22.8 percent, while enrollment in plans that allowed patients to exit the network for a price grew by 57 percent. Traditional HMOs increased their coverage at less than one-fifth the rate of HMOs that allowed patients to leave the network. Jensen *et al., supra* note 38 at 127. See also Haugh, *supra* note 29 at 39, noting that "Open-access plans are growing much faster than traditional HMOs. PPOs added 44 million members in the last five years, compared with the 30 million who joined HMOs. Even HMOs are adding point-of-service options." Terry, R. H. K., "Hang On — The Ride's Going to Get Rougher," *Med. Econ.,* 76.7 (Apr. 12, 1999): 176–178.

[68]Conventional fee-for-service insurance without utilization review declined from 40 percent in 1987 to 5 percent in 1990. See Hacker, *supra* note 2 at 15.

[69] See Magnus, S. A., "Physicians' Financial Incentives in Five Dimensions: A Conceptual Framework for HMO Managers," *Health Care Manage. R.*, 24.1 (Winter 1999): 57–72, arguing that "the growing popularity of financial incentives may indicate that they are becoming the method of choice for influencing physician behavior;" Sussman, A. J., D. G. Fairchild, and T. A. Brennan, "PHOs and Risk: Aligning Incentives with Internal Subcapitation," *Health Care Financ. Manage.*, 53.8 (Aug. 1999): 42–46; "Capitation Contracts Continue to Grow Among Both Physicians and Hospitals," *Health Care Strategic Manage.*, 17.5 (May 1999): 7, "According to an annual survey, Managed Care Indicator, conducted by Evergreen Re, both US hospitals and physicians are continuing to increase their numbers of capitated contracts. The survey found that the trend to use capitation is likely to continue in the coming years."

[70] See Blendon, *supra* note 4.

[71] See Families USA Foundation, "The Best from The States II: The Text of Key State HMO Consumer Protection Provisions," Oct. 1998; Families USA Foundation, "Hit and Miss: State Managed Care Laws," Jul. 1998 (updating Families USA Foundation, "HMO Consumers at Risk: States to the Rescue," Jun. 1996); Dallek G., *et al.*, "Consumer Protections in State HMO Laws," (Center for Health Care Rights), Nov. 1995.

[72] *Id.* at 2.

[73] For a description of state legislative efforts to protect emergency room patients from problems caused by "managed care," *see* Hoffman, D. E., "Emergency Care and Managed Care — A Dangerous Combination," *Wash. L. Rev.*, 72 (1997): 315, 368–380.

[74] See, e.g., 1998 Colo. Sess. Laws, ch. 238, §10-16-704(2).

[75] See, e.g., Ala. Code §27-49-4 (Supp. 1997).

[76] See, e.g., Vt. Stat. Ann. tit. 8, §4089f (Supp. 1998).

[77] See, e.g., Fla. Stat. Ch. 641.60(2) (1998).

[78] See, e.g., Kan. Stat. Ann. §40-46-04 (Supp. 1997); R.I. Gen. Laws § 23-17.13-3(B)(8) (Supp. 1997).

[79] See, e.g., Tex. Civ. Prac. & Rem. Code Ann. §88.001-§88.003 (West 1998).

[80] Families USA Foundation, "Hit and Miss: State Managed Care Laws 4," Jul. 1998.

[81] *Id.* at 5–7.

[82] *Id.* at 4.

[83] *Id.* at 19. "Only two states — Texas and Missouri — have passed laws exempting managed care corporations from their laws against suing corporations for malpractice. Only Texas, however, has taken the additional step of creating a cause of action so individuals can sue their health plans." Texas' law, Tex. Civ. Prac. & Rem. Code Ann. §88.001-§88.003 (West 1998).

[84] Pub. L. No. 93–406, 88 Stat. 829(1974); 29 U.S.C.S. §§1001-1461.

[85] H.R. 2723, "Bipartisan Consensus Managed Care Improvement Act of 1999," sponsored by Rep. Charlie Norwood, passed 275-151 (roll no. 490) on 7 October 1999.

[86] S. 1344, "Patients' Bill of Rights Act of 1999," sponsored by Sen. Trent Lott, passed 53-47 (roll no. 210) on 15 July 1999. As of this writing (October 1999), it remains unclear what will emerge from the House-Senate conference and be sent to President Clinton for his signature.

[87]See generally Blendon *et al.*, *supra* note 4.

[88]*Id.* at 90.

[89]See, e.g., Ross, E. C., "Regulating Managed Care: Interest Group Competition for Control and Behavioral Health Care," *J. Health Pol., Pol'y, & L.*, 24.3 (June 1999): 599–625.

[90]There have, however, been some attempts to understand these issues. See, e.g., Declercq, E. and D. Simmes, "The Politics of Drive-Through Deliveries: Putting Early Postpartum Discharge on the Legislative Agenda," *Milbank Quarterly*, 75 (1997): 175, analyzing the process by which the issue of early hospital discharge of mothers and new babies moved quickly onto the agenda of decision makers and resulted in new state laws.

[91]See, e.g., Morrisey, *supra* note 27 at 1.

[92]See generally Anders, *supra* note 16.

[93]Congressional Budget Office (CBO), Cost Estimate: S. 6, Patients' Bill of Rights Act of 1999, 23 April 1999, http://www.cbo.gov/costextend.shtml (visited 10/9/1999).

[94]See Kagan, R. A., "Adversarial Legalism and American Government," *J. Pol'y Anal. Manage.*, 10.3 (Summer 1991): 369.

Medical Care and Public Policy: The Benefits and Burdens of Asking Fundamental Questions†

T. R. Marmor* and D. Boyum**

This article questions two assumptions that regularly appear in discussions of what a fundamental discussion of medical care policy choices should include. First, we review skeptically the presumption that explicit specification of the scope of publicly financed medical services is a crucial step in improving policy making in the health and medical care arenas. Second, we question the appropriateness in many, if not most, contexts of explicit rationing, the belief that being clear about who gets what (and who does not) constitutes proper public policy. The article proceeds by looking back on the grounds for universal access to medical care, discusses the disputes about how to set limits on care, and illustrates its argument with references to Dutch debates about explicit choice, the Oregon experiment with priority setting, and the appeals to "healthy public policy" as a standard for sensible policy reform. The article closes with a brief discussion of the spread of assumptions about health reform as they move across national borders.

I. Introduction

The subject of this article — "fundamental questions about the future of health care" — is easy to describe, but much harder to treat in genuinely illuminating ways. Our central aim is this: to review the grounds for the collective financing of medical care, the plausible limits to that commitment, and the implications of both the commitment and the limits to resource allocation. More specifically, we address the question: "What health services should be a collective responsibility and thus accessible to all?"[1]

Our response to this question calls for at least an initial disclaimer, because we may well disappoint those who posed it for us. All questions proceed from underlying or implicit assumptions. In this instance, two are especially noteworthy. First, the question presumes that defining the scope of socially guaranteed medical services is important to advancing the current understanding of, or the public discourse about, health and medical care policy. Second, the question also presumes that choices about medical care should be made explicitly.

We do not share these presumptions. In our view, unresolved questions about the range of publicly financed medical services are not, in most cases, principal obstacles to medical care reform. Nor do we believe that any unresolved questions should be answered in a categorical (and quite explicit) fashion. So rather than trying to delineate and justify a particular basic benefits package, we will try to explain why efforts to do so are liable to be counterproductive. We will further argue that the "fundamental questions" are symbolic of several larger developments in the cross-national commentary about medical care, about which we are also less enthusiastic. These developments in the international discussion of health policy include the insistence that difficult questions of public policy be settled openly and definitively, an increased focus on reducing wasteful services and augmenting preventive ones, a blurring of traditional distinctions between medical care and public health policy, and the portrayal of "health care reform" as a global phenomenon.

It should be clear that we are not opposed to the dialogue of change. We are opposed, however, to those policy remedies that depend on fundamental reevaluation of prevailing health policy purposes and programs. This is what we call policy panaceas. Our conviction is that such panaceas represent misdirected energy; hence, our essay moves beyond the central question *to* this broader set of policy prescriptions.

II. Back to Fundamentals: The Case for Universal Access to Basic Medical Care

The arguments for universal access to basic medical care range widely over the philosophical landscape. All begin with the assumption that serious medical need should not be addressed like an ordinary market good. But, from there on, the reasoning for why that is so, the range of medical care to which that justification applies, and the conception of what constitutes a fair result all differ. Some start with the premise that health is the most basic and fundamental of all human needs, and argue from there that the appropriate criterion for the distribution of medical care is medical need.[2] Since natural endowments and the risks of ill-health differ, pursuing this conception requires active redistribution of resources from the well to the sick, from the lucky to the unlucky, and from the more prudent to the less prudent.

Others have argued that health, like nourishment, is perhaps best seen not as a "basic need," but rather as central to the capability and freedom of individuals to pursue their lives as they would like.[3] As Amartya Sen notes, "If people do desire a life without hunger or malaria, the elimination of these maladies through public policy does enhance their liberty to choose to live as they desire."[4]

This is but one of many arguments that sees good health (or freedom from preventable illness) as instrumental to other important values. Another view, associated prominently with Norman Daniels, is that a reasonably egalitarian distribution of initial health status is a precondition for "fair equality of opportunity."[5] The reason we should give more attention and resources to the birth of children with higher risks of injury, chronic illness, or deformity, on this view, is simple. Otherwise, the outcomes of these children's lives would be foreordained by the unfortunate circumstances of their birth and that would be, in principle, unfair. After all, through no fault of their own, these children enter a world where differences in income and status are supposed to represent work and effort, not bad luck.

Alan Buchanan has linked medical care (and decent health status) to free economic participation. His grounds are that market-based rewards are justifiable only if people are sufficiently healthy to participate on fair terms in the economy.[6] J. Donald Moon has maintained that a reasonable level of health is a prerequisite to the exercise of political freedoms.[7]

These are the questions that social and political philosophers have raised throughout the 20th century when discussing the proper distribution of medical care (and health). Indeed, there is a fascinating literature that sets out these various grounds for redistribution, that links those grounds to broad or narrow definitions of what collective financing of care covers and, in more recent times, to the question of how those views are affected by differing views of the determinants of the health status of large populations.[8]

There is, however, what might seem a paradoxical case for largely bypassing this set of basic issues when dealing with "fundamental questions about the future of healthcare." Might we not simply begin by acknowledging that most OECD countries proceed from the assumption that universal access to basic medical services is a widely shared value. Despite widespread assaults on the legitimacy and affordability of many welfare state programs over the past quarter century, no industrial democracy has challenged this view by substantially changing longstanding entitlement to medical care.

Put another way, the case for distributing medical care in ways different from what market processes alone would produce has many types of justifications. One could advocate universal medical coverage on the basis of any of the philosophical arguments noted above, but also on more practical grounds as well, such as compassion or altruism[9] or the need to correct the various market failures inherent in medical insurance markets.[10] But given the broad consensus for universal access to basic medical care, it is not obvious to us that abstract argumentation about the divergent roads to that consensus will help provide discrete answers to pressing policy questions.

III. How Should Limits be Determined?

Having stated this, however, there are immediate issues to face. The values that universal access to basic medical care express will conflict with other important values. There is no escaping the constraints of scarce resources. If adequate medical care were as inexpensive as adequate clothing, health reform would not be as high on the agenda of industrial democracies — as it is.

So, health policy inevitably involves placing limits on the collective financing of medical services. But how should these limits be determined? Increasingly, it seems to us, scholars, physicians, and public officials are insisting that difficult choices about the scope of public provision of medical care be debated openly and decided definitively. While we cannot prove this claim in any statistical sense, consider a few telling anecdotes.

Most obvious was the effort of Oregon to construct a list for ranking the comparative value of all medical procedures. The stated aim of the Oregon plan was to determine which medical services would be reimbursable under the Medicaid program, the state-administered program for some of Oregon's poor. The purposes of that exercise, according to Oregon's reformers, were to save on expensive, low-benefit care so as to extend the coverage of their Medicaid program to the poor and near poor who were not currently insured. As it happened, Oregon both expanded coverage of Medicaid and expended 20 percent more than expected, but the internationally noteworthy feature of its controversy was the effort to ration explicitly by services[11] and to do so through a fairly open process of public deliberation and debate.

There are, of course, many other examples. In 1990, the Dutch Ministry of Welfare, Health, and Cultural Affairs set up a special committee (see later), which a year later issued its widely publicized report, "Choices in Health Care." That such a committee was convened is revealing in itself. Typically, government committees are titled according to the problem they are supposed to address. But the Ministry of Welfare, Health, and Cultural Affairs did not name a "Committee on Medical Costs" or a "Committee on Access to Medical Services." Instead, they named the "Committee on Choices in Health Care." In other words, the Committee title expresses a particular perspective on health policy. The title presumes (or implies) that the difficulties inherent in the collective financing of medical services are best dealt with by highlighting implicit policy tradeoffs.

This viewpoint is expressed even more clearly by the Committee's report. There are, according to the Committee, only three ways to address the problem of increasing demand for medical care: (i) make more money available for care; (ii) avoid wasting money now available; and (iii) make explicit choices about care.[12]

Setting aside the question of whether this list of alternatives is complete (it certainly is not), it is plain that the Committee has framed the problem of rising medical costs in a way that points directly toward open restrictions on care as the only feasible contemporary solution.

Consider another example. The Canada Health Act of 1984 requires that provinces provide "comprehensive" insurance coverage for all "medically necessary" services in order to be eligible for federal grants. However, neither the federal government nor any of the provinces has ever defined the terms "comprehensive" or "medically necessary." As a result, there is some variation in covered services across provinces.[13]

Several provinces have responded to escalating medical costs with efforts at delimiting covered services. (Not only have Canadian medical costs reached nearly 10 percent of GDP, but the federal share of Medicare spending, which was 50 percent in 1977, has declined to 22 percent.) The provinces have decided, in concert with their medical associations, to define the scope of basic services and to de-insure services not found to be "medically necessary." At the same time, both Alberta and the Canadian Medical Association (CMA) have requested that the federal government develop a list of officially sanctioned "core services."

These developments, like the Committee on Choices in Health Care in the Netherlands, reveal a widely shared viewpoint about how public policy can and should work to constrain medical costs. Growing numbers of Canadians appear to believe that carefully defining covered benefits will be effective in curtailing costs. They also seem to believe that choices should be made as openly and clearly as possible. In a recent policy statement, for example, the CMA stated this position bluntly: "CMA advocates a systematic and transparent decision-making framework for determining which services are considered core and comprehensive health care services."[14]

At first glance, it is difficult to object to the CMA stance. What's wrong with being systematic and transparent? Who would argue that a democracy ought to make important choices in a disorderly and covert manner?

The trouble is this. Both the CMA and the Committee on Choices in Health Care apparently treat choices about public health coverage as if they were deciding purely technical questions: Which treatments, at what cost, will prevent which diseases, for what benefit? But the public finance of medical services is an intensely political matter, with the actual results of programmatic action of utmost importance. One implication of this is that decisions can only be evaluated in the context of real-life implementation, not just policy pronouncements. Expressing the right values in medical care — however important for political support and social cohesion — is an insufficient basis for program evaluation. After all, were medical care programs to pursue broadly accepted values in grossly inefficient or unpopular ways, there would be substantial grounds for complaint. On this line of reasoning, it is the design, implementation, and administration of relevant laws and regulations that constitute the "fundamental" contemporary issues in health policy — both in action and in analysis.

Assume for the moment, then, that the implementation of health and healthcare policy should be our focus. What, then, follows? First, recall our earlier point that despite the range of philosophical arguments cited above, one can distill a core consensus among western industrialized nations both philosophically and practically. That consensus is that citizens should have ready access (without serious financial burdens) to adequate medical care.

There is far less consensus, of course, about the means of achieving this objective. For example, Norwegian citizens are likely to be more accepting of direct governmental provision than are Americans. To make the same point another way, health policies (and medical care programs) are likely to be different in different OECD settings despite a common core of objectives. Differences in economic, social, and political circumstances will be part of the explanation, especially the legacy of past commitments and institutional arrangements. Social norms also play an important role in determining what is desirable and possible and will continue to do so. Consider, for instance, the extent of "voluntary" health insurance purchase in the Netherlands, a degree of coverage that to the American policy analyst seems extraordinary.

Given these considerations, what can be said about the allocational decisions that modern societies face in medical care and health policy? First, that there are no easy, new, or universal answers available. All advanced industrial democracies will continue to struggle with the costs and distribution of medical services, and the appropriate strategies for reconciling competing goals will differ across and within countries. Second, there is no reason to presume that open confrontation of difficult allocational choices will facilitate this process. For one thing, part of what citizens want from medical insurance is the reassurance that they will be competently cared for, and not bankrupted, when sick. In our view, this kind of discourse — championed by, among others, Oregon's defenders, the CMA and the Committee on Choices in Health Care — is misleading. It labels medical care as "covered" and "uncovered" in binary fashion; it is likely to encourage needless social conflict and undermine public confidence in the collective medical care system.

Moreover, allocational decisions about medical care can be made in a variety of ways. Alberta, the CMA, and the Committee on Choices in Health Care all want choices to be made by government fiat. But such an approach, while theoretically consistent, leaves little room for the kind of discretion that recognizes the variety of circumstances present in medical treatment. As Diane Marleau, the then Canadian Health Minister, said last year in rejecting Alberta's call for a regimented list of core services: "What's absolutely essential for one person may not be absolutely essential for the other one."[15] Nor are top-down decisions likely to be sufficiently adaptive. It took years and several iterations for Oregon to develop its rank list; yet every week, medical journals report studies that would, in principle, require Oregon to rerank some procedures. And, in any event, the decisions about where the line should be drawn has, in practice, been far less important in Oregon's financial experience with Medicaid than was advertised or understood internationally. In short, considerations of both justice and flexibility suggest that allocational decisions should be made in varied ways, through the interaction of patients, physicians, hospitals, insurance companies, and public officials and of the groups that represent them.

IV. The Push for "Rational" Health Policy Analysis

What is the intellectual genesis of efforts like the Oregon Medicaid plan or the Committee on Choices in Health Care? In large part, they seem to arise from an aspiration to bring rational policy analysis to decisions about the allocation of medical care. It is well known among health policy scholars that the effectiveness of most medical treatments is limited at best, and that the distribution of care is arbitrary, reflecting local practice doctrines and economic incentives more than the dictates of medical effectiveness.[16] Such an apparent squandering of public resources is anathema to policy analysts, and it is no surprise that they urge the "rational" allocation of medical services as a response.

Both the Oregon Medicaid plan and the Committee on Choices in Health Care are clear manifestations of the desire to "rationalize" medical care. A closely related development is the attack on waste. The perpetrators are obvious: excess capacity, useless bureaucratic hassle, medical malpractice, and defensive medicine (particularly in the United States), not to mention the unnecessary tests and procedures resulting from all this and on which most commentators tend to focus.

It may be the case, as many scholars claim, that the medical profession does an inadequate job of evaluating the effectiveness of procedures. But there will always be procedures that, while of unproven benefit, nonetheless offer the possibility of help. And it is unlikely that any set of rules we design can significantly change this dynamic. However untested, therapies will always be sought by patients wanting to improve their lives, while doctors themselves will want to employ them. Monetary incentives certainly play a role, but physicians are also guided by a special professional ethic. Like lawyers who have a duty to do whatever it takes to serve their clients, doctors are committed to doing whatever they can to assist their patients. In the absence of a strong medical consensus about the efficacy of a particular procedure — we rarely perform tonsillectomies any more, and radical mastectomies are increasingly open to question — there is little likelihood that either of the intimate partners in the doctor–patient relationship will ever perceive a significant proportion of medical treatments as simply "wasteful."[17]

Another fact about medical care well known by health policy scholars is that most serious illness and premature death is causally related to individual behavior. So it is hardly surprising that many advocate prevention as a cure to the ailments of our health system. But what if we all ate more wisely, exercised more regularly, abstained from smoking and excess drinking, and led less stressful lives? Certainly we would tend to be healthier. We might even be happier. But the inference that we would, as a result, drastically reduce medical expenditures is, according to scholars who have investigated the possibility, without solid evidence.[18] The point is that prevention can, and has, changed the incidence of disease, but, at best, it can only delay death and dying. Indeed, although preventive practices have served to improve our health record — and there is good evidence that they have in the instances of heart disease and stroke — they have also brought onto the health policy agenda new issues of long-term care and frailty.

Ironically, these advocates of "rational" health policy are not engaging in good policy analysis. Cost-benefit analysis is an important part of policy analysis, but all too often analysts forget that policy analysis also involves making realistic judgments about political institutions, organizational and professional norms, and patterns of individual behavior. Those who predict substantial benefits from a focus on waste are overlooking some of these dimensions of policy analysis, as are those who forecast large savings from prevention.

V. Is "Healthy" Public Policy the Answer?

As noted, many policy analysts, noting the close links between lifestyles and diseases, have argued that prevention should be a central aim of reform in health policy. From there, it is only a small logical step to recognize that many areas of public policy, not just health care policies, can have significant effects on the health of a population. Education and poverty policies perhaps come first to mind. But it takes little effort to expand the list substantially. Environmental laws, automobile safety regulations, drunk driving laws, workplace safety rules, tobacco and alcohol taxes, and gun control — all are plainly relevant to the health of the public. The question this raises is clear: if all these different policies impact health, is not the traditional focus of health policy — the cost, availability, and quality of medical services — too narrow? Should not we redefine health policy as "healthy public policy?"

What does one mean by healthy (or healthier) public policy anyway? Abstractly, the concern is with the impact of public action (constraints and inducements) on actors, settings, and actions that in turn affects the health status of a defined population. So, if the health status of pregnant women is the relevant measure, healthy public policy would mean interventions that increased the healthiness of such women, whatever those might be. In this context, healthy public policy is set off from health care policy; changes in the latter may or may not be core elements in the former. It would all depend upon what policies could improve the health of pregnant women. For example, prenatal checkups and decent midwifery at birth, apart from adequate nutrition during pregnancy, freedom from threats to the baby's health from poverty, drugs, alcohol, and freedom from work-related hazards constitute the most important determinants of variation in the health of the newborn. Healthy public policy would in this instance be easy to comprehend, however difficult in practice it might be to effect the changes that would make a substantial difference. These practical political difficulties — so important in their own right — do not raise conceptual problems.

But there are conceptual problems, nonetheless, in other formulations of what constitutes healthy public policy. Health as understood in the example of newborns is thoroughly conventional and its measurement — rates of infant mortality, morbidity, birthweight, deformity, and the like — involves nothing unorthodox. The attention to causes beyond the individual medical care of the pregnant woman — such as the threats from low income or the environment of work — does widen the focus from a zone of conventional medical care to one that might be labeled the field of health. But the broadening here is exclusively one of causation of ill health, not of conceptions of healthiness.

The political movement for "healthy public policy" has in fact been redefining what one means by health (or healthiness) itself. For example, WHO emphasizes that not only do safer cities and salubrious physical environments make for "healthier" citizens in obvious ways, but that greater political participation by citizens is part of what one means by a healthier policy. It is at this conceptual point that serious difficulties arise.[19]

One may identify a wide range of dimensions of health. Mortality is at one end of the spectrum. This seems to be unambiguous; but even here there is a question. Causes of death of those living to 90 usually do not raise issues of health policy. A quiet death in one's sleep at that age causes no problems other than the understandable loss of those who were emotionally close to the person. On the other hand, premature mortality seems a sure sign of unhealthiness, but it is not clear whether we should consider deaths from drug wars or ethnic hostility in Northern Ireland primarily issues of health policy. That seems odd at the very least. But societies with comparatively high mortality rates for particular subpopulations are appropriate targets for health policy intervention; likewise with morbidity — or sickness — conceptions of health. Preventable morbidity — which the antibiotic revolution did so much to reduce — raises few conceptual problems. While complex and dynamic, the determinants of mortality and morbidity patterns raise all sorts of complexities, but not with respect to what one means by health.

The more broadly defined notions of health and function do, however, generate puzzles. Disease refers to what one reports as discomforting, troublesome, and disquieting. Indeed, depending upon whether one pronounces the term with emphasis on the first or second syllable, the meaning changes from a non-medical to a medical term. Dis-ease normally refers to a condition that experts label, for example, the cardiovascular difficulties that present themselves to sufferers as shortness of breadth, pain of angina, and similar symptoms. It is interesting to notice that in other cases, some conditions that might be worrisome can be transformed from a questionable personal disease to a medical disease. A good example is the labeling shift from gluttony to eating disorder.

The same holds true for what is called functional capacity. A substantial proportion of the population has one or another condition that is chronic, that stays with them over a very long time. Arthritis is an example of a chronic condition that is, in general, incurable. Means to reduce the pain of tasks of everyday life constitute the current agenda of intervention for this condition. It hardly needs emphasizing that coping with these concerns are desperately important to those who suffer from arthritis (or any other chronic condition that is painful and hampers independent living).

The issue is this: what follows if one conceptualizes functional capacity as a measure of healthiness, not as an independent objective? There is no question that the disease arthritis threatens functional capacity. In other words, the cause is diagnostically part of the specialized world of medical care. But the measure of improvement — when cure and reduction of the disease's severity is not possible — widens the scope of what some mean by healthiness. One could, for example, perfectly well say that Jane Jones was not very healthy, but coped very well, lived well, and, indeed, was happier than those with far less burdensome disease conditions. What do we gain by saying that the means by which Ms. Jones deals successfully with the disease she has — the coping mechanisms — are health matters or that she is healthier despite being sicker than someone else? In many chronic conditions, psychological resilience and practical aids constitute more important elements of improvement than can be expected from the world of medicine. Or, to put the matter in population terms, a society that helps people cope better with chronic conditions is better off. What, we should ask, is gained by saying that such a society is healthier? Widening the definition of health to include functional capacity also widens the responsibilities of health policies into an almost unlimited area.

If one extends healthiness to living well, the problems of establishing the borders of health policy become quite serious. It poses an overriding importance of living well. Renaming something as an element of healthiness does not in itself constitute a conceptual advance. One does not say something about wisdom, decency, or competence in living by the change of terms. It is worth asking what explains the broadening of the health concept so considerably. Much of the literature on the determinants of health actually investigates the causes of ill health, not the dimensions of health itself.

The broadening of the concept of health requires more explanation than simply noting the increased interest in the complex and dynamic determinants of health more conventionally understood. This in itself is a large subject in the politics of advanced industrial societies. What we offer here is commentary on one obvious theme: the extent to which the incorporation of social objectives into health is a mechanism to increase support for purposes that, for one reason or another, are less easily supported on traditional grounds.

It is important to emphasize the broadening of what health means, because there is no necessary connection between advocating healthier public policies and widening the definition of health. It would be perfectly possible to treat healthier public policies as those that reduced the incidence and severity of ordinary circumstances of ill health — mortality and morbidity rates, degrees of painful suffering, and so on. Why then tack on healthiness to the wish to make cities more humane, less given to crime, and less frightening to their inhabitants? Why make the case for political participation when it is very difficult to link improvements in this measure of an improved society to conventionally measured progress in health status?

Put this way, the question immediately suggests an answer. Improving — or at least maintaining — the health of populations is a governmental responsibility with long-established legitimacy. The domain of classic public health, understood as health threats to the whole collectivity, is commonplace. Controlling contagion is nowhere challenged as a responsibility of government even if particular efforts are criticized as inadequate, wasteful, or inefficient; not so with objectives like increasing citizen participation in governance, an aim that is in fact deeply contentious. Likewise, improvements in the amenities of urban life — as desirable as they may be in principle — take on greater apparent urgency if associated with impacts on health conventionally understood. And closely related to the legitimacy of health objectives for public policy is the enormous scale of the public budget now distributed to health and health care programs. Our speculation, which we cannot substantiate from either interviews or other data, is that advocates of a widened conception of healthy public policies imagine that substitution of health for medical care program expenditures will be easier than advancing their policy objectives more directly.

It is worth reflecting on this topic as a matter of intellectual history. In the postwar period, industrial democracies moved from the realm of medical research to massive efforts to bring conventional medical care to their entire populations. The Lalonde Report of 1974 was Canada's version of the claim that this effort had achieved much of what could be achieved through the instruments of conventional medical care. The report suggested that greater attention should be paid to personal habits (lifestyle), to the work and general environment, and to other elements in what was defined as "the health field" to produce gains in mortality or morbidity. The target of health status was unchanged; the objects of intervention were considerably broadened. What is interesting (and depressing to note) is that such broadened conceptions of the causal factors implicated in remediable ill health caused very little reallocation of resources in public medical programs within advanced industrial democracies. We need to understand why that was the case before reasserting the need to look more widely at the causes of ill health and to define health more broadly.

Let us put the point more sharply. A movement has taken shape that has as its objectives the improvement of modern societies by simultaneously redefining health more expansively and holding political authorities responsible for improvements in collective health status so understood. This has taken place despite the failure to understand why the priorities of modern governments in the medical care area were so little transformed by the last round of new perspectives in the 1970s. And even where change has taken place — as with improvements in water quality, and, to a lesser extent, air quality — it has taken place through the guidance not of health leaders, but of environmentalists using health arguments in part. Why should a further widening of subject matter advance the cause of either health narrowly understood or healthiness more widely conceived? It may, but the evidence from the impact of the earlier "new perspective on health" is not obviously supportive.

It is naive to assume that identifying a cause of ill health — like poverty — does much in itself to mobilize action against economic want. After all, the basis for broad mobilization around classic public health concerns like contagious diseases is precisely the threat such conditions represent for the bulk of a jurisdiction's population. Self-interest and public action are linked in the threat posed by contagious diseases; coercive regulation is necessary to prevent free-riders from undermining remedies whose beneficent effects depend on generalized compliance. (And, even given that basis, the 19th century's experience with public health measures was one of enormous controversy over the deprivation of freedom that vaccination, sanitation, and other measures threatened.) Not so with poverty in modern societies, where a minority faces low income and where the majority's concern (if it exists at all) arises from grounds other than common health threat. Indeed, if poverty causes ill health and illness care is publicly financed, it might well be that antipoverty means would more efficiently spend funds allocated to health care to the poor. But that is a calculation of the relative effectiveness of prevention versus care. And we are fully aware that prevention is harder to advance politically than programs for care, except when the public is thoroughly scared, as was the case with, for instance, the polio threats of the 1950s or the cancer wars of more recent decades.

It is the assignment of responsibility that lies at the core of the difficulties in translating the insights of epidemiology, not public policy. The wider the set of causes of ill health to which attention is paid, the less the concentration on any one by an accountable official. Moreover, even where accountable officials are alert to the diversity and complexity of causes, the dispersion of the groups whose interests will be harmed (or helped) by public policy intervention makes their tasks more difficult. On the one side, the experts in the causes of trouble are not organized by their common health concern. Their links arise from the specializations involved in studying, quite separately, the dynamics of water pollution (and purification), air pollution (and improvement), slum development (and redevelopment), and so on. Whatever the facts are with respect to health status, this intellectual link to health is not obviously translatable into enduring coalitions; the degree of overlap in health concerns competes with the specializations that everywhere defeat easy exchange among experts, let alone nonexperts.

This much is and has been true for threats to health conventionally understood. Environmental commissioners may welcome support that comes more easily when they add improved health to their list of gains from a cleaner environment. But they do not concede priorities on their agenda to health ministers, even ones who rank the environmental threats to health as terribly important.

Put another way, the constituencies that develop around public programs do not go away or get transformed by intellectual redefinitions of either the causes or consequences of ill health. For the very same reason, officials who feel certain that fewer poor people would mean less sickness cannot be expected to win support among their hospital constituencies for massive reallocation of funds from hospital care to income transfers, let alone legal authority to do so. The competition for funds means that programs already organized around the matter of interest — whether water or air conditions, income or medical care deficits, social services to the elderly, or nursing home operations — are the places where incremental adjustments can be made most easily. The alternative is the starting of new agencies whose purpose reflects the changed perspective. That gives the impetus of organizational survival to the public policy reform. But it also makes the initial innovation the key obstacle to getting started, not the difficulty of convincing those tangentially involved that they should help in the process of improving the health of citizens whose air quality, water quality, or whatever is the prime concern of the relevant official. In short, there is a very small constituency on behalf of health improvement itself, as opposed to particular parts of the world of health and health care that more easily convert into political demanders.

All of this is to suggest why it is hopelessly naive to believe that identifying causes of ill health is sufficient to get changes in public policy. But, while sophisticated conceptions of health and the causes of its improvement and decline are neither the necessary nor the sufficient conditions of public policy reform, they are not irrelevant either.

There is still another way in which the "healthy public policy" movement is terribly naive. If the goal is to coordinate public policy in the pursuit of health, why not, we might ask, merge the equivalent of the Department of Health and Human Services (HHS) and the Environmental Protection Agency (EPA)? After all, not only do the established missions of these governmental organizations overlap, meaning there is currently some unnecessary duplication of tasks, but in a larger sense both organizations should have the same purpose: to improve well-being, however that is defined. To such questions, the healthy public policy movement has no answers. Yet there are sound reasons for keeping organizations like HHS and EPA separated.

For starters, such distinctions help us to understand and make sense of the world of public policy. As cognitive psychologists stress, the human mind understands concepts as much by identifying differences among them as by recognizing similarities. Distinguishing physics from chemistry makes it easier for people to understand science, even though Mother Nature would find the distinction puzzling. For similar reasons, it is helpful to classify public policy as health, education, environmental, and so on.

There are also managerial reasons for keeping HHS and EPA separate. By and large, organizations are more easily and effectively managed when they have, in effect, fewer lines of business. To be sure, consolidation can eliminate redundancies or realize economies of scale. But on balance, very large organizations appear to be less successful than ones of moderate size. Consider that in 1980, the sales of the Fortune 500, a list of America's largest industrial companies, represented over 60 percent of the GDP; today, the share is less than 40 percent.

What we are suggesting is that advocates of healthy public policy ignore the limitations inherent in all human endeavors. Of course, in some sense it would be more rational if the actions of HHS and EPA were perfectly coordinated in pursuit of the common good. But public policy must be organized with the recognition that because citizens possess finite intelligence, skill, and trustworthiness, so too will their institutions. The separation of HHS and EPA, not to mention the various divisions within these organizations, represents a concession to this reality. It is a concession that strikes the healthy public policy movement as irrational; in our view, it is wise and, indeed, inevitable.

VI. Global Health Policy Reform: Misleading Mythology or Learning Opportunity?

In the previous sections, we discussed several trends in the analysis of and commentary on health policy. One of the features shared by these various trends is a propensity to analyze health policy problems and advocate health reform strategies without reference to particular social or political contexts. In this section, we explore another trend cut from this same cloth — the tendency to treat health reform as if it were a coherent global trend.

"Countries everywhere," according to a European newsletter on health policy, "are reforming their health care systems. There cannot be a country in the world," it is claimed, "which is not at least raising questions about the cost of delivery of health care." Moreover, we are told, "what is remarkable about this global movement is that both the diagnosis of the problems and the prescription for them are virtually the same in all health care systems."[20] Within this brief paragraph are two central, but highly questionable assumptions of the group we call "globalists" in health care policy. First, the globalists take for granted that the diagnoses and remedies associated with the so-called "health reform" share the same meaning in different settings. (This view is, *a priori*, implausible, and, as a number of studies show, empirically unsustainable.) Secondly, there is the presumption that, since the problems are similar and the remedies at least analogous, cross-national learning is largely a matter of "establishing a database and information network on health system reform." This trivializes both the need to understand the differing contexts of health policy making and the real threats of mislearning that make appeals to easy cross-national transfer of experience seem so naive.

There is little doubt, however, that there has been globalization of commentary in the world of health care. As Rudolf Klein noted in 1995, none of us can escape the "bombardment of information about what is happening in other countries."[21] Yet, in the field of health policy, there is now a substantial imbalance between the magnitude of the information flows and the capacity to learn useful lessons from that information. Indeed, we suspect that the speed of communication about developments abroad actually reduces the likelihood of sensible learning from those developments. Why might that be so?

There is no doubt about the salience of health policy on the public agenda of EU countries — and, indeed, of most industrial democracies.[22] Canada, whose universal insurance program has been a model for many over the last quarter century, has had a majority of its provinces set up Royal Commissions within the last few years so as to chart adjustments. The United States was an obvious example of a nation struggling with health policy disputes in the early 1990s. Dutch disputes about health policy change have been on-going for nearly a decade and the international interest in the Dutch experience is unprecedented — at least in the United States — in extent if not comprehension.[23]

One could obviously go on with examples of health policy controversies in Germany (burdened by the fiscal pressures of unification), in Great Britain (where criticisms of the Tory Government's policies contributed to its recent defeat in 1996), in Sweden (with fiscal and unemployment pressures of considerable seriousness), and so on. Yet, in our view, the real puzzle is less why medical care is everywhere on the agenda of discussion than why international evidence (claims, reports, caricatures) has been so much more prominent in this most recent round of "reform" debates than, for example, during the fiscal strains of the 1970s. Globalization of inquiry and commentary has undeniably taken place. Times of policy dispute do sharply increase the demand for new ideas — or at least new means to old ends. Over the past 10 years, interest in cross-national experience has increased as has communication of impressions about that experience. Just as many American analysts turned to Canadian and German experience, so did Canadian, German, Dutch, and other intellectual entrepreneurs turn more to international models in recent years.

Despite the increase in cross-national commentary and citation, however, most policy debates in most countries are (and will remain) largely parochial affairs. The debates emphasize national problems; they emphasize national evidence — historical and contemporary — and embody quite different visions of what policies particular countries should adopt. Only rarely are the experiences of other nations — and the lessons they embody — seriously investigated and considered. When cross-national claims are employed in such debates, their use is typically that of policy warfare, not policy understanding and careful lesson-drawing. And, one must add, there are fewer knowledgeable critics at home of ideas about "solutions" abroad, which is both an inducement to use cross-national evidence less carefully and a source of skepticism as well.

VII. Conclusion

We hope this paper would be helpful as well as provocative. We have tried to establish the following major claim, namely, that there are a series of hard questions that must be faced in modern medical care finance, delivery, and organization — even if there turns out to be no new, very bright, or very easy answers. These include:

(i) How to raise the funds to pay for a decent level of medical care?

(ii) How to distribute this financial burden fairly?

(iii) How to place defensible borders on whatever is spent?

(iv) How to assure results that are reasonably reliable and acceptably administered?

Our paper's central question was whether a reconsideration of the fundamental arguments for the social provision of medical care will help in such an exercise. And our subordinate question was whether there are any new answers to these basic questions — answers like redefining the scope of basic medical care services that are collectively financed, eliminating waste and ineffective care, promoting prevention, or, more hopefully, recasting the purpose of the exercise from collective financing of medical care to the more efficient pursuit of what some call "healthy public policy."

In surveying these approaches, we reached two principal conclusions. First, none of these "new" approaches is likely, in practice, to transform how governments address the challenges of contemporary health care policy. That should not be interpreted to mean that concern about ineffective care, wasteful services, prevention, or health promotion is trivial. Rather, understood as panaceas — or even promising new approaches — these policy prescriptions have been oversold in national and international intellectual exchanges. Second, we regard the proliferation of these various policy "solutions" as products of a disturbing trend in the analysis of health and health care programs. That trend can be understood as the widespread belief among many scholars and public officials that public health policy can be radically reformed in ways that would make it much more rational. As we have attempted to demonstrate, this is hopelessly naive in the absence of understanding the critical (and sometimes unique) context in which reform is attempted. But, if the context is crucial and the scope for adjustment is modest, then going back to fundamentals is not naive, but misdirected. In this respect, our paper has reaffirmed the conclusions of broader work on the welfare state. We identified a number of ways not to think about the welfare state, specifying at the same time some simple rules of thumb for what to avoid. One of those rules of thumb addresses the persistence in American social welfare debates of the view that revolutionary, fundamental change was really at hand — whether in welfare, medical care, old age pensions, etc. Our suggestion then, as applicable here to the wider welfare state debates, is that "fundamental change is almost never on the agenda" of modern democracies.[24] To the extent this homily applies, the European Union countries ought to attend to more modest reform suggestions. The dreams of broad transformations — whether covering only "basic services" or the appeal to "healthy public policies" — are not likely to be as helpful as they often appear. Defensible reform is likely to unfold slowly, incrementally, and often without a grand design. It is an evolutionary process, not a revolutionary one. But, precisely because of that, sensible policy commentary should focus principally on the advantages and disadvantages of incremental adjustments, not fundamental reconsiderations.

Endnotes

[†]Originally published in *Health Policy*, Volume 49, Issue 1, Pages 27–43, 1999, © Elsevier Science.

[*]Theodore R. Marmor, Professor of Public Policy & Management, Professor of Political Science, Yale School of Management, New Haven, Connecticut, USA.

[**]David Boyum, Postdoctoral Fellow, Yale University, USA.

[1]This paper was originally prepared for the Dutch Science Council and their inquiry into fundamental questions about the future of health care in the Netherlands. We appreciate their support and the helpful comments of the discussants, M. McKee and P. J. van der Maas.

[2]See, e.g., Williams, B., "The Idea of Equality," in *Problems of the Self* (Cambridge University Press, 1973): 240.

[3]Sen, A., *Inequality Reexamined* (Cambridge: Harvard University Press, 1992).

[4]*Id.* at 67.

[5]Daniels, N., *Just Health Care* (Cambridge: Cambridge University Press, 1985).

[6]Buchanan, A., "The Right to a Decent Minimum of Health Care," *Philosophy and Public Affairs*, 13 (1984): 55–78.

[7]Moon, J. D., "The Moral Basis of the Democratic Welfare State," in *Democracy and the Welfare State*, ed. A. Gutmann (Princeton: Princeton University Press, 1988).

[8]Frank, J. W. and J. F. Mustard, "The Determinants of Health from a Historical Perspective," *Dædalus* 123.4 (Fall 1994): 1–19; Evans, R. G., M. Barer, and T. R. Marmor, eds., *Why Are Some People Healthy and Others Not: The Determinants of the Health of Populations* (New York: Aldine de Gruyter, 1994).

[9]Saas, H.-M., "Justice, Beneficence, or Common Sense?: The President's Commission's Report on Access to Health Care," *Journal of Medicine and Philosophy*, 8.4 (1983): 381–388.

[10]Arrow, K. J., "Uncertainty and the Welfare Economics of Medical Care," *American Economic Review*, 53 (1963): 941–973.

[11]The interested reader can follow some of the Oregon controversy through a series of summer 1991 articles in *Health Affairs*. For a largely neutral effort to describe the Oregon effort, see Fox, D. M. and H. M. Leichter, "Rationing Care in Oregon: The New Accountability," *Health Affairs* (Summer 1991): 8–27; for a scathing critique of the presumptions of the Oregon Plan, see Brown, L. D., "The National Politics of Oregon's Rationing Plan," 28–59. For an effort to answer this critique, see the letter by Oregon officials, "Policy Analysis or Polemic on Oregon's Rationing Plan," and Brown's answer (Winter 1991): 307–312. The irony of all this is that the realities of what Oregon actually has done is nowhere in the policy literature crossing borders. In an evaluation of their "innovation" for a Harvard University program, Jacobs, L., J. Oberlander, and I have discovered this striking fact, see *Journal of Health, Politics, and Law*, 24.1 (Feb. 1999).

[12]Government Committee on Choices in Health Care, *Choices in Health Care* (Rijswijk, Netherlands: Ministry of Welfare, Health, and Cultural Affairs, 1992): 43.

[13]For those readers unfamiliar with the structure of Canadian national health insurance, the following sketch may be helpful. By constitutional dictate, Canadian provinces are dominant in the administration of social policies, including health insurance. The federal role, established first with universal hospital insurance in the late 1950s, and its medical insurance counterpart in the late 1960s, was initially one of financing on average 50 percent of the nation's health expenditures, more in some lower income provinces, less in others. Those transfers came, however, with strings: constraints expressed as the Canada Health Act's principles: universal coverage, comprehensive benefits, public administration, and accessible (including the prohibition of private insurance for publicly financed services). Over time, that federal financing role has diminished and there is constant clamoring about whether national standards can be maintained in the presence of diminished federal fiscal help.

[14]"CMA Policy Summary: Core and Comprehensive Health Care Services," *Canadian Medical Association Journal*, 152 (1995): 740A–740B.

[15]Gray, C., "Public Versus Private Care: Philosophy, Not Economics, Is Shaping the Debate," *Canadian Medical Association Journal*, 153 (1995): 453–455.

[16]The work of John Wennberg has been particularly influential in this regard. See, e.g., Wennberg, J. E., J. L. Freeman, R. M. Shelton, and T. Bubolz, "Hospital Use and Mortality among Medicare Beneficiaries in Boston and New Haven," *New England Journal of Medicine*, 321.17 (26 Oct., 1989): 1168–1173.

[17]For an extended discussion of the conflicting notions of waste, see Blustein, J. and T. R. Marmor, "Cutting Waste by Making Rules: Promises, Pitfalls, and Realistic Prospects," in *Understanding Health Care Reform*, ed. T. R. Marmor (New Haven: Yale University Press, 1994), Ch. 5, 86–106.

[18]Russell, L., *Is Prevention Better Than Cure?* (Washington, D.C.: The Brookings Institution, 1986).

[19]Kickbusch, I., "Healthy Public Policy: A Strategy to Implement the Health for All Philosophy at Various Governmental Levels", in *Healthy Public Policy at the Local Level*, ed. A. Evers (Frankfurt/New York: Campus/Westvie, 1989): 1–6.

[20]Hunter, D., "A New Focus for Dialogue," *European Health Reform: The Bulletin of the European Network and Database*, 1 (Mar. 1995): 1.

[21]Klein, R., "Background Paper" for the Four Country Conference on Health Policy, February 23–27, 1995, Ministry of Health, The Netherlands.

[22]Readers may be puzzled by our reluctance to refer to "reform" simply. The parade of substitutes — health policy, health concerns, and health worries — reflects our discomfort with the marketing features of how the expression is used. "Reform" would be more accurate, the simple description of change without the connotation of necessary improvement. That there are pressures for change in health policy is obvious. Understanding them is part of our gathering's purpose, but actual policies called "reform" can be a benefit, a burden, or, in some cases, beside the point.

[23]Interestingly, the first bulletin of the European newsletter on health reform cited above has a report on "Why the Dutch Health Care System Is Now in Chaos and Confusion," *supra* note 21 at 8.

[24]Marmor, T. R., J. L. Mashaw, and P. Harvey, *America's Misunderstood Welfare States: Persistent Myths, Continuing Realities* (New York: Basic Book, 1992) Ch. 7.

Medicare and Political Analysis: Omissions, Understandings, and Misunderstandings†

T. R. Marmor*, S. Martin** and J. Oberlander***

I. Introduction

The focus of this chapter requires some explanation. It is not a recapitulation of the patterns of Medicare's politics from enactment in 1965 to the present (2003). That is the subject of Jonathan Oberlander's other article in this issue. Nor is the main focus on projections of Medicare's future politics, a daunting topic addressed only briefly here. Instead, the chapter aims to make sense of the scholarly literature on the Medicare program and its politics by distinguishing among (and discussing) three categories of commentary:

(i) program and policy discussion without political analysis: the literature of straightforward omission;
(ii) program and policy discussion with serious political analysis: the literature of commendable commission;
(iii) program and policy evaluation that purports to incorporate political analysis, but fails to do so credibly: the literature of regrettable misunderstanding.

Why focus on the existing Medicare scholarship and, in particular, the quality of political analysis in that literature? Our fundamental premise is that the Medicare program is regularly misunderstood through ignorance of its political history, confusion about its fundamental values, and distortion of the program's choices by unsubstantiated presumptions about what Medicare's purposes were supposed to be. The future of Medicare is certain to be a matter of political concern in the decade ahead. Prudent reform depends crucially on clarifying what the program does and does not do. That, in turn, requires attention to Medicare's central social aims, actual historical experience, and recognizable political identity. Our literature search revealed serious difficulties on all three counts.

Our survey of the Medicare literature illustrates just how often Medicare is misunderstood and how rare cogent analysis of its politics is. If the public debate on Medicare is to be improved in these respects, we need to identify and understand common misconceptions about the program and explain their apparent staying power. That is the aim of this chapter.

II. The Literature of Straightforward Omission: Program and Policy Discussion Without Political Analysis

The dominant literature on Medicare is what many call health services research.[1] The great majority of researchers working on Medicare understand the program predominantly from the perspective of systematic policy analysis and consequently view public policy largely as collective problem solving. Often trained in economics, they have produced a vast literature on the impact of Medicare payment policies, the structure of its benefit package, and the economic behavior, demographic characteristics, and financial state of Medicare beneficiaries.[2] This line of scholarship suggests that if there were more factual understanding of Medicare's circumstances, the quality of problem solving would improve. And this work presumes that public policy can and should be studied as a matter of objective, technical inquiry.

Health services research rests on the assumption that policy is separable from politics. This is, as we will argue, in most respects an unsustainable division. The technocratic perspective has at least three consequences for understanding Medicare politics that we want to highlight. The first is that the politics of Medicare is willfully ignored. Since the two phenomena of policy and politics are presumed to be distinct, the analysis of policy, as a matter of division of labor, need not explicitly attend to political analysis. Medicare policy in this tradition is discussed independently of American political institutions, interests, and ideologies.

The literature on Medicare's reform of its system for paying physicians is an illuminating case in point. In 1989, the federal government replaced the existing method of paying physicians retrospectively for their costs with a prospectively determined fee schedule. The fee schedule — officially the Resource Based Relative Value Scale or RBRVS — was organized around the relative values assigned to all services that physicians provided. These valuations in turn were based on estimates of the resources (e.g., time, training, complexity) required by each service.

Health services researchers seriously debated whether the new payment scale accurately reflected differences in physician effort and if it represented an efficient means of reimbursement.[3] They never, however, raised obvious questions about the politics of the payment scheme: how did it change the balance of power in Medicare policy making?; which interests and institutions did it advantage?; what were the implications for democratic accountability of adopting a highly complex payment system dependent on bureaucratic expertise?; why had the United States cloaked a fee schedule for Medicare in such highly technical terminology when other nations such as Canada and Germany did so via straightforward political bargaining and negotiation between providers and payers?[4] In short, the evaluative literature largely ignored the political implications of payment reform.

Marilyn Moon's *Medicare: Now and in the Future* provides another clear illustration of the literature of omission.[5] Moon's intent is to provide an overview of the program since its enactment in 1965. She aims to explain this "fascinating and complex health care program" on the presumption that it is "often not well understood."[6] In this task, Moon succeeds brilliantly, providing a lucid account of the policy challenges confronting Medicare.

A striking feature of this volume is its mix of clear description and political inattention. So, for example, Moon deftly describes the program's expansion of beneficiaries in the 1970s from an elderly constituency to both the disabled and those suffering from renal failure. Her book uses Medicare's fiscal realities to criticize two myths that appear regularly in Medicare debates. She notes correctly that after 1985, Medicare's annual rate of increase in per capita expenditures fell below that of private health insurance outlays for comparable coverage. Second, she debunks the claim that increasing numbers of Americans above 65 years of age "must be a major factor in Medicare's growth."[7] With the number of beneficiaries at that time increasing by 1.1 percent per year, aging could not possibly account for the much larger annual growth in Medicare's expenditures. Moon's book is a financial and demographic account that sets the record straight on many key topics.

What Medicare spent, to whom and for whom, is what this book illuminates best. Moon's analysis is a comprehensive and compelling account of policy issues in Medicare reform, past and present. Yet, when discussing Medicare's possible future, Moon's analysis proceeds as if one were discussing the United States as a person, someone facing a set of future developments and wondering what would be best to do. Indeed, this mode is hardly restricted to Moon's volume, but rather is characteristic of the great bulk of contemporary policy analysts. The political world in which programs operate is acknowledged, but not analyzed, and sophisticated policy analysis is not matched by the same commitment to political analysis. Instead, the approach is to start with the nation as a person, ask what are the problems at present, and assume that rational agents will review options and choose sensible means to agreed-upon ends. Moon, like others in this craft tradition, knows this is unrealistic. (In fact, she uses the term "messy" to describe the fight over catastrophic coverage in 1988–1989.)[8] But, that does not carry over into explicitly taking the political advantages and disadvantages of options — past, present, or in the future — into account.

Not surprisingly, the citations of work in this policy analysis tradition overlook most of the political analysis of Medicare that has been published. As justification, analysts like Moon might well contend that disciplinary specialization has important benefits and that economists like her should write about what they know best. After all, it is better to leave out misunderstandings than, as we shall see in the discussion later, to generate political myths. As noted, Moon is not at all atypical in her inattention to political analysis. Indeed, it is possible to pick almost any health services research journal and find articles on the past, present, or future of Medicare that exhibit the same pattern. Consider, for example, the 1999 article, "Restructuring Medicare for the Next Century: What Will Beneficiaries Really Need?," by Christine Cassel *et al.*[9] This exercise in futurology notes the "tight political and fiscal constraints surrounding Medicare reform," but leaves the matter there.[10] It describes unrealistically only two choices (for the nation?). One option would allow current and future generations to enter the existing system of fragmented and poorly prioritized care, which has proved to impose heavy cost burdens on families and society. The other would structure health care policy in a way that promotes healthy and successful aging, enabling older adults to remain productive and independent.[11]

This dichotomy is a rhetorical device. It is neither a realistic choice nor a forecast of the political and economic circumstances in which the favored direction might be actually chosen. The aim is to defend one particular policy option, not to estimate what it might take to have that option adopted or implemented. As a vision of what Medicare might be, this normative stance is perfectly understandable. As a policy option whose prospects are understood, it lacks the understanding of what political context might favor the proposed change in Medicare's operations.

A second consequence of the technocratic perspective embodied by health services research is that the assumption that policy analysis should be undertaken separately from political analysis occasionally slips into the analytic assumption that policy is made — and therefore can be explained — without politics. Medicare policy is interpreted as technical responses to technical problems; efficiency substitutes for politics as an explanation of how policy change occurs. To wit, in Arnold Epstein and David Blumenthal's account of physician payment reform, the "[r]ecognition of deficits in the CPR methodology" motivates policymakers to reform Medicare.[12] The authors dubiously cite methodological deficiencies as more important to the adoption of payment reform than the federal budgetary deficits that propelled policymakers' interests in Medicare during the 1980s.

If analysts explain Medicare primarily as a rational process of responding to the imperatives of efficiency, they overlook critical questions: how do issues come to be considered policy problems?; how do we account for the timing and form of policy proposals? and what explains the relative political attractiveness of policy solutions? These are questions about the politics of ideas and the construction of policy issues and alternatives that a rationalist perspective on Medicare cannot answer, and usually does not ask.

A final consequence of the separation of policy from politics is the normative conclusion that policy should be separated from politics. Policy analysts often deplore the distorting impact of politics on their carefully designed policy solutions. There is palpable frustration that the political world will not accept the expert advice that the policy world offers. Policies are interpreted as failing to achieve their goals, because politics prevents their adoption in the required form or ruins its implementation.

As a result, the policy prescriptions of health services researchers sometimes seek to quarantine policy from politics. Thomas Rice and Jill Bernstein exemplify this tendency in their 1990 discussion of an ideal reimbursement system for Medicare. They explain that "creation of an objective, fair way to establish performance standards [for setting limits on Medicare payments to hospitals and physicians] would minimize political influence," while the task remains of "ensuring that this formula rather than political influence is the driving force behind the standards and fee updates."[13] Medicare, in other words, must be isolated from politics if it is to operate efficiently. This conclusion leads the authors to favor a payment policy controlled by formula rather than by politics.

The attraction of policy analysts to politically-immune policies is grounded in economic understandings of politics. Economists tend to see public policies as the product of the preferences of social interests whose political power is in turn a function of their economic power.[14] Political institutions do not occupy a prominent place in these scholars' analyses, and there is little consideration given to the independent potential of government actors to act apart from and even against the agenda of social interests. Nor is there attention to the role of ideas in the policy process. Policy making is instead understood as driven by the pathologies of interest group politics. In the language of political economy, rent seeking economic interests influence governmental policy in order to maximize their financial welfare. The result is widespread skepticism about government regulation, preference for market solutions, and, where politics do reside within the government's sphere, preference for policies and institutions that are shielded from political influence.[15]

The failure, then, of much of the Medicare literature to attend to politics is not simply a failure of explanation. If prescription is the aim of policy commentary on Medicare, it is difficult to justify ignorance of the political institutions and circumstances through which policies are chosen and implemented. Useful policy analysis ultimately depends on political analysis, just as good political analysis must be informed by policy analysis. The disjunction between Medicare policy and politics is intellectually unsustainable. An understanding of Medicare requires knowledge of its politics because what has taken place and will take place emerges from the central political institutions of American government.

Indeed, there is an argument that policy studies should take as their aim the narrowing of disagreement about what are the actual states of affairs, the elucidation of competing values represented in alternate courses of action, and the sensitizing of policymakers and other audiences to complex considerations that lie below the noise of policy warfare. "The contribution [to shaping public policy] is likely to come through more informed debate, more substantial argument, and more reasoned limits on unrealistic alternatives, not wholesale transformation of the processes of policy making."[16]

III. The Literature of Commendable Commission: The Political Analysis of Medicare

This category of commentary is much less extensive than the apolitical approaches just discussed. One striking feature of the scholarship on Medicare's politics is the sharp disjunction between the substantial attention paid to the program's origins and the relative inattention to the politics of Medicare in operation. In the decade of the 1960s, a number of books discussed the legislative battle over what came to be known as Medicare.[17] In the three decades and more since, few books have sought to reinterpret the story of how Medicare came to legislative enactment. Sheri David's 1985 account is one, and Lawrence Jacobs's 1993 comparative study of the role of public opinion in the birth of Medicare and the British National Health Service is the other.[18] Both raise issues worth attending to in contemporary discussions of Medicare reform.

David contends that "[b]efore [the United States] can sensibly proceed to solve present and future health care problems," there must be an examination of the "choices, options, and compromises made during the entire Medicare debate."[19] An ample documentary account of those debates, David's book does not, however, make a persuasive case that understanding Medicare's origins is the necessary precondition for righting the wrongs of contemporary American medical care.

Jacobs's book is directly relevant to the politics of contemporary Medicare. His is a case study of the important role that public preferences and understandings play in creating health policy.[20] Jacobs relies on primary research to substantiate claims that the central political figures in the Medicare legislative struggle took (what they regarded as) public opinion into account.[21] Jacobs thus challenges the argument in the work of both Oberlander and Marmor that the mass public plays a minor (and largely restraining) role in the details of Medicare policy making.

Jacobs's findings, which were based on archival and interview sources, improve the understanding of developments that other commentaries ignore. He found, for example, important splits between the architects of Medicare in the Department of Health, Education, and Welfare (HEW) and fiscally cautious leaders in the Bureau of the Budget. The former favored conciliation and accommodation with American medical care providers — especially using private insurance companies as fiscal intermediaries — so as to make the road to their national health insurance dreams more likely. The latter — the federal budget officials — regarded the control of expected inflation as primary and thought the direct federal administration of Medicare would control costs more reliably. That was a fateful policy choice — a victory for HEW's accommodation policy. And, Jacobs's book reveals a hidden part of Medicare's administrative birth that remains an important issue today.

The political analysis of Medicare in operation has been modest in amount, almost all article length, and much less connected to the general features of American politics than was the case with the fight over the program's enactment. Jonathan Oberlander's book, published in 2003, is a recent development, and his bibliography provides the basis for our generalization about the literature.[22]

There are nonetheless a number of illuminating accounts of why the Medicare program has developed as it has. Timothy Jost's account of the administrative politics of Medicare — while concentrating on the role of courts — parallels the understandings of both the Marmor and Oberlander volumes about the patterns of policy making. These include the congressional domination of much of Medicare's policy making, the prominence of fiscal politics in the period since 1983, and the relative weakness of public opinion in expanding Medicare's benefits and its relative strength in constraining large-scale reductions of benefits.[23] The importance of all three considerations in what Medicare's fate will be in the future makes this kind of work especially relevant to contemporary policy analysis.

Broader accounts of American politics in the 1990s provide additional understanding of the forces that shape Medicare's fate now and in the future. The work of Mark Peterson on changing patterns of congressional decision-making is one example.[24] Equally relevant is Lawrence Jacobs's and Robert Shapiro's recent scholarship on public opinion, which confirms the important role of the views of the mass public in constraining efforts to restrict Medicare's benefits and its lesser impact on other features of Medicare policy making in the decade.[25] Also important is an article by Lawrence Brown in the *Health Care Financing Review* that explicitly addresses the theme of this essay, namely, the relative ease with which policy analysts describe the "problems" that "need" fixing and the truly complicated politics of Medicare reform in the first half of the 1990s.[26]

The purpose of this section is not to review the entire field of useful analysis of Medicare's politics. Rather, it is to sharply distinguish efforts that take politics into account and those that do not. David Smith's new book, *Entitlement Politics*, illustrates well the former category,[27] in dealing, for example, with how to explain the character of the Breaux–Thomas Bipartisan.

Commission on the Future of Medicare in the late 1990s, Smith relies on the roles, personnel, and prior commitments of the actors.[28] He concentrates on explaining the commission, though he addresses the evaluation of policy options as well. The commission "as an exercise in bipartisan collaboration. . . was a dismal failure that, at best, provides cautionary lessons for the future."[29] Never "a serious effort to come together in a genuine bipartisan way," the commission, Smith rightly argues, was an "episode in the continuing struggle over the future of Medicare."[30] [M]ost of the [commission's] appointees were, in fact, "major players in that conflict, with strong political and program commitments of their own."[31]

Any appeal to bipartisan commissions in the future should attend to such a cautionary analysis. The same applies to interpreting the persistent appeal in contemporary Medicare debates to the advantages of "competition" in reforming the program. Smith's summary is contestable, but calls for serious analysis. "Despite the lack of systematic evidence or even persuasive argument," he contends, "confidence in the efficacy of market competition to constrain the costs of managed care plans seems to be an unexamined belief based upon occasional behavior, a few regional examples, or faith."[32]

Jonathan Oberlander has written the most comprehensive and extended account of what Medicare's politics have been like.[33] He divides the policies and politics into three categories: (i) disputes about benefit policies, with a pattern of what might be termed nondistributive politics;[34] (ii) financing policy issues, where the pattern has been one of recurrent crisis politics;[35] and (iii) federal payment policies, where the politics have centered on Medicare's impact on the federal budget.[36] Again, the point is not to explore the content of the patterns; Oberlander's article does that. Rather, it is to highlight the absence of such portraits in the conventional treatment of Medicare policy making.

IV. The Literature of Regrettable Misunderstanding: Program and Policy Evaluation with Misleading Political Analysis

The current discussion of Medicare, like its history, includes considerable disagreement, with frustrating gaps between claims and evidence.[37] Here, we emphasize an especially important source of distortion, namely policy commentary that reflects careless and misleading political analysis. This problem is unmistakable in the arguments voucher proponents made in the debate over Medicare's future during the late 1990s.[38] In this section, we address four aspects of what we regard as myth-ridden debate: (i) the unsubstantiated invocation of public opinion to justify policy judgments; (ii) misplaced confidence in long-term forecasts and inattention to the interaction of economic and political factors in forecasting; (iii) contestable claims presented as "conventional wisdom"; and (iv) explicit political analysis without understanding. We rely on arguments for vouchers to illustrate the problematic use of public opinion and the limits of political forecasting. Addressing misconceptions in the conventional wisdom and limited political analysis broadens our focus beyond vouchers. But, throughout, we aim to clarify the Medicare debate by approaching these topics as political scientists, a perspective too often absent from the larger national debate.

A. How Not To Use Public Opinion

Enthusiasm for converting Medicare into a system of voucher payments culminated, as noted, in the majority-supported proposal of the Breaux–Thomas Commission and its subsequent introduction as legislation.[39] To see how voucher advocates have justified these plans analytically, we turn to the work of economists Henry Aaron and Robert Reischauer, whose writings on vouchers have been especially extensive, if in the end still disappointing. The reputation for thoughtfulness of these scholars makes the imprecision of their Medicare political analysis all the more troubling. Their 1995 *Health Affairs* article, "The Medicare Reform Debate: What Is the Next Step?,"[40] is a particularly revealing illustration of misleading political analysis.

The scope of their article is quite broad: the proposal to convert Medicare "from a 'service reimbursement' system into a 'premium support' system."[41] They liken this proposal to "many that are now reshaping private employer-based insurance."[42] They purport not only to describe the technical issues that "cannot be solved quickly" and "preclude quick budget savings," but also to provide a brief history of Medicare and why it is unsustainable in its present form.[43] In short, they engage in historical characterization, political analysis, policy evaluation, and program forecasting. They also take pains to caution readers that "[t]he history of reforms in United States social policy is replete with exaggerated claims of the benefits the reform will produce. To muster enthusiasm, supporters of reform paint rosy pictures of the marvelous benefits that will ensue if only their recommendations are adopted."[44] They could have added that reform advocates regularly invent political analysis to bolster their claims of expertise. Aaron and Reischauer have many sensible things to say about how Medicare has operated and why cost savings are difficult under any implementable reform. However, their characterization of Medicare's political history and contemporary political circumstances is simply misleading.

The most striking feature of this kind of analysis is misplaced analytical confidence. Here, we will summarize and focus on a subset of factual claims and their supposedly obvious "implications" to illustrate the weaknesses of this sort of political analysis.[45] The claim that Medicare's "popularity" is not only "overwhelming" but well deserved, because the program has achieved all its designers' major objectives"[46] is clearly contestable. The authors cite no evidence to support their claims about the breadth and depth of the public's views.[47] While the work of Larry Jacobs and other public opinion scholars establishes that Medicare enjoys broad approval, that same work undercuts the easy connection between knowledge of the program (especially the extent to which objectives are understood to have been satisfied) and support for the program.[48] To the extent Medicare is broadly popular, that support mostly reflects a relatively superficial understanding of Medicare's role in helping America's elderly with large medical expenses.[49] Other than that, the public is largely uninformed.[50]

Nor can it be the case that the public is satisfied, because the major objectives of Medicare's designers have all been achieved. That, of course, is one of the major conclusions of the program's history: the key objective of expansion has not been achieved.[51] The original hope was that Medicare would grow into universal health insurance, not coverage only for the elderly, the disabled, and those suffering from renal failure.[52] Moreover, the reformers anticipated that Medicare would largely remove financial fearfulness from the lives of older Americans facing sickness, injury, and other medical burdens.[53] That, as Marilyn Moon and others have aptly demonstrated, has not been accomplished for a variety of reasons.[54] Because the claims are factually false, so are the causal connections.

Moreover, if Aaron and Reischauer's factual claims about politically relevant factors are questionable, the "implications" drawn are equally suspect. None of them are "straightforward"[55] in the sense that reasonable analysts could not find grounds for questioning their normative plausibility or predictive accuracy. Consider one claim where the grounds for objection are quite obvious: the assertion that "congressional reforms will — and should — bring Medicare more in line with the structure of health care financing and delivery that is evolving to serve the non-Medicare population."[56]

Underlying this claim is the view, later made explicit, that Medicare should be adapted to what itself is "evolving" as a practical matter of avoiding resentments.[57] This claim assumes, but does not substantiate, the belief that Medicare's operation should resemble the health insurance practices other Americans confront, irrespective of any demonstrated superiority of the "evolving" practices and public support for them. That assumption ought to invite skepticism on nonnative grounds, but the more important point for present purposes is an empirical one. Simply put, there is no credible evidence for the prediction that voucher enthusiasm will arise from resentment about the elderly having a broader set of choices than younger Americans. By our reading, the existing evidence actually suggests just the opposite.

To understand the public's likely response to such ideas, one must recognize that Medicare vouchers presume a large shift to managed care organizations.[58] The interpretation of resentment by voucher enthusiasts thus requires a groundswell of support for moving the elderly into managed care. But therein lies an immediate puzzle. How can that be reconciled with the evidence about the public's critical views of the managed care industry? A managed care backlash has by now become a well-established finding in research on the public's views on health care.[59] The evidence of a backlash against managed care reflects considerable frustration with constraints on patient choice.[60] But, it is not at all obvious that such frustration has led to any resentment of Medicare's benefits. Indeed, the opposite seems more plausible. If the reactions embodied by the efforts to legislate a "patient's bill of rights" are any indication, the general public's dissatisfaction with "choice" will more likely produce more vigorous efforts to make private health care more like "traditional" Medicare.[61]

What explains such ill-supported claims of resentment? Two accounts come to mind. The first (and, we hope, least likely) possibility is that voucher proponents, as trained economists, see little value in the systematic study of public opinion. In this view, appealing to public opinion is often little more than storytelling, a sort of fanciful speculation about what sorts of attitudes might exist that would justify a particular overhaul of Medicare. Casual speculation is not, however, a basis for credible policy analysis. The second, more generous interpretation, is that these claims rest on a distinctive reading of the available data. It is true, for instance, that younger cohorts typically express less support for Medicare and greater skepticism about the program's future than do older cohorts.[62] To note these differences is one thing. To interpret them as evidence of generational resentment is quite another.[63] In this case, the inferential leaps do not withstand serious scrutiny. In the first place, they require stability in cohort-specific preferences over time that is unlikely. Second, they disregard the likelihood that the preferences of younger cohorts may largely reflect their relative ignorance of Medicare's operation.

If the problems with Aaron and Reischauer's treatment of public opinion were idiosyncratic, there would be no point belaboring them. Unhappily, the weakness of their approach is representative of many Medicare analysts. The failure to attend seriously to public opinion research on Medicare reflects a troubling tendency in much health services scholarship. In this sense, Aaron and Reischauer exemplify a broader problem. Economists, in particular, all too frequently practice a strain of policy analysis that treats the "political" part of political economy as barely more than an afterthought.[64] To be sure, one might expect a tilt toward a scholar's home discipline.[65] In our view, however, the emphasis on economic analysis at the expense of politics needs rebalancing.

That rebalancing requires eliminating casual appeals to mass attitudes, and, instead, substituting attention to the existing research on public opinion. This research makes clear that the mapping of attitudes expressed in public opinion surveys onto specific policy proposals is rarely straightforward.[66] Substantial uncertainty and unclear preferences can be masked in responses to questions about policies as removed from public understanding as is Medicare.[67] Moreover, as Ion Oberlander has argued, public opinion has, at moments, stopped Medicare reform, but it has never driven it.[68] It typically has a more negative impact on policy making, serving to constrain policy options rather than create them.[69] To the extent it has been influential, it has set limits on efforts to transform Medicare, particularly serving to constrain program cutbacks.[70] Insofar as voucher proposals can be seen as an attempt to cut back public benefits indirectly, there is no demand for them from the public.[71] As congressional Republicans learned during the 104th Congress, Medicare cutbacks are extremely difficult to achieve in the absence of clear public mandates for change.[72]

Public opinion, properly understood, may doom voucher reforms. But it did not produce them, and it provides little support for making Medicare into a system of vouchers. There may well be a defensible rationale for vouchers, but it cannot be found in the evidence available from research on American public opinion.[73]

B. The Perils of Prediction

Another issue raised by politically presumptive writing concerns predictions about the political agenda over time. The commentary on Medicare, as with other programs, is regularly accompanied by claims about what the future will be like years and decades into the future.

Our contention is that configurations of partisan balance and economic circumstances cannot be easily anticipated, and that all-to-common overconfidence in speculation on these subjects is, at the very least, unwarranted. Aaron and Reischauer provide a reminder of the importance of prudent political analysis with the boldness of theft claims about the future. Take, for instance, the assertion that "the cost of providing Medicare benefits is projected to rise very rapidly and will exceed projected revenues by ever larger amounts."[74] It was obvious in 1995 that Medicare's projected costs were rising and that the revenues would likely rise less rapidly than the forecasted costs. But, that merely illustrates a truism: Forecasts are not so much serious predictions as conditional claims whose truth depends entirely on the accuracy of the premises.[75] By 2000, the view that Medicare's costs would continue to rise at 10 percent per year into the indefinite future[76] seemed odd indeed.

Likewise, the prediction that comprehensive health care reform would remain off the "political agenda... for years to come,"[77] illustrates easy extrapolation rather than serious forecasting. In 1995, Washington insiders, reeling from the Clinton reform debacle, were predisposed to think that health care reform was over for as far as the eye could see.[78] They turned out to be wrong, as health care issues returned to the agenda in limited form.[79] Indeed, by 2000, health reform issues arose again in connection with that year's election. Both candidates seeking the Democratic presidential nomination unveiled serious proposals for health care reform — this on top of months of congressional attention to reforms of the health insurance industry embodied in the so-called "Patients' Bill of Rights."[80] According to a November 1999 poll by the *New York Times* and *CBS News*, health care topped the list of issues the public most wanted Congress and the president to address.[81]

The reappearance of health care reforms on the national agenda is a reminder that political forecasting is always an exercise fraught with uncertainty. Scholars of agenda-setting have established that the ebbs and flows of political agendas are a complex product of many forces. Each of these forces is subject to considerable uncertainty at any given time, and their combination is even more difficult to predict.[82] Periods of continuity can coexist with sudden and large changes in policy agendas.[83] While agenda scholars understand the families of factors that affect both the incremental and dramatic dynamics of policy debates, they are incapable of anticipating the precise timing and consequences of these factors as they interact. As a result, one should view point predictions of future political agendas with great skepticism.[84]

The futurology of Aaron and Reischauer, as with their use of public opinion, is important because it conforms to wider practices that have long plagued Medicare policy analysis. Medicare's harshest critics have regularly engaged in a form of "future dread," where they dress up projections of Medicare's financial status decades into the future with an unjustifiable certainty.[85] Such long-range projections are notoriously sensitive to even slight changes in their underlying components. Witness, for example, the difference between HCFA's 1995 projection that kick-started the current debate over massive changes and its report just four years later that projected an additional 13 years of "solvency."[86] For good reason, sensible analysts approach long-range forecasts with caution. But, the same logic that recommends caution in projecting a program's financial future also requires restraint in using those very same projections to make the case for major changes from current policy.

To do otherwise, as when proponents of restructuring Medicare forecast a future of certain crisis, is to misuse such long-range projections. The need for an honest recognition of the limits of forecasting increases in the case of Medicare, where the environment is marked by frequent technological change and is embedded in a larger and changing world of private and public health care.[87] Of course, this point is not lost on analysts as experienced as Aaron and Reischauer. Indeed, Aaron himself recently issued similar cautions, going so far as to assert that "a fog of fundamental unknowability shrouds projections of Medicare costs beyond just a few years?"[88]

The uncertainty about Medicare's future costs is but one limitation on confident forecasting. It is compounded by the dependence on such forecasts in the service of promoting current proposals for reform. Too often, the desire to rationalize policy prescriptions masks inherent risks of long-range forecasts — a danger that even the most thoughtful analysts face. When such impulses are combined with a failure to recognize the even greater difficulty in forecasting politics (as opposed to demographics or economics), the dangers of what we have described as unfounded futurology are maximized. The result is all too often fear-mongering masquerading as forecasting, a practice that distorts one's understanding of Medicare's current problems and future possibilities.[89]

C. Confusions of Conventional Wisdom

Another source of confusion in the Medicare debate arises from claims reported as current conventional wisdom about the program's future. One such mistaken view asserts that, because Medicare faces financial strain, the program requires dramatic transformation.[90] The experience of the 1980s and much of the 1990s showed that Medicare's administrators, when willing and able, could limit the pace of increase in the program's costs.[91] Consider, also, that Medicare controlled its spending growth more tightly than did private health insurance during most of the last two decades[92] — even though private insurance was undergoing massive changes aimed at controlling costs during this period.[93] To be sure, controlling the program's future costs poses undeniable challenges to policymakers just as it has before. Mustering the political will to implement cost-control measures is no small feat. But, it is worth remembering that policy makers have managed the task in the past without having to reshape Medicare radically.[94]

The very language used to define the financial problems Medicare undoubtedly faces is another source of distortion. Republican as well as a number of Democratic critics continue to use the fearful language of insolvency to describe Medicare's future.[95] That future, according to this group, is a dreaded one in which the program's trust fund will be literally "out of money."[96] This language represents the unfortunate triumph of metaphor over thought.[97] Thinking that Medicare's trust fund is its crucial fiscal variable is analogous to thinking that a thermometer's reading constitutes a heat wave or a freeze.[98] The program's hospital 'trust fund' refers to an accounting term, a conventional way to describe earmarked revenue and spending."[99]

The very notion of a public trust fund combines the language of trust with the funding-source reality of payroll taxes to underscore the solidity of commitment to finance promised benefits in social insurance programs.[100] The appeal to "insolvency" as a danger needs to be recognized for its symbolic and strategic value in framing the debate over Medicare. Such symbolic framing can be politically consequential.[101] For that very reason, though, policy analysts should guard against misleading symbols. Whatever its psychological and political importance, the trust associated with the fund is a fiscally neutral element in the goods and services Medicare finances. Congress can change the taxes that finance Medicare if it has the will. Likewise, it can change the benefits and reimbursement provisions of the program. Or it can do some of both, as it has at different times in Medicare's operational history. Channeling the program's revenues through something called a "trust fund" changes nothing in the real political economy. Thinking so is the cause of much muddle, unwarranted fearfulness, and misdirected energy.[102]

D. Explicit Political Analysis Without Sufficient Evidence

A final category of regrettable misunderstanding of Medicare is analysis that is explicitly political in its aims, but that proceeds without sufficient appreciation of Medicare's actual experiences. Here, political and programmatic analysis rests on deductive reasoning, economic assumptions, and theories about the behavior of government and political actors that substitute for empirical analysis of Medicare.

This type of analysis follows a predictable script with government programs portrayed as inefficient, financially uncontrollable, constraining of individual choice, and ineffective. The market is alternatively cast as efficient, effective at controlling the costs of medical care, and promoting choice. The irony of this tale is that its widespread prevalence in health economics contrasts with its amazing lack of veracity as a framework for accurately understanding health policy or describing modern health systems.[103] To name but one of many problems with this perspective, the presumption that market competition controls medical care spending coexists with the reality that the United States has more market competition in its health system than any other industrial democracy, and yet, far and away spends the most on medical care. This seeming conflict does not prompt rethinking the role of markets in medical care, because the political economy conclusion stems not from empirical analysis but from unsupported presumption. Health economist Roger Feldman thus scolds his fellow economists for not doing enough to prove the obvious by offering "a cogent analysis of why government control of health care does not work."[104]

This conflation of normative values with political analysis is abundantly evident in the literature of positive political economy on Medicare. So, for example, Ronald Vogel, a public choice analyst, presumes it is entirely predictable that "Medicare began with structural flaws and continues to contain structural flaws. . ."[105] What is left unsaid is that from this perspective all government social programs are, a *priori*, presumed to be inherently flawed, because they disrupt the virtues of the competitive market. Accordingly, Vogel dismisses the ability of federal payment policies such as DRGs to control Medicare spending. Incredibly, he does so by citing a single study that is not primarily concerned with Medicare and without reference to the work of Marilyn Moon and others documenting Medicare's success in cost control relative to private insurance.[106] This illustration is an unfortunately egregious one of normative commitments masquerading as analysis, thereby producing conclusions based on presumption rather than careful engagement with the evidence.

Mark Pauly offers another illustration of explicit political analysis without understanding. Pauly sets out to explain, from a political economic perspective, "why the United States provides mixed public (Medicare) and private (Medigap) insurance for the elderly."[107] Finding that "there is no definitive efficiency rationale" for this phenomenon, Pauly alternatively notes that there is a positive political economy explanation that suggests that. . . majority rule voting could lead to the choice of a mixed government and market system. The disturbing implication of this important finding is that outcomes from politically chosen mixes schemes are not necessarily efficiency improving. . . The only rationale for the public program is that it might have avoided more adverse selection problems in the private insurance market.[108]

What is striking about Pauly's explanation for the development of Medigap policies alongside public Medicare is that it is not based on any examination of Medicare's political history. There is no attempt to describe the origins of Medicare or how its benefit structure developed over time. Nor does Pauly cite any of the Medicare politics literature, instead choosing to focus on theories of majority rule voting. In Pauly's view, there is no need to attend to the actual reasons why supplemental insurance developed, because once again, deductive reasoning is presumed to be an adequate basis for political analysis. Outcomes are simply taken to be reasonable grounds to assume intent and purpose, precluding the necessity to study legislative origins and policy history.

V. Conclusion

Medicare, a major program of American public life, continues to be systematically misunderstood. The serious literature on Medicare's politics is not available to most of the public, is not recognized in the writing of those who generate the bulk of policy proposals, and is underrepresented in health services research. Furthermore, much of that research is premised on the assumption of unanimous agreement about what Medicare should do, leaving to be resolved only the question of what will work.

Our commentary has been sharply critical of the omission of systematic attention to Medicare politics in policy analysis.[109] Too much of this literature maintains an indefensible separation between policy making and politics. Yet, simply engaging in political analysis is not the same as conducting sound political analysis. We are also sharply critical of a particular type of thinking about Medicare's politics, that of regrettable misunderstanding discussed in the preceding section. This sort of casual political analysis undermines the authority of careful policy analysis. The remedy for it is a mix of self-restraint and more serious attention to what political science can (and cannot) tell us about Medicare's likely future.[110] It hurts rather than helps public understanding of what should and can be done in American policy making to substantiate program evaluation with politically superficial judgments. This is particularly important where the political analysis is presented as scholarship, but not bolstered by evidentiary support or defensible inferences. We do not argue that scholars should hide their normative preferences. They should state them clearly. Nor do we suggest that political scientists have a monopoly on commentary about American political realities (or Medicare's). Rather, our claim is that scholarly standards should apply to claims about politics by those invoking analytical authority for their policy conclusions.

This is especially so given the stakes involved in reforming Medicare as the baby-boom generation approaches retirement. If the fixture of Medicare depends on clarifying policy choices and values, we can ill afford to have a commentary on Medicare that is dominated by misunderstanding and mythology.

Endnotes

†Originally published in the *Washington and Lee Law Review*, Volume 60, 2003.

*Theodore R. Marmor, Professor of Public Policy and Management at the Yale School of Management, Professor of Political Science, and former Director of the Robert Wood Johnson Foundation's postdoctoral program in Health Policy from 1993–2003. Graduate of Harvard University and Wadham College, Oxford. This work was supported in part by the Robert Wood Johnson Foundation. The views expressed are those of the authors and do not imply endorsement by the Robert Wood Johnson Foundation.

**Spencer Martin, M.D., M.S., postdoctoral fellow in health policy and politics at Yale's School of Management.

***Jonathan Oberlander, Associate Professor of Social Medicine, University of North Carolina-Chapel Hill. The author gratefully acknowledges the support of the Greenwall Foundation for this research.

[1]This section on health services research draws on Oberlander, J., "Medicare and the American State: The Polities of Federal Health Insurance, 1965–1995," (1995): 14–20. Dissertation, Yale University, on file with the author.

[2]Major works on Medicare policy include Blumenthal, D., *et al.*, *Renewing the Promise: Medicare & Its Reform* (New York: Oxford University Press, 1988); Davis, K. and D. Rowland, *Medicare Policy: New Directions for Health and Long-Term Care* (Baltimore: Johns Hopkins University Press, 1986); Moon, M., *Medicare: Now and in the Future*

(University Press of America, 1993); Pauly, M. V. and W. L. Kissick, eds., *Lessons from the First Twenty Years of Medicare* (Philadelphia: University of Pennsylvannia Press, 1988); and Rettenmaier, A. J. and T. R. Saving, eds., *Medicare Reform: Issues and Answers* (University of Chicago Press, 1999).

[3]Hsiao, W. C., *et al.*, *Final Report: Resource Based Relative Value Scales of Selected Medical and Surgical Procedures in Massachusetts* (Boston: Harvard School of Public Health, 1985).

[4]See Glaser, W. A., "Designing Fee Schedules by Formulae, Politics, and Negotiations," *Am. J. Pub. Health*, 80 (1990): 804, 806–808, pointing out the inherent limitations of the Harvard RBRVS.

[5]See generally Moon, *supra* note 2, providing an overview of Medicare's finances and programmatic development since 1967.

[6]*Id.* at XV.

[7]*Id.* at 23. See also Moon, M., *Medicare Now and in the Future*, 2nd ed. (Urban Institute Press, 1996): 25, updating the data on aging. Between 1982 and 1996, the number of Medicare beneficiaries rose at a rate of 1.9 percent, suggesting that the aging of the population is not a major contributor to Medicare's growth. *Id.*

[8]Moon, *supra* note 2 at xvi.

[9]Cassel, C. K., *et al.*, "Restructuring Medicare For the Next Century: What Will Beneficiaries Really Need?," *Health Affairs* (Jan./Feb. 1999): 118, 118–131.

[10]*Id.* at 119.

[11]*Id.*

[12]Epstein, A. and D. Blumenthal, "Physician Payment Reform: Past and Future," *Milbank Quarterly*, 71 (1993): 193, 196. "CPR" refers to Medicare's original system of paying physicians on the basis of their customary, reasonable, and prevailing charges. *Id.* at 194.

[13]Rice, T. and J. Bernstein, "Volume Performance Standards: Can They Control Growth In Medicare Services?, *Milbank Quarterly*, 68 (1990): 295, 310.

[14]See Pauly, M. V. "Positive Political Economy of Medicare, Past and Future," in *Lessons from the First Twenty Years of Medicare*, *supra* note 2 at 49, 49–71, developing an economic perspective on Medicare politics.

[15]But see Rice, T., *The Economics of Health Reconsidered* (1988): 3, arguing against the majority of American health economists who privilege market based health policies and contending that "one of the main reasons for the belief that market-based systems are superior stems from a misunderstanding of economic theory as it applies to health;" Evans, R., *Strained Mercy: The Economics of Canadian Health and Care* (Toronto: Butterworth, 1984): 5, providing an example of how, outside the United States, faith in market-based systems of healthcare is less homogeneous.

[16]See Marmor, T., "Policy Analysis", *J. of Pol'y Anal. & Mgmt.*, 6 (1986): 112, 114, reviewing three books on policy analysis; see generally MacRae, D. and J. A. Wilde, *Policy Analysis for Public Decisions* (Duxbury Press, 1979), Ch. 6, discussing the conditions under which a policy alternative is likely to be enacted and implemented.

[17]See generally, e.g., Marmor, T. R., *The Politics of Medicare*, 2nd ed. (New York: Aldine De Gruyter, 2000), discussing the debate over Medicare; Skidmore, M. J., *Medicare and the*

American Rhetoric of Reconciliation (Tuscaloosa: University of Alabama Press, 1970), same; Corning, P. A., *The Evolution of Medicare . . . from Idea to Law* (US Social Security Administration, Office of Research and Statistics, 1969), same; Somers, H. and A. Somers, *Medicare and the Hospitals: Issues and Prospects* (Washington: The Brookings Institution, 1967), same; Feingold, E., *Medicare: Policy and Politics* (San Francisco: Chandler Publishing, 1966), same; Greenfield, M., *Health Insurance for the Aged: The 1965 Program for Medicare* (Institute of Governmental Studies, University of California at Berkeley, 1966), same; Harris, R., *A Sacred Trust* (New York: New American Library, 1966), same; Somers, H. and A. Somers, *Doctors, Patients, and Health Insurance: The Organizing and Financing of Medical Care* (Washington: The Brookings Institution, 1961), same.

[18]See generally David, S. I., *With Dignity: The Search for Medicare and Medicaid* (Westport Connecticut: Greenwood Press, 1985), interpreting Medicare's history; Jacobs, L. R., *Health of Nations: Public Opinion and the Making of American and British Health Policy* (Ithaca: Cornell University Press, 1993), same.

[19]David, *supra* note 18 at 156–157.

[20]Jacobs, *supra* note 18 at 4.

[21]See *id.* at 32–38, finding that papers in the John F. Kennedy and Lyndon B. Johnson Presidential library files document the institutionalization of a public opinion apparatus in presidential decision making.

[22]See generally Oberlander, J., *The Political Life of Medicare* (University of Chicago Press, 2003), providing comprehensive political analysis of the development of Medicare since its enactment in 1965.

[23]Jost, T. S., "Governing Medicare," *ADMIN. L. Rev.*, 51 (1999): 39, 40.

[24]Peterson, M. A., "The Politics of Health Care Policy; Overreaching in an Age of Polarization," in *The Social Divide: Political Parties and the Future of Activist Government*, ed. M. Weir (The Brookings Institution, 1998): 181–229.

[25]See generally Jacobs, L. R. and R. Y. Shapiro, *Politicians Don't Pander: Political Manipulation and the Loss of Democratic Responsiveness* (University of Chicago Press, 2000), discussing the "partisan duel" over social policy in the 1990s.

[26]See Brown, L. D., "The Politics of Medicare and Health Reform, Then and Now," *Health Care Fin. Rev.*, 18 (1996): 163, 164–168, analyzing the political struggles that have shaped the debate over Medicare, past and present.

[27]See generally Smith, D. G., *Entitlement Politics: Medicare and Medicaid 1995–2001* (New York: Aldine De Gruyter, 2002), examining partisan approaches to the future of federal healthcare entitlements.

[28]*Id.* at 350–351.

[29]*Id.*

[30]*Id.*

[31]*Id.* at 353.

[32]*Id.* at 354.

[33]See generally Oberlander, *supra* note 22, providing a comprehensive study of Medicare politics.

[34]See *id.* at 36, noting the lack of expansion in Medicare benefits.

[35]See *id.* at 74, discussing the various financing crises faced by Medicare.

[36]*See id.* at 107, discussing Medicare's payment practices and budget issues.

[37]This section draws extensively on Marmor, T. R. and G. J. McKissick, "Medicare's Future: Fact, Fiction and Folly," *Am. J. L. and Med.*, 26 (2000): 225, 238–248.

[38]See Marmor, T. and J. Oberlander, "Rethinking Medicare Reform," *Health Affairs*, (Jan./Feb. 1998): 52, 53, analyzing the proposed voucher plan. Under the Republican proposal, Medicare beneficiaries would receive a voucher to purchase health insurance from the private insurance market and this would replace the government-organized insurance Medicare currently provides. *Id.*

[39]See National Bipartisan Commission on the Future of Medicare, "Building a Better Medicare for Today and Tomorrow," http://thomas.loc.gov/medicare/bbmtt31599.html (Mar. 6, 1999), recommending changing Medicare into a premium support system, on file with the *Washington and Lee Law Review*.

[40]See generally Aaron, H. J. and R. D. Reischauer, "The Medicare Reform Debate: What is the Next Step?," *Health Affairs*, (Winter 1995): 8, illustrating misleading political analysis.

[41]*Id.* at 20.

[42]*Id.* at 8.

[43]See *id.* at 9–12, using the history of Medicare to bolster their argument.

[44]*Id.* at 27–28.

[45]The claims we will analyze derive from two of the opening paragraphs of Aaron and Reischauer's examination of the Medicare reform debate in 1995. "Five central facts," the reader is told, "will shape the debate on the future of Medicare."

> First, Medicare enjoys overwhelming support among the American electorate, a popularity that is well deserved because the program has achieved all of its designers' major objectives. Second, the cost of providing Medicare benefits is projected to rise very rapidly and will exceed projected revenues by ever larger amounts. Third, legislative reform of the entire health care system is now off the political agenda and likely will remain so for *years* to come. Fourth, there exists a strong and broad consensus against raising taxes. Fifth, dramatic changes are taking place in the way health care is financed and delivered for the non-Medicare population.
>
> The implications of these facts are straightforward. First, before changes are made in Medicare, policymakers will have to assure the general population and beneficiaries alike that the reforms will not compromise the attributes of the program that the public values so much. Second, Congress will have to act soon to restore Medicare's financial viability. Third, the measures that Congress adopts will not be part of any major legislative effort to reform the overall health care system. Fourth, most, if not all, of the budgetary savings on Medicare will come from reducing federal payments to providers and raising costs to

beneficiaries, not from raising Medicare payroll taxes. Fifth, congressional reforms wilt — and should — bring Medicare more in line with the structure of healthcare financing and delivery that is evolving to serve the non-Medicare population.

Id. at 8–9.

[46] *Id.* at 8.

[47] See Marmor, T., "How We Got to Where We Are: American Health Care Politics, 1970 to 1990," in *Understanding Healthcare Reform*, ed. T. Marmor (Yale University Press, 1994): 21, 28–30, criticizing public financing economists for not consulting public opinion findings or qualitative work on social beliefs from anthropology or social psychology.

[48] See Jacobs, *supra* note 18 at 191–193, noting widespread support for Medicare despite little public understanding of the program; Jacobs, L. R., *et al.*, "The Polls — Poll Trends: Medical Care In the United States—An Update," *Pub. Opinion Q.*, 57 (1993): 394, 394–395, giving the results of public opinion polls regarding health care issues in the 1992 presidential campaign; see generally Bowman, K., "Public Opinion and Medicare Restructuring: Three Views," in *Medicare: Preparing for the Challenges of the 21st Century*, eds. R. D. Reischauer *et al.* (Brookings Institution Press, 1998): 281, examining the significance of public support and public opposition to Medicare reforms.

[49] See Jacobs, *supra* note 18 at 191–193, noting Medicare's broad popularity.

[50] See Public Agenda, Medicare: Red Flags, http://www.publicagenda.org/(Mar., 1997), displaying the results of a 1997 Washington Post/Kaiser Family Foundation/Harvard University poll that found a full 53 percent of respondents willing to admit they knew "very little" about Medicare, on file with the *Washington and Lee Law Review.*

[51] See Marmor and McKissick, *supra* note 37 at 227–230, relating the expectation of incremental program expansion to Medicare's origins.

[52] See Marmor, *supra* note 17 at 6–10, providing a narrative history and more extensive analysis of Medicare's origins and operations.

[53] See *id.* at 12, examining the factors that limited senior citizens' access to health insurance before Medicare.

[54] See Moon, M. and J. Mulvey, *Entitlements and the Elderly: Protecting Promises, Recognizing Reality* (Urban Institute Press, 1996): 35, 89–93, discussing the limited expansion of Medicare.

[55] See Aaron and Reischauer, *supra* note 40 at 8, "The implications of these facts are straightforward."

[56] *Id.*

[57] Aaron, H. J. and R. D. Reischauer, "Rethinking Medicare Reform Needs Rethinking," *Health Affairs,* (Jan./Feb. 1998): 69, 69.

[58] See Marmor and Oberlander, *supra* note 38 at 59, noting rosy predictions of rapid managed care growth.

[59]See generally, "The Managed Care Backlash," *J. Health Pol., Pol'y L.*, 24 (1999): 860, devoting its entire October 1999 issue to the reasons for and implications of the managed care backlash; see also Blendon, R. J., *et al.*, "Understanding the Managed Care Backlash," *Health Affairs*, (Jul./Aug. 1998): 80, 80–85, reporting a 1998 Harris poll that illustrates the ill regard with which the public views the managed care industry. In that poll, managed care firms ranked second from the bottom in terms of the public's positive feelings about them; only tobacco companies ranked lower. *Id.* See also Jacobs, L. R. and R. S. Shapiro, "The American Public's Pragmatic Liberalism Meets its Philosophical Conservatism," *J. Health Pol., Pol'y & L.*, 24 (1999): 1021, 1024–1025, discussing poll results on America's reaction to managed care; Press Release, Kaiser Family Foundation, "National Survey Suggests Need for Broad Public Debate About Medicare Reform," http://www.kff.org/medicare/1442-index.cfm (Oct. 20, 1998), presenting public opinion on managed care providers, on file with the *Washington and Lee Law Review*.

[60]See generally Wilensky, G. R., "What's Behind the Public's Backlash?," *J. Health Pol. Pol'y & L.*, 24 (1999): 873, providing further analysis on the backlash against managed care; Jacobs and Shapiro, *supra* note 59 at 1021, same; Blendon, *et al.*, *supra* note 59 at 80, same.

[61]When one considers the character of some of the other policy changes that the managed care backlash has helped produce, such as restrictions on insurers' ability to limit hospital stays after routine births, the odds increase that this alternative reaction will occur. See Ginzberg, E. and M. Ostrow, "Managed Care—A Look Back and a Look Ahead," *New Eng. J. Med.*, 336 (1997): 1018, 1020, highlighting the public's dissatisfaction with managed care. Combine a general antipathy toward managed care firms with sympathetic target groups (new mothers, vulnerable patients) and the impulse toward restricting the practices of insurers fits with our general understanding of the ways in which lawmakers respond to public opinion. See generally Arnold, R. D., *The Logic of Congressional Action* (Yale University Press, 1990), discussing ways in which politicians anticipate and respond to the preferences of constituents and *worry* about the incidence of costs and benefits distributed across groups of voters. Despite the efforts of generational equity enthusiasts to paint the elderly as "greedy geezers" senior citizens remain, as a group, closer to the new mothers/vulnerable patients end of the scale than to the greedy insurers end. Jacobs and Shapiro, *supra* note 59 at 1024–1025, finding a lack of public confidence in managed care plans, HMOs, and health insurance companies; Kaiser Family Foundation, *supra* note 59, reporting the generational differences in views on Medicare, showing support for Medicare in cohorts above and under the age of 65.

[62]Note that Medicare is still quite popular among even the youngest cohort. See Kaiser Family Foundation, *supra* note 59, showing strong support for the preservation of Medicare. To say that younger voters are less supportive of Medicare is not to say that they are unsupportive of it. See *id.* at 10, displaying public opinion data. Solid majorities remain for the program, even among young adults. As for the measures of skepticism about the program's future, it is harder to say what such expressions of doubt mean. After all, one may like a program and still have doubts about its future. See *id.*, showing that a majority

of those polled believed that Medicare was headed toward a crisis. In that sense, expressions of skepticism do not provide meaningful direction for policy-making in the way that expressions of support and opposition do. As Karlyn Bowman has argued, concern about a program's future and talk of crisis may be "simply a way for people to say to their elected legislators: pay attention. This issue is important to me." Bowman, K., "Public Opinion and Medicare Restructuring: Three Views," in *Medicare: Preparing for the Challenges of the 21st Century*, eds. R. D. Reischauer *et al.* (Brookings Institution Press, 1998): 283. With these caveats in mind, we simply note that young adults show up as more skeptical than older adults. But skepticism among the latter age group is easy to find in the survey data as well. What the skepticism means remains open to debate, a debate that in our view is unlikely to be resolved without richer data. Robert J. Blendon has written a recent study that reports greater skepticism among other younger cohorts. See generally Blendon, R. J., "Public Opinion and Medicare Restructuring: Three Views," in *Medicare: Preparing for the Challenges of the 21st Century*, eds. R. D. Reischauer *et al.* (Brookings Institution Press, 1998): 288. He found, for instance, that the under 30 cohort was the only one in which a majority of individuals predicted bankruptcy for Medicare. See *id.* at 290, discussing public opinion data.

[63]It is also the case that neither the size nor the direction of the differences has operated in the past as the resentment advocates would claim. According to one scholar of public opinion and the elderly, based on survey data from the National Election Study through 1988, "the nonelderly were consistently more likely to say the federal government spends too Little on Social Security and health care, Medicare, or care for the elderly." Rhodebeck, L. A., "The Politics of Greed? Political Preferences Among the Elderly," *J. Pol.*, 55 (1993): 342, 350. Given the increased conservatism of younger cohorts in recent years, we do not want to make too much of the patterns found by Rhodebeck. See Abramowitz, A. I. and K. L. Saunders, "Ideological Realignment in the US Electorate," *Pol.*, 60 (1998): 634, 639–642, noting a trend toward the Republican party among younger cohorts. It is enough for our purposes simply to note that, in the not too distant past, younger cohorts seemed perfectly willing to support programs for the elderly.

[64]See Marmor, *supra* note 17 at 185–191, discussing the tendency of economists to avoid political concerns; see also "Challenges of Leadership and Politics: Four Views," in *Medicare: Preparing for the Challenges of the 21st Century*, eds. R. D. Reischauer *et al.* (Brookings Institution Press, 1998): 280, 285, same. But see Reinhardt, U. E., "A Primer for Journalists on Medicare Reform Proposals" (April 2003), unpublished manuscript, on file with the author, providing an exception to economists' tendency to avoid political concerns and, instead, offering a good illustration of combining economic, political, and policy analysis.

[65]Given the benefits of specialization it is hardly surprising — and it may even do some good — that economists tend to approach these questions by putting economics front and center. For a more extended discussion, see Marmor, *supra* note 17 at 185–191.

[66]See Marmor, *supra* note 47 at 28–30, discussing the role of public opinion in Medicare policy-making.

[67]See Jacobs and Shapiro, *supra* note 59 at 1022–1026, discussing public perceptions of managed care; see generally Jacobs and Shapiro, *supra* note 25, arguing that politicians often produce — rather than respond to — public opinion, strategically manipulating polls and question wording to, in effect, create mass "preferences" consistent with their policy objectives.

[68]See Oberlander, *supra* note 1 at 250–254, discussing the role of public opinion in Medicare policy-making.

[69]See *id.*, discussing Medicare's lack of growth despite mass support for expanded benefits.

[70]See *id.*, noting the absence of cutbacks on Medicare benefits.

[71]One experienced public opinion analyst characterizes the available evidence on the public's support for vouchers this way:

A voucher system described in various ways in various polls seems to attract the support of about 30 percent of the population. It is not clear from the data I have seen exactly how fine that support is. Do these respondents reject the system we have now? Is the response simply a message to do something to save the system? Or is the 30 percent a measure of actual support for a voucher system or some alternative? I am not sure that we know the answers judging from the current questions in the public domain.

Bowman, *supra* note 48 at 285.

[72]See Peterson, *supra* note 24 at 201–219, discussing Republican strategies to enact healthcare reform.

[73]See generally Marmor and Oberlander, *supra* note 38, providing a deeper discussion of the many reasons not to support voucher plans. But see generally Aaron and Reischauer, *supra* note 57, responding to Marmor and Oberlander's arguments and a defense of vouchers; Butler, S. M., "Medicare Price Controls: The Wrong Prescription," *Health Affairs,* (Jan./Feb. 1998): 72, 73, same.

[74]Aaron and Reischauer, *supra* note 40 at 8.

[75]See Marmor, T. R., *et al., America's Misunderstood Welfare State: Persistent Myths, Enduring Realities* (Basic Books, 1990): 216–218, discussing the inherent fallibility of long-term cost prediction.

[76]See Aaron and Reischauer, *supra* note 40 at 10, predicting long-term cost growth.

[77]*Id.* at 8.

[78]See Toner, R., "Health Care Autopsy: Plenty of Targets to Blame for Failure," *Phoenix Gazette* (Sep. 27, 1994): A1, discussing the collapse of the healthcare reform agenda.

[79]See Toner, R., "The Hard Lessons of Health Reform," *N.Y. Times* (Jul. 4, 1999): Section 4, 1, discussing President Clinton's 1999 Medicare reform proposal.

[80]Patients' Bill of Rights, S.1256, 105th Cong. (1999).

[81]See Wilentz, S., "For Voters, the 60's Never Died," *N.Y. Times* (Nov. 16, 1999): A27, noting continued public support for health care reform and other traditionally liberal issues.

[82]See generally Kingdon, J. W., *Agendas, Alternatives. and Public Policies* (Longman Publishing Group, 1984), discussing how political agendas depend on a confluence of problem recognition, policy solutions, and political conditions; Baumgartner, F. R. and B. D. Jones,

Agendas and Instability in American Politics (University of Chicago Press, 1993), proposing a punctuated equilibrium model of policy change, tracing the history of policy change in 20th century America, and analyzing the long-term changes in the structures and context of American political institutions.

[83]See Baumgartner and Jones, *supra* note 82 at 57, proposing a punctuated equilibrium model of policy change and agenda setting.

[84]See generally Marmor, T. R., "Forecasting American Health Care: How We Got Here and Where We Might be Going," *J. Health Pol., Pol'y and L.,* 23 (1998): 551, providing a more extensive discussion of the dangers of forecasting.

[85]See Marmor, *et al., supra* note 75 at 137, refuting pessimistic projections of Social Security's future.

[86]See Aaron, H. J., "Budget Estimates: What We Know, What We Can't Know, and Why It Matters," in *Policies for an Aging Society,* eds. S. H. Altman and D. I. Shactman (Johns Hopkins University Press, 2002). See Table 3.1 on projections of Medicare outlays.

[87]For similar points about the consequences of Medicare's complex environment, see Kassirer, J. P., "Managing Managed Cares Tarnished Image," *New Eng. J. Med.,* 337 (1997): 338–339; Aaron, *supra* note 86 at 16.

[88]Aaron, *supra* note 86 at 70–71, 77.

[89]See *id.* at 63–64, 68–70, discussing the misuse of long-range projections.

[90]See Marmor, *supra* note 17 at 189–191, describing "politically presumptive writing."

[91]See Moon, *supra* note 7 at 19, noting Medicare's superior ability to control costs through the early 1990s.

[92]See Moon, M., "Beneath Me Averages: An Analysis of Medicare and Private Expenditures" (The Henry J. Kaiser Family Foundations, Report No. 1505, 2000): 13.

[93]Moon, *supra* note 7 at 19.

[94]Doubts about policymakers mustering the political will required to impose fiscal discipline on the program through marginal adjustments stand curiously at odds with radical reformers' strong faith in these same policymakers' willingness to summon the political courage to make fundamental changes to the program's design.

[95]"Remarks on Returning without Approval to the House of Representatives the Taxpayer Refund and Relief Act of 1999," *Weekly Comp. Pres. Doc.,* 35 (Sep. 23, 1999): 1793.

[96]"President Touts Successes in Remarks to LR Chamber," *ARK. Democrat-Gazette,* (Dec. 12, 1999): A21.

[97]See generally Marmor, *supra* note 17, describing further the ironies of the political evolution of Medicare's trust fund. The same social-insurance financing of hospital services that was so critical to gaining political support for Medicare in the first place has, through its artifact, the trust fund, ironically become one of its greatest political vulnerabilities and the nominal foundation to support the attacks oldie program's harshest critics; see also Oberlander, *supra* note 1, at 129–150, arguing that Congress adopted the Medicare trust fund to assure political stability, but it has actually turned out to be a source of instability. But see generally Patashnik, E. and J. Zeliza, "Paying for Medicare: Benefits, Budgets, and Wilbur Mills's Policy Legacy" (1999), unpublished

manuscript, on file with author, disputing the view that this development is an ironic legacy of the trust fund device. Patashnik and Zelizer argue instead that fiscal conservatives understood the implications of the trust fund mechanism from inception, and its ability to impose discipline on Medicare's budget was crucial to their willingness to support the program. *Id.*

[98] Another analogy is useful here. When the United States declares war, no one shouts that the Department of Defense will run out of money. There is, of course, debate over the wisdom of the military engagement and disputes over the willingness of Congress to pay for the additional war-related expenses. However, no one would contend that the increased expenses due to a new military engagement will "cause" the Department of Defense to become bankrupt.

[99] Marmor, *supra* note 17 at 135.

[100] See generally Patashnik, E. M., *Putting Trust in the Federal Budget: Federal Trust Funds and the Politics of Commitment* (Cambridge University Press, 2000), describing federal trust funds.

[101] See generally Edelman, M., *The Symbolic Uses of Politics* (University of Illinois Press, 1964), exploring the symbolic processes underlying political claims; Elder, C., and Cobb, R., *The Political Uses of Symbols* (Longman, 1983), examining the importance of symbols as a basis for political activity; McKissick, G. J., "Defining Choices: Interest Group Lobbying and the Framing of Policy Alternatives," (2000), unpublished manuscript, on file with author.

[102] The oddity of worrying about a Medicare bankruptcy is also apparent when one considers the different political responses to the funding shortfalls for Medicare's hospitalization coverage (Part A), on the one hand, and the shortfalls for its coverage for physician services (Part B), on the other. Hospitalization insurance alone is financed by payroll taxes earmarked for Medicare's Part A trust fund. This is a mechanism designed explicitly to echo the same social-insurance principles as Social Security pensions. In contrast, when Congress tacked on physician services as Part B of the 1965 Medicare bill, premium payments from current beneficiaries and from general federal tax revenues were to finance physician expenses. Because general tax revenues can only run short, but not out, projected shortfalls in paying for physician services have simply been covered by additional general revenues, by increased premiums, or by cutbacks in expenditures. As a consequence, there have never been Medicare-Part-B crises of the form associated with Part A. It is only the projected shortfalls in the hospital trust fund that have triggered the recurrent crisis over Medicare and the use of bankruptcy language. Thus, the experience with the trust fund demonstrates how important the funding mechanisms can be for the politics of a program. In that sense, the use of a trust fund is more than an accounting term of art. It has very real political implications and consequences. For a cogent discussion of the different "crisis" politics of Medicare's component parts, see Oberlander, *supra* note 1. For an insightful analysis of the politics of government trust funds, see Patashnik, *supra* note 100.

[103] See generally Rice, *supra* note 15, providing an excellent critique of these assumptions in health care economics.

[104]Feldman, R. D., *American Health Care: Government, Market Processes and the Public Interest* (The Independent Institute, 2000): 2–3.

[105]Vogel, R. J., *Medicare: Issues in Political Economy* (University of Michigan Press, 1999): 3. Political choice perspective refers to an application of microeconomic theory to politics.

[106]*Id.* at 17.

[107]Pauly, M. V., "The Medicare Mix Efficient and Inefficient Combinations of Social and Private Health Insurance For U.S. Elderly," *J. Health Care Fin.*, 26 (2000): 26, 26–37.

[108]*Id.* at 29.

[109]This paragraph draws on Marmor and McKissick, *supra* note 37 at 248.

[110]What should one expect from those who are experts on the details of Medicare's programmatic operation who commit the conceptually distinct sin of leaving out political analysis altogether? For this sin of omission, the answer is this: a clear acknowledgment of the limitations of such assessments for either predicting Medicare's future prescribing reforms at my particular time. Such work makes a valuable contribution in providing careful attention to the programmatic details of Medicare's history. Nevertheless, the caution about limits remains.

Comparative Perspectives and Policy Learning in the World of Health Care†

T. R. Marmor*, R. Freeman** and K. Okma***

The main point of this chapter is to explore the methodological questions raised by weaknesses in international comparative work in the field of health policy. The core question is how competent learning from one nation to another can take place. The chapter argues that there is a considerable gap between the promise and the actual performance of comparative policy studies. Misdescription and superficiality are all too common. Unwarranted inferences, rhetorical distortion, and caricatures — all show up too regularly in comparative health policy scholarship and debates.

The chapter first describes the context of the health and welfare state reform debates during the past three decades. In almost all industrialized democracies, rising medical expenditures exacerbated fiscal concerns about the affordability of the mature welfare states. In reaction to pressure for policy change in health care, policy makers looked abroad for promising solutions of domestic problems. The following section takes up the topic of cross-national policy learning. Then, it critically reviews recent debates about health care reforms and addresses the purposes, promises, and pitfalls of comparative study in health policy. The next section categorizes existing comparative health policy literature to highlight the character, possibilities, and limits of such work. The concluding section returns to the basic theme: the real promise of comparative scholarship and the quite mixed performance to date.

None of us can escape the "bombardment of information about what is happening in other countries".[1] Yet, in the field of health policy that is the subject here, there is an extraordinary imbalance between the magnitude and speed of the information flows and the capacity to learn useful lessons from them.[2] There is, moreover, a considerable gap between promise and performance in the field of comparative policy studies. Misdescription and superficiality are all too common. Unwarranted inferences, rhetorical distortion, and caricatures — all show up too regularly in comparative health policy scholarship and debates. Why might that be so and what does that suggest about more promising forms of cross-national intellectual exchange? The main point of this chapter is to explore the methodological questions raised by concerns about the above weaknesses in international comparison in health policy. The core question is how competent learning from one nation to another can take place in health care policy.

To address that question, this chapter first describes the political context of health and welfare state reform debates during the past three decades. The first section argues that in almost all industrial democracies, rising medical expenditures exacerbated fiscal concerns about the affordability of mature welfare states. These concerns turned into increased pressure for policy change in health care and with that, the inclination to look abroad for promising solutions of domestic problems. The second section takes up the topic of cross-national policy learning more directly, addressing some of the promises and methodological pitfalls of such work. The third section focuses on recent debates about health reform and skeptically reviews the claims of convergence among OECD health care systems, and explains the growth of scholarship on comparative health policy. The fourth section addresses the purposes, promises and pitfalls of comparative study in health policy. The fifth section groups the works in categories that highlight the character, possibilities and limits of the comparative health policy literature. The concluding section returns to the chapter's basic theme: the real promise of comparative policy scholarship and the quite mixed portrait of the performance to date.

I. The Political Context: Welfare State Debates and Health Reforms 1970–2000

There is little doubt about the prominence of health policy[3] on the public agenda of most if not all of the industrial democracies. Canada's universal health insurance is a model of achievement for many observers, the subject of considerable intellectual scrutiny and the destination of many policy travelers in search of illumination. Yet, both the national government and a majority of its provinces in recent years have felt sufficiently concerned about the condition of Canadian Medicare to set up advisory commissions to chart adjustments. The United States has been even more obvious about its medical care worries, with crisis commentary a fixture for decades on the national agenda. Fretting about medical care costs, quality, and access is not limited to North America. Disputes about reforming Dutch medical care have been on-going for decades. Any review of the European experience would discover persistent policy controversies in Germany (burdened by the fiscal pressures of unification), in Great Britain (with recurrent debates about the NHS), and in Italy and Sweden (with great fiscal and unemployment pressures).[4]

The puzzle is not whether or why there is such widespread interest in health policy, but why now. And why has international evidence (arguments, claims, caricatures) seemed more prominent at the turn of the 21st century than, say, during the fiscal strains of the mid-1970s or early 1980s? What can be usefully said not only about the substance of the experience of different nations, but about the political processes of introducing and acting upon policy change in a national context?

There is a simple answer to these questions that, one hopes, is not simple minded. Medical care policy came to the forefront of public agendas for one or more of the following reasons. First, the financing of personal medical care everywhere became a major financial component of the budgets[5] of mature welfare states. When fiscal strain arises, policy scrutiny (not simply incremental budgeting) is the predictable result. Second, mature welfare states, as Klein and Higgins[6] argued in the late 1980s, face restricted capacity for bold fiscal expansion in new areas. This means that managing existing programs in changing economic circumstances necessarily assumes a more prominent place on the public agenda. Third, there is what might be termed the wearing out (perhaps wearing down) of the post-war consensus about the welfare state. We see the effects of more than two decades of fretfulness about the affordability, desirability, and governability of the welfare state.[7]

Having begun in earnest during the 1973–1974 oil shock, with high levels of unemployment and persistent stagflation, bolstered by electoral victories (or advance) of parties opposed to welfare state expansion, critics assumed a bolder posture. Mass public increasingly heard challenges to programs that had for decades seemed sacrosanct.[8]

From Mulroney to Thatcher, from New Zealand to the Netherlands — the message of serious problems requiring major change gained support. Accordingly, when economic strain reappears, the inner rim of programmatic protection — not just interest group commitment, but social faith — weakens and the incentives to explore transformative but not fiscally burdensome options become relatively stronger. These factors help to explain the pattern of welfare state review — including health policy — over the past three decades across the industrialized world. But, even accepting this contention, there still remains the question of why these pressures gave rise to increased attention to other national experiences.[9]

Recent experience illustrates how times of policy change increase the demand for new ideas — or at least new means to old ends. Klein once argued, "no one wants to be caught wearing yesterday's ideas."[10] Everywhere, policy makers and analysts looked increasingly across the border to look for the latest policy fashion. Just as some American reformers turned to Canada's example, so a number of Canadian, German, Dutch, and other intellectual entrepreneurs reviewed American, Swiss, and Swedish experience in recent years. In the 1990s, many conferences followed this pattern. Conferees were interested in getting better policy answers to the problems they faced at home. For example, participants in one such conference held in the Netherlands in the mid-1990s were explicit about their aspirations for cross-border learning: how to find a balance between "solidarity and subsidiary," how to maintain a "high quality health system in times of economic stress," and even an optimistic query about "what are the optimum relations between patients, insurers, providers, and the government."[11] Understood as simply wanting to stretch one's mind — to explore what is possible conceptually, or what others have managed to achieve — this is unexceptionable. Understood as the pursuit of the best model, absent further exploration of the political, social, and economic context required for implementation, this is wishful thinking.

Others saw the opportunity for an informational version of this intellectual stretching: quests for "exchange of policy information" of various sorts without commitment to policy importation, "exchanging views with kindred spirits," and explicit calls for stimulation. All of this is the learning anthropologists have long extolled — understanding the range of possible options and seeing ones own circumstances more clearly by contrast.

But what about drawing policy lessons from such exercises? What are the rules of defensible conduct here and are they followed? The truth is that, whatever the appearances, most policy debates in most countries are (and will remain) parochial affairs. They address national problems, emphasize national developments in the particular domain (pensions, medical finance, transportation), and embody conflicting visions of what policies the particular country should adopt. Only occasionally are the experiences of other nations — and the lessons they embody — seriously examined.[12] When cross-national experiences are employed in such parochial struggles, their use is typically that of policy warfare, not policy understanding and careful lesson-drawing. And, one must add, there are few knowledgeable critics at home of ideas about "solutions" abroad. In the world of American medical debate, the misuse of British and Canadian experience surely illustrates this point. The National Health Service was from the late 1970s the specter of what "government medicine" or "socialized medicine" and "rationing" could mean. In recent years, mythmaking about Canada has dominated the distortion league tables in North America.[13]

The reasons are almost too obvious to cite. Policy makers are busy with day-to-day pressures. Practical concerns incline them, if they take the time for comparative inquiry, to pay more attention to what appears to work, not academic reasons for what is and is not transferable and why. Policy debaters — whether politicians, policy analysts, or interest group figures — are in struggles, not seminars. Like lawyers, they seek victory, not illumination. For that purpose, compelling stories, whether well-substantiated or not, are more useful than careful conclusions. Interest groups, as their label suggests, have material and symbolic stakes in policy outcomes, not reputations for intellectual precision to protect.[14] Once generated and communicated, however, health policy ideas are adopted more readily in some contexts than in others. These patterns of adoption and adaptation have to do with the machinery of government, as well as with local cultural understandings. The autonomy and authority of government in parliament in the UK, for example, as well as its position at the apex of a nationalized health service, means that, "ideas can make a difference more quickly in Britain than in America." [15] It may be, too, that policy ideas transfer more easily between similar types of health systems. Institutional similarity — however notional — seems to have facilitated the spread of managed competition ideas among the national health services of northern and southern Europe.[16]

This argument must be qualified, however. Lessons from abroad often meet strong local cultural resistance. Giaimo and Manow, for example, observe that "while the market has won in international terms, the national answers to the economic pressures resulting from economic globalization demonstrate that national 'markets for ideas' have yet to be fully liberalized."[17] Morone[18] similarly remarks of Canada's experience with universal health insurance:

> It is difficult to imagine a lesson that is more foreign to the American experience. Instead of hard conscious choices, we have sought painless automatic solutions. Rather than explicit programmatic decisions Americans prefer hidden, implicit policies. Rather than centralize control in governmental hands, we would scatter it across many players. In short the Canadian lessons... are not just different — they challenge the central features of American political culture, at least as they have manifested themselves in health care policy.

It is not clear, then, whether what matters is administrative infrastructure as such or the values and assumptions it appears to embody. For it matters a lot, not only how systems are configured in organizational terms, but also how they are construed mentally.[19] This probably amounts to something more than ideas and values as such, pointing to the significance of ways of thinking or "framing." Different national policy communities — however well networked internationally — simply see problems differently.

For all this, the field of health policy is notable for the absence of studies which set out to investigate the process of transfer or learning in any specific instance. Bennett refers to the "paucity of systematic research that can convincingly make the case that cross-national policy learning has had a determined influence on policy choice in a particular jurisdiction at a particular time."[20] But, paucity of studies on policy learning does not apply to cross-national studies of policy origins, implementation, and change. Indeed, for that broader field of work, there are large and growing clusters of quite different sorts of scholarship and advocacy that address medical care cross-nationally.

None of these considerations are new — or surprising. But the increased flow of cross-national claims in health policy — both in the world of academia and politics — generates new reasons to consider the meaning of cross-national policy learning.

II. The Promise and Perils of Cross-National Comparative Policy Research

The presumptions of such cross-national efforts are important to explore, even if briefly. One is that the outside observer can more easily highlight features of debates that are missed or underplayed by national participants. The other is that comparative commentary may bring some policy wisdom as well as illuminating asides about national debates. The common assumption is that cross-cultural observation, if accurate and alert, has some advantages. It brings a different, "foreign" and arguably illuminating perspective to the debate.

A similar rationale lies behind much of the enthusiasm for contemporary comparative policy studies. Welfare state disputes — over pensions and medical care, most prominently — are undoubtedly salient on the public agendas of all industrial democracies. There is in fact a brisk trade in panaceas for the various (real and imagined) ills of welfare states. As will be obvious in later comments on the comparative literature, however, many cross-national investigations are not factually accurate enough to offer useful illumination, let alone policy wisdom. But, properly done, studies that compare what appear to be similar topics have two potential benefits not available to the policy analyst in a single nation inquiry.

First, how others see a problem, how options for action are set out and evaluated, and how implementation is understood and undertaken — all offer learning opportunities even if the policy experiences of different polities are not easily transplantable as "lessons." Second, where the context is reasonably similar, comparative work has features of a quasi-natural experiment. So, for instance the adaptation of reference prices for pharmaceuticals in Germany and in the Netherlands — two countries with very similar institutional arrangements in health care — provide an interesting example of policy learning. The reference pricing constraints outlay in the short term. But these gains are somewhat dissipated as the actors strategically adapt to the new policy reality.[21]

Cross-national sources of information have proliferated to the extent that it has become almost impossible for a policy maker in any given country not to know something about what is going on elsewhere. But know what, exactly? What part can and should comparative policy analysis play in these debates? Ruud Lubbers, the former Dutch prime minister, provides a striking example of trying to draw lessons from American experience, apparently without much understanding of its policy realities.[22] In a 1997 article for the *International Herald Tribune*, Lubbers contrasted what he called the "lean welfare state... with rapid job growth" of the United States with "costly social welfare system[s] with persistently high unemployment in most of Europe." He went on in the rest of the article to laud Holland's "third way", one that "tackled" the unemployment problem while "remaining within the European tradition that emphasizes quality of life rather than growth at any cost." This rather self-congratulatory theme seems odd in comparison with contemporary Dutch complaints. But, the point here is that the United States functions as a poorly analyzed symbol of a type of welfare state to avoid. Citing President Clinton as his source, Lubbers went on to write most of the article about the so-called Dutch miracle: a more flexible workforce, less unemployment, and a somewhat more restrained welfare state, all the result of the famous corporatist Wassenaar Agreement of 1982.

The American example is in fact hardly discussed, treated mostly as a negative symbol of what the Dutch have avoided.[23] Nowhere is there any recognition that the American welfare state is in fact quite extensive fiscally, concentrated on its older citizens, and with spending levels that — when properly accounted for in tax expenditures, direct program outlays, and the like — are hardly lean. Indeed, the point of recent books like Hacker's *The Divided Welfare State*[24] is precisely to set aside this common, but mistaken impression of American social policy as concentrated on the poor; miserly in its levels of benefits; and, depending on one's ideology, splendid or horrible in its social and economic results.[25]

The paradox is that the post-1970 decades witnessed the rapid expansion of public policy research, of which a significant proportion claimed provide comparisons across countries as a base for drawing lessons. But most of these studies, in fact, consisted of mere statistical and descriptive portraitures of health systems, ignoring the methodological issues of comparison. So, the argument here underlines the truism that policy making and policy research are often — if not always — pursued with little reference to each other. Nevertheless, the question remains as why that truism should apply so fully in this particular, costly area of public policy: health care. Why are claims about system convergence so widespread in the face of persistent patterns of continuity in national models of health care?

III. Convergence in the Health Reform Debate: Claims and Realities

The bulk of the ideological and fiscal debates about health reform took place within national borders, largely free from the spread of "foreign" ideas. To the extent similar arguments arose cross-nationally, that mostly represented what might be described as "parallel thinking." That is to say, the common questioning of health policy reflects similarities in circumstances and problem definition. This was obvious in the common preoccupation with rising medical care costs. Figure 1 portrays the upward pressure of medical care expenditures in four OECD nations since the early 1970s. Even while the four countries' health expenditure rose steadily, they also varied in the growth rates over time. Obviously, some countries, in some periods, were more successful than others in reigning in health costs. This raises the question whether — and if so, to what extent — common pressure will cause system convergence.

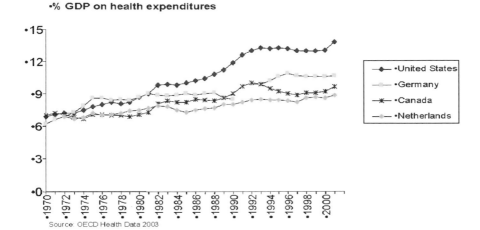

Figure 1. Health expenditure in The Netherlands, Germany, Canada, US, 1970–2000 (percent of GDP).

One can think of convergence as "a kind of soft technological determinism," the logic of which is that, across systems, "the common features will increase at the expense of the differences."[26] This sense of convergence has intensified by the emergence in the late 1980s and 1990s of active international and supranational actors in both general welfare state disputes and, in particular, health policy. These actors include the European Union (EU), the World Health Organization (WHO), the Organisation for Economic Co-operation and Development (OECD), and the World Bank. Yet, however powerful these institutions are in some areas, their role in domestic policy making within the OECD world remains indirect and limited. The European Commission has established a policy competence in public health and has become a sponsor of biomedical research. Yet, recent rulings of the European Court of Justice have had important spill over effects on national healthcare policies. EU legislation designed originally to ensure the freedom of goods, people, capital and services across borders no longer exempts the domain of health care.[27] The WHO struggles to lead health policy discussions, but remains a minor actor in the funding of medical care. And the World Bank, particularly powerful in the transformation of health care in Eastern Europe, expresses some of the reform ideas found in the western industrial democracies, but does not wield its influence there. Finally, OECD reports certainly affect the discussion of welfare state issues, but at one step removed from policy decision-making. But in spite of their limited direct role in health policy, the international agencies have become platforms for debate and carriers of policy ideas across borders.

Almost everywhere, health care became relatively more expensive as public budgets were more constrained — but how much more expensive and how much more constrained has varied substantially between countries. These pressures, in turn, are mediated by different sets of actors and institutions. It is important to note that debates over controlling health care expenditures took place everywhere, regardless of actual levels or growth rates of health spending. In short, the apparently common pressures on health systems are themselves uneven and indirect. And this is the essential difficulty in taking convergence as a framework for studying — or advocating — reforms in health policy. Quite simply, there is as much evidence of continued difference (or divergence) in national arrangements for the finance, delivery, and regulation of health care as there is of increasing similarity. As a former official of the OECD's health policy unit claimed, "[T]he delivery and finance of healthcare vary between nations more than any other public policy."[28] One does not have to agree with Poullier's conclusion to see that reducing variation has been neither the purpose nor the effect of health reform in the past decades. In health care no more than in other areas of public administration are there good arguments or evidence that "one size fits all".

To be fair, this variation is one of degree rather than of kind. At the most general level, it seems perfectly clear that some countries with roughly similar constellations of political interests, economic and political institutions, and resources develop broadly comparable arrangements for health care. And so, in turn, when social structures, patterns of economic organization, and expressions of political interest begin to change, health care arrangements will face pressures to change also. But what matters is what that formulation leaves unsaid. While there is value in pointing to the structural and technological context of health policy, policy makers face not only with multiple pressures but also with myriad proposals for change, tend to choose options that are politically feasible in the short term. To them, an appeal to convergence seems anodyne, reductionist or superficial. Conditions are not determining. They explain only why there should be pressure for reform, but not whether or not change will indeed occur, let alone what shape or direction it will — or should — take.

Nonetheless, these conditions do help to explain why — if not when or where or how — cross-national trade in policy ideas should be going on and why it is increasing. For the more similar countries become in general, the more they may believe they can learn from each other. Getting it right in health policy — ensuring universal access to high quality health care without breaking the bank — makes for significant competitive advantage in the domestic political arena as well as in the international economy. Convergence in circumstances creates opportunities for learning, as well as an increased interest in applying lessons from abroad. Convergence theory, then, offers useful clues about why adaptive change might take place. It says much less, however, about the form it takes, about why one solution to a problem should be preferred over others. And for that topic, the next section addresses the purposes, promises, and pitfalls of comparative studies in health policy.

IV. Purpose, Promise, and Perils of Comparative Inquiry in Health Policy

The emphasis in this part of the discussion is on the following, perhaps obvious distinctions among the purposes comparative analysis in health policy can serve: learning about national health arrangements and how they operate, learning why they take the forms they do, and learning policy lessons from these analyses. While these distinctions should be obvious to scholars of the subject, much of the comparative commentary on health care neither clarifies the different modes of comparison nor addresses the difficulties of drawing policy lessons from the experience of other countries.

First, there is the goal of learning about health policy abroad. Comparative work of this sort can illuminate and clarify national arrangements without addressing causal explanation or seeking policy transplantation, as aims. Its comparative element remains for the most part implicit: in reading (or writing) about them, we make sense of other systems by contrasting them with our own and with others we know about. The process of learning entails, what is obvious once noted: appreciation of what something is by reference to what it is like or unlike. This is the gift of perspective, which may or may not bring explanatory insight or lesson drawing.

The second fundamental purpose served by comparison is to generate causal explanations without necessarily seeking policy transplantation, that is, learning why policies develop as they do. Many of the historical and developmental studies of healthcare fall into this category. This approach uses cross-national inquiry to check on the adequacy of nation-specific accounts. Let us call that a defense against explanatory provincialism. What precedes policy making in country A includes many things — from legacies of past policy to institutional and temporal features that "seem" decisive. How is one to know how decisive as opposed to simply present? One answer is to look for similar outcomes elsewhere where some of these factors are missing or configured differently. Another is to look for a similar configuration of precedents without a comparable outcome.

A third and still different approach is to treat cross-national experience as quasi-experiments. Here one hopes to draw lessons about why some policies seem promising and doable, promising but impossible, or doable but not promising. All of these approaches appear in the comparative literature. And, with the growth of such writing, there was widespread optimism about the promise of lesson drawing from comparative policy analyses. But is that optimism justified?

One useful starting point to address this question is a cross-national generalization that at first sight seems misleading but, upon reflection, helps to clarify differences in the framing of policy problems. A 1995 article on European health reform, for example, claims that "countries everywhere are reforming their health systems."[29] It asserts that "what is remarkable about this global movement is that both the diagnosis of the problems and the prescription for them are virtually the same in all health care systems." These globalist claims, it turns out, were mistaken.[30] But the process of specifying more precisely what counts as national healthcare problems — whether cost control, poor quality of care, or of fragmented organization of services — turns out to be quite clarifying. In this instance, the comparative approach first refutes the generalization, but then helps to discipline the process of describing national health "problems." So, to illustrate further, the European researcher coming to investigate Oregon's experiment in health care rationing would soon discover that it was neither restrictive in practice nor a major cost control remedy in the 1990s.[31] To do so is to see the issue of rationing more clearly.

Offering new perspectives on problems and making factual adjustments in national portraits are not to be treated as trivial tasks. They are what policy craftsmen and women might well spend a good deal of time perfecting. All too many comparative studies are in fact caricatures rather than characterizations of policies. A striking illustration is the 2000 WHO report mentioned above on the ranking of the performance of health systems across the globe. Not only was the ambition itself grandiose, but its execution evoked sharp criticism by serious scholars.[32] That criticism in itself should not serve as a deterrent to serious scholars who seek to compare experiences. But it is a warning against superficiality.

An often cited advantage of comparative studies is that they serve as an antidote to explanatory provincialism. An example from North American health policy provides a good illustration of how to and how not to proceed. Some policy makers and academics in North America regard universal health insurance as incompatible with American values. They rest their case in part on the belief that Canada enacted health insurance and the US has not because North American values are sharply different. In short, they attribute a different outcome to a different political culture in the US. In fact, the values of Canada and the United States, while not identical, are in fact quite similar.[33] Like siblings, differences are there, sure, but Canada's distribution of values is closer to that of the United States than any other modern, rich democracy. In fact, the value similarities between British Columbia and Washington State are greater than those between either of those jurisdictions and, say, New Brunswick or New Hampshire along the North American east coast. Similar values are compatible with different outcomes, which in turn draw one's attention to other institutional and strategic factors that distinguish Canadian from American experience with financing health care.[34] One can imagine many other examples of such cautionary lessons, but the important point is simply that the explanatory checks are unavailable from national histories alone.

The third category of work is directly relevant to our inquiry. Drawing lessons from the policy experience of other nations is what has financially supported a good deal of the comparative analysis available. The international organizations have this as part of their rationale. The WHO, as noted, is firmly in the business of selling "best practices." The OECD regularly produces extensive, expensive, hard to gather, statistical portraits of programs as diverse as disability and pensions, trade flows and the movement of professionals, education, and health care. No one can avoid using these studies, if only because the task of collecting data and discovering "the facts" in a number of countries is so daunting. But the portraiture that emerges requires its own craft review. Does what Germany spends on spas count as public health expenditure elsewhere or does it fall, as in the United States, under another category? Often, the same words do not mean the same things. And different words may denote similar phenomena.

For now, it is enough to restate that learning about the experience of other nations is a precondition for understanding why change takes place, or for learning from that experience. Looking at the large and growing volume of comparative studies in health policy, we found that the vast majority of studies do not deliver on their claim to provide a sound base for drawing lessons from the experience of other countries. The section below categorizes the studies in four groups, each with their distinct purpose and applications. This grouping shows that the majority of reports and studies available (the first and second categories) provide, at best, a sound base for further analysis but hardly any ground for learning from experience abroad. The few studies that are based on more solid analysis (the third and fourth group) are less frequent, less wide in their geographical application and more modest in their claims about policy lessons.

V. Comparative Health Policy Analysis: Clusters of Writing

Health policy in the OECD world is, at the same time, a matter of insistent national debate, a frequent topic of descriptive, statistical portraiture for international organizations, a sometime subject of publication in the comparative journals, and only very infrequently in its cross-national comparative form, the object of book length treatment. For many years, readers had to turn to Anderson's[35] treatment of Swedish, British, and American medical care developments in the post-World War II period for acute, well-informed judgments.[36] There were many other individual country studies, but few if any that employed a systematic, comparative method of policy analysis. In contemporary debates about Dutch health care, for instance, there appears little evidence of detailed understanding about German — or American — policy experience with health care reform in the 1990s. What is true for medical care applies just as well to other fiscally important areas of the welfare state. So, for example, American discussions of disability policy in the early 1980s drew very little from Dutch experience, though there were knowledgeable scholars in both countries who sought to have influence.[37]

By the end of the 1980s, political scientists — particularly North American ones — had become interested in comparing relations between the medical profession, as a particular kind of interest group, and the state[38]. Their theoretical focus was by and large on the institutions of government and the different ways in which they shape health care politics. Slowly, the field began to produce genuinely comparative political analyses of substantial industry and competence.

The ten years and more since then have witnessed a rapid expansion of cross-national health policy literature. The quality of these works varies enormously — whether measured by the standard of intellectual rigor, theoretical perspective, descriptive accuracy, or concern for systematic policy learning across borders. There are, roughly speaking, four separable but not mutually exclusive categories of such writing.[39]

The first includes the well-known statistical, largely descriptive documents that provide data on a number of countries assumed to constitute a coherent class. It also includes more specialized surveys that deal with public opinion, health care and health policy.[40] In that way they supply much of the basic information that policy commentators explore. The OECD Health Data series has become a staple of both academic and more applied analyses alike. These studies typically neither provide behavioral hypotheses nor test explanations for why certain patterns exist. Nor do they, generally speaking, explicitly deal with the promises and pitfalls of cross-border learning. In a wider sense, the recent efforts to rank systems, countries, or institutions by means of benchmarking techniques belong to this group, too. In a much-discussed report, the WHO used its comparative data to rank the performance of national health care systems.[41]

The second category of comparative studies — by far the largest number — includes collections of international material, that we label as "parallel" or "stapled" national case studies. Examples of this kind of cross-national study are the volumes by Ham *et al.* (1990), OECD (1992, 1994), Wall (1996), Altenstetter and Bjorkman (1997), Ham (1997), Raffell (1997) and Powell and Wessen (1999)[42] as well as the series Health in Transition booklets of the WHO European Observatory. These are usually country reports bound together, accompanied by an editorial introduction and summary conclusion. For the most part, the authors are intent on setting out "how things work" in whichever country they are writing about. They are mostly descriptive, but with some assessment of performance and the flagging of issues prompting political concern. As such, they represent a qualitative correlate of the quantitative statistical studies described above. Done carefully, they are an invaluable resource for cross-national understanding. In many cases, they leave readers to find what is relevant and, as far as policy learning is concerned, leave them to do the work.

Third, there are books about a number of individual countries that employ a common framework of analysis, usually addressing a particular theme in health policy, for example, competition or privatization. That means, in principle, that comparative generalizations are possible, though not all such works actually draw them.[43]

Fourth, there are cross-national studies with a fundamental theoretical orientation that take up a specific medical care theme or question as the focus of analysis.[44] One of the interesting features of this fourth category of comparative studies is that there appears a necessary trade-off between theoretical depth and the number of nations studied. The disciplined treatment of broad topics by a single author almost inevitably addresses a more limited set of countries.[45]

In this latter category, Tuohy's *Accidental Logics*[46] offers both a theoretical and empirical analysis of policy change and continuity in three English speaking nations. The book addresses a limited range of countries but combines theoretical sophistication with command of the relevant factual data, and causal analysis in addressing the quite different patterns of policy change during the post-World War II years in Britain, Canada, and the United States. The likelihood of major policy changes, for Tuohy, differs according to each nation's particular "institutional mix." By that, she means the degree of governmental hierarchy, market forces and professional collegiality in medical decision-making and the "structural balance" between the state, medical providers, and private financial interests. Directed at understanding, Tuohy's work is of clear relevance to policy makers concerned with questions of timing for reform initiatives.

Works in this fourth category of scholarship typically use comparative methods to explore and to explain policy developments. Their practical limitations for policy makers include the relatively restricted range of countries studied and, to some degree, to their considerable reliance on the theoretical perspective known as historical institutionalism. There is some irony in the fact that the most careful cross-national analyses tend to have reinforced a sense of the contingency and specificity of the way things work out at different times in different places. This kind of comparison seems to ignore (if not implicitly deny) the cross-national exchange of information and ideas in health policy that is so much part of the very intellectual environment in which it has been produced. The most powerful studies are at the same time the most academic; the practical learning which might result from comparison is largely left implicit. Often, these books do not reach the desk of policy makers. There is much less here which speaks directly to the policy maker seeking to use evidence and experience from elsewhere in any straightforward way. Nonetheless, in the course of little more than a decade, the comparative analysis of health policy became a specialized field of academic inquiry, highly developed and successful in its own terms, but limited so far in its policy impact. So, we turn back to the evaluative question: how should we evaluate the purposes and performance of comparative policy research?

Perhaps the most important lesson we can draw from the overview in the current literature is that the development of a serious body of comparative work takes more time and effort than health policy makers are willing to spend. They feel pressures to take action and feel they cannot wait. At the same time, policy errors based on misconceptions of the experience abroad can be costly. The eagerness of some health ministers to embrace and import policy models from the US like the managed care models, the benchmark methodology, or the medical savings idea without a proper assessment of how these ideas and models worked out in practice may lead to policies that will require repair action soon, can force politicians to reverse policies altogether, and can erode the popular support for health policy altogether. The unwillingness of some politicians to delay action in order to study experience with similar policy elsewhere contrasts sharply with the practice of some Asian countries that have spent much time and attention before adjusting certain measures to their own national policy environments. The good news is that the last two decades have brought a large body of comparative study that can serve as the base for the next generation of studies that take the above warnings into account. The statistical data are there, the materials are there, the experience in drawing portraitures of individual countries is there, and all of that are necessary conditions for the next phases of policy learning about causalities and the transfer of policy experience.

VI. Summary and Conclusions

The last decades have seen a growing body of comparative study in health policy, but this growth was not matched by a growing understanding of the processes of policy learning from the experience of other countries. There is, in fact, little attention to methodological questions of this learning process.

The confluence of economic, demographic, and ideological factors that led to extensive debate about the future of the welfare state also created pressure to reform health care systems. Fiscal strains and declining political support for an active role of the state undermined support for welfare state expansion, and that strain also affected health policy. There was, indeed, growing pressure to seek for new policy solutions abroad. That pressure also gave rise to a new body of research within national research communities as well as international agencies like the World Bank, OECD, WHO and European Union. However, to date most of that research consists of merely descriptive studies of health care systems and policy measures within national boundaries. The studies pay little attention to the question what experience can be applied in another country under what circumstances. Institutional and cultural factors are important elements in the policy context as determinants of successful reception and implementation of ideas.

In practice, there is much mislearning and misrepresentation by omission. Policy makers and politicians feel pressured to change, but have little or no time (or willingness) to critically assess claims about policy experience across the border.

Potentially, comparison can bring learning opportunities as other countries can serve as natural experiments, in particular when the policy contexts are similar. Some lessons apply across many countries. Similar pressure can create opportunities for learning, and international organizations serve as platform for debate and potential sources for comparative studies. Existing studies largely ignore the important difference between the process of learning about other countries' experience, learning why certain change takes place, and the process of drawing lessons from that experience. But the basic ingredients for improved policy learning are there: the statistical database, the first generation of descriptive country studies and the experience of academics and international organizations.

Endnotes

---

†Originally published in the *Journal of Comparative Policy Analysis,* Volume 7, Issue 4, Pages 331–348, December 2005, © JCPA. This essay won the Best Article Prize for 2005 awarded by JCPA and the ICPA-Forum.

*Theodore R. Marmor teaches politics, law, and management at Yale University.
**Richard Freeman teaches government, health policy, and political research at the University of Edinburgh, Scotland.
***Kieke Okma works as an international consultant in health care, health finance and health law.

[1] Klein, R., "Learning from Others: Shall the Last be the First?," *Journal of Health Politics, Policy and Law*, 22.5 (1997):1267–1278.

[2] This skeptical argument is advanced, with Anglo-American examples from medical care and welfare, in Marmor, T. R. and W. Plowden, "Rhetoric and Reality in the Intellectual Jet Stream: The Export to Britain from America of Questionable Ideas," *Journal of Health Politics, Policy and Law*, 16.4 (1991):807–812. On the other hand, there is very rapid communication of scientific findings and claims, with journals and meetings regarded as the proper sites for evaluation. As of yet, there is no journal in the political economy of medical care that has enough authority, audience, or acuteness to play the evaluative role assumed in the medical world by *The New England Journal of Medicine, Lancet, BMJ*, or *JAMA*.

[3] Readers may be puzzled by our reluctance in this note to treat "reform" as the object of commentary. This paragraph's parade of substitutes — health policy, concerns, worries, etc. — reflects discomfort with the marketing connotations of the "reform" expression. That there pressures for change is obvious and understanding them is part of our gathering's point, but re-forming can obviously be a benefit, a burden, or beside the point.

[4] In the 1990s work in English on health policy learning was for the most part concerned with a single topic, "managed competition." This topic dominated reform discussion across countries between the mid-1980s and the mid-1990s. However, the focus was largely on the transatlantic relationship between the US and the UK: Klein, R., "Risks and Benefits of Comparative Studies: Notes from Another Ahore," *Milbank Quarterly* 69.2 (1991): 275–291 and Klein, *supra* note 1; Marmor and Plowden, *supra* note 2; Mechanic, D., "The Americanization of the British National Health Service," *Health Affairs*, (Summer 1995): 51–67; Marmor, T. R., "Global Health Policy Reform: Misleading Mythology or Learning Opportunity," in *Health Policy Reform, National Variations, and Globalization*, eds. Altenstetter, C. and J. W. Bjorkman (Basingstoke: Macmillan, 1997); Marmor, T. R. and K. G. H. Okma, "Cautionary Lessons from the West: What (Not) to Learn from Other Countries' Experiences in the Financing and Delivery of Health Care," in *The State of Social Welfare*, International Studies on Social Insurance and Retirement, Employment, Family Policy and Health Care, eds. Flora, P., P. R. De Jong, J. Le Grand and J. Y. Kim (Aldershot: Ashgate, 1998); O'Neill, F., "Health: The 'Internal Market' and Reform of the National Health Service," in *Policy Transfer and British Social Policy*, ed. Dolowitz, D. (Buckingham: Open University Press, 2000). There were complementary treatments of Western Europe: Freeman, R., "Policy Transfer in the Health Sector," European Forum conference paper WS/35 (Florence: European University Institute, 1999); Southern Europe: Cabiedes, L. and A. M. Guillen, "Adopting and Adapting Managed Competition: Health Care Reform in Southern Europe," *Social Science and Medicine*, 52.8 (2001): 1205–1217; and New Zealand: Jacobs, K. and P. Barnett, "Policy

Transfer and Policy Learning: A Study of the 1991 New Zealand Health Services Taskforce," *Governance*, 13.2 (2000): 229–257.

[5]Technically, this is not strictly true of course, as is evident in the sickness fund financing of care in Germany, the Netherlands, and elsewhere. But, since mandatory contributions are close cousins of "taxes," budget officials must obviously treat these outlays as constraints on direct tax increases. Moreover, the precise level of acceptable cost increases is a regulatory issue of great controversy.

[6]Klein, R. and M. O'Higgins, "Defusing the Crisis of the Welfare State: A New Interpretation," in *Social Security: Beyond the Rhetoric of Crisis*, eds. Marmor, T. R. and J. Mashaw (Princeton, NJ: Princeton University Press, 1988): esp. 219–224.

[7]The bulk of this ideological struggle took place, of course, within national borders, free from the spread of "foreign" ideas. To the extent similar arguments arose cross-nationally, as Kieke Okma has noted, mostly that represented "parallel development." See Report Four Country Conference, "Health Care Reforms and Health Care Policies in the United States, Canada, Germany and the Netherlands," Amsterdam, February 23–25 (The Hague: Ministry of Health, Welfare and Sports, 1995). But, there are striking contemporary examples of the explicit international transfer and highlighting of welfare state commentary. Some of this takes place through think tanks networks; some takes place through media campaigns on behalf of particular figures; and, of course, some takes place through academic exchanges and official meetings. Charles Murray — the controversial author of *Losing Ground* (Basic Books, 1984) and co-author of *The Bell Curve* (Free Press, 1994) — illustrates all three of these phenomena, as our British conferees can attest. The medium of transfer seems to have changed in the post-war period. Where the Beveridge Report would have been known to social policy elites very broadly, however much they used it, the modern form seems to be the long newspaper or magazine article and the media interview.

[8]This is the argument developed in Marmor, T. R., J. Mashaw, and P. Harvey, *America's Misunderstood Welfare State: Persistent Myths, Enduring Realities* (New York: Basic Books, 1990): esp. Ch. 3. The wider scholarly literature on the subject is the focus of a review essay, Marmor, T. R., "Understanding the Welfare State: Crisis, Critics, and Countercritics," *Critical Review*, 7.4 (1993): 461–477.

[9]The turning to US health policy experience for lessons about cost control or insurance coverage seems particularly puzzling to American scholars preoccupied with health care problems at home.

[10]Klein, R., "Commentary at Second Annual Meeting of the 4 Country Conference on Health Policy," Montebello, Canada (1996).

[11]Report Four Country Conference, *supra* note 7.

[12]Some readers have suggested this article is too pessimistic about the field of cross national policy learning. And it is certainly true that some cross national investigations have been enormously illuminating and helpful. For example, the 1964 Royal Commission on Health Services was an exemplary investigator of the experience of other countries. In the 1990s comparative policy investigations by Japanese and German analysts were important in nursing home reforms in both countries.

[13]For an elaboration of this point, see Marmor, T. R., "Patterns of Fact and Fiction in the Use of the Canadian Experience," in *Understanding Health Care Reform* (New Haven.: Yale University Press, 1994): Ch.12. A particularly careful and extensive treatment of the North American experience is the review article by Evans, R. G., M. L., Barer, and C. Hertzman, "The 20-Year Experiment: Accounting for, Explaining, and Evaluating Health Care Cost Containment in Canada and the United States," *American Review of Public Health*, 12 (1991): 481–518.

[14]The political fight over the Clinton health plan vividly illustrates these generalizations. The number of interest groups with a stake in the Clinton plan's fate — given the nearly one trillion dollar medical economy — was enormous; there were more than 8,000 registered lobbyists alone in Washington and thousands more trying to influence the outcome under some other label. The estimates of expenditures on the battle are in the hundreds of millions; one trade association, The Pharmaceutical Manufacturer's Association, spent $7 million on "public relations" by 1993. The most noted effort was that of the Health Insurance Association of America, who produced the infamous Harry and Louise add. Washington was awash in interest group activities during the health care reform battle of 1993–1994, but the character, impact, and meaning of those activities are far from clear.

[15]Marmor and Plowden, *supra* note 2 at 810.

[16]Freeman, R., "Competition in Context: The Politics of Health Care Reform in Europe," *International Journal for Quality in Health Care*, 10.5 (1998): 395–401.

[17]Giaimo, S. and P. Manow, "Institutions and Ideas into Politics: Health Care Reform in Britain and Germany," in *Health Policy Reform, National Variations and Globalization*, eds. Altenstetter C. and J. W. Bjorkman (Basingstoke: Macmillan, 1997): 197.

[18]Morone, J. A., "American Political Culture and the Search for Lessons from Abroad," *Journal of Health Politics, Policy and Law*, 15.1 (1990): 41.

[19]Freeman, *supra* note 4.

[20]Bennett, C. J., "Understanding Ripple Effects: The Cross-National Adoption of Policy Instruments for Bureaucratic Accountability," *Governance*, 10.3 (1997): 213–233.

[21]Report Four Country Conference, "Pharmaceutical Policies in the US, Canada, Germany and the Netherlands" (Amsterdam: Four Country Conference, 2000).

[22]Lubbers, R., "In Seeking a Third Way, The Dutch Model is Worth a Look," *International Herald Tribune* (Sep. 9, 1997).

[23]One of the Dutch policy commentators on a chapter dealing with cross-national perspectives on the Dutch welfare state and its health system strikingly illustrates how one can oddly justify not learning much from comparative policy studies. "Comparative studies," he writes, "are generally backward looking, so don't always provide us with the right answers for the future." The restrictive definition of the purpose of comparative inquiry — getting the "right answers" — limits greatly what this Dutch public servant would consider useful.

[24]Hacker, J., *The Divided Welfare State: The Battle over Public and Private Benefits in the United States* (New York: Cambridge University Press, 2002): 7.

[25]As Hacker rightly points out, the "share of the US economy devoted to social spending is not all that different from the corresponding portion in even the most generous of European welfare states." The "sources" of the spending — tax expenditures and employment-benefits especially — are what distinguishes the American case. The same myth of the "lean" American welfare state was the object of criticism in a book published a decade earlier, see Marmor, Mashaw and Harvey, *supra* note 8.

[26]Field, M. (ed.), *Success and Crisis in National Health Systems: A Comparative Approach* (New York: Routledge, 1989): 13.

[27]"Report of Workshop on EU Law and National Health Policy" (The Hague: Ministry of Health, Welfare and Sports, 2004).

[28]Poullier, J. P., "Managing Health in the 1990s: A European Overview," *Health Service Journal,* (27 Apr., 1989): 6.

[29]Hunter, D., "A New Focus for Dialogue," *European Health Reform: The Bulletin of the European Network and Database,* 1 (Mar. 1995).

[30]Jacobs, A., "Seeing Difference: Market Health Reform in Europe," *Journal of Health Politics, Policy and Law,* 23.1 (1998): 1–33.; Marmor, T. R., "The Rage for Reform: Sense and Nonsense in Health Policy," in *Health Reform: Public Success, Private Failure,* eds. Drache, D. and T. Sullivan (London: Routledge, 1999): 260–272.

[31]Jacobs, L., Marmor, T. M. and J. Oberlander, "The Oregon Health Plan and the Political Paradox of Rationing: What Advocates and Critics Have Claimed and What Oregon Did," *Journal of Health Politics, Policy and Law,* 24.1 (1999): 161–180.

[32]The 2000 WHO report seeks to rank health systems across the globe. The WHO posed good questions about how health systems work: are they fair, responsive to patient needs, efficient, and do they provide good quality health care. But it answered those questions without the much attention to the difficulties of describing responsiveness or fairness or efficiency in some universalistic and reliable manner. What is more, the report used as partial evidence the opinions of WHO personnel to "verify" what takes place in Australia, Oman, Turkmenistan, or Canada. Moreover, while the report claims to provide data in order to improve health systems across the globe, it is hard to see how a health minister of a country ranked, say, at place 125 on the ranking order, has any stake to climb the ladder. Predictable, most of the uproar about the report was the battle between the countries that ranked high but not highest. Many journalists and members of parliament quoted the report as a critical comment on the failures of the national health system whereas predictable, the French minister saw the number one ranking of his country (that in the end turned out to be based on a calculating error) as proof of effectiveness of his policy. With comparatives like that, one can easily understand why some funders of research regard comparative policy studies as excuses for boondoggles. But that should not drive out the impulse for serious cross-national scholarship and learning. Williams, A., "Science or Marketing at WHO? A Commentary on World Health 2000," *Health Economics,* 10.2 (2000): 93–100.

[33]Lipset, S. M., *Continental Divide: The Values and Institutions of the United States and Canada* (New York: Routledge, 1990).

[34]Maioni, A., *Parting at the Crossroads: The Emergence of Health Insurance in the United States and Canada* (Princeton, NJ: Princeton University Press, 1998); White, J., *Competing Solutions: American Health Care Proposals and International Experiences* (Washington, DC: The Brookings Institution, 1995).

[35]Anderson, O., *Health Care: Can There Be Equity? The United States, Sweden and England* (New York: John Wiley, 1972).

[36]For a retrospective appreciation of Anderson, see Freeman, R. and T. Marmor, "Making Sense of Health Services Politics Through Cross-National Comparison," *Journal of Health Services Research and Policy*, 8.3 (2003): 180–182.

[37]Wilensky, H. L., *Rich Democracies: Political Economy, Public Policy, and Performance* (Berkley: University of California Press, 2002). There is a rich scholarly disability literature, with a good deal of knowledgeable commentary on comparative policy developments. See especially Aarts, L. and P. De Jong, "Able to Work? How Policies Help Disabled People in 20 OECD Countries," (Paris: OECD, 2003).

[38]Tuohy, C., "The Political Attitudes of Ontario Physicians: A Skill Group Perspective," Ph.D. thesis (New Haven, CT: Yale University Department of Political Science, 1974); Stone, D., *The Disabled State* (Philadelphia: Temple University Press, 1984); Freddi, G. and J. W. Bjorkman (eds.), *Controlling Medical Professionals. The Comparative Politics of Health Governance* (London: Sage, 1989); Wilsford, D., *Doctors and the State: The Politics of Health Care in France and the United States* (Durham, NC: Duke University Press, 1991); Immergut, E. M., *Health Politics Interests and Institutions in Western Europe*, Cambridge Studies in Comparative Studies (Cambridge: Cambridge University Press, 1992); Pierson, P., *Dismantling the Welfare State? Reagan, Thatcher and the Politics of Retrenchment* (Cambridge: Cambridge University Press, 1994).

[39]Marmor, T. R. and K. G. H. Okma, "Review Essay: Health Care Systems in Transition," *Journal of Health Politics, Policy and Law*, 28.4 (2003): 747–755.

[40]Blendon, R. J. and M. Brodie, "Public Opinion and Health Policy," in *Health Politics and Policy*, eds. Litman, T. J. and L. S. Robins (Albany, NY: Delma, 1997).

[41]World Health Organization, "The World Health Report 2000, Health Systems: Improving Performance" (Geneva: World Health Organization, 2000).

[42]Ham, C., R. Robinson and M. Benzeval (eds.), *Health Check: Healthcare Reforms in an International Context* (London: King's Fund Institute, 1990); OECD, "The Reform of Health Care. A Comparative Analysis of Seven OECD Countries," Health Policy Studies (Paris: OECD, 1992); OECD, "The Reform of Health Care. A Review of Seventeen OECD Countries" (Paris: OECD, 1994); Wall, A. (ed.), *Health Care Systems in Liberal Democracies* (London: Routledge, 1996); Altenstetter, C. and J. W. Bjorkman (eds.), *Health Policy Reform, National Variations and Globalization* (Basingstoke: Macmillan,1997); Ham, C. (ed.), *Health Care Reform: Learning from International Experience* (Buckingham: Open University Press, 1997); Raffell, M. W. (ed.), *Health Care and Reform in Industrialized Countries* (University Park: Pennsylvania State University Press, 1997); Powell, F. and A. Wessen, *Health Care Systems in Transition* (Thousand Oaks, CA: Sage, 1999).

[43]Good examples are Freddi and Bjorkman's *Controlling Medical Professionals* (London: Sage, 1989) and Ranade's *Markets and Health Care* (Harlow: Longman, 1998); another is White's *Competing Solutions* (Washington: Brookings Institution, 1995), written at the Brookings Institution to draw lessons from OECD experience for the universal health insurance debate in the United States. Sometimes journals present work of this kind: see the case studies of priority setting in *Health Policy*, 50.1–2 (1999), for example, and the *Journal of Health Politics, Policy & Law*, 26.4 (2001) for international commentary.

[44]A good example of this genre is the book edited by Bayer, R. and E. Feldman, *Blood Feuds: Aids, Blood and the Politics of the Medical Disaster* (Oxford: Oxford University Press, 1999) on the politics of contaminated blood in Germany, France, Japan, Canada, Denmark, and the United States. The theme is taken up in Bovens, M., P. t' Hart and B.G. Peters (eds.), *Success and Failure in Governance: A Comparative Analysis of European States* (Cheltenham: Edward Elgar, 2002) which also looks at medical professions and health care reform.

[45]For instance, Pierson (1994) compares retrenchment politics in Reagan's America and Thatcher's England; Immergut (1992) compares the disputes over national health insurance in France, Switzerland, and Sweden in the early part of the twentieth century; Maioni (1998) compares the different paths to national health insurance taken in Canada and the United States; Moran, in *Governing the Health Care State* (Manchester: Manchester University Press, 1999), assesses the political economy of health care in Britain, Germany and the United States; Freeman, in *The Politics of Health in Europe (*Manchester: Manchester University Press, 2000), assesses the politics of health care in five European countries.

[46]Tuohy, C., *Accidental Logics* (Oxford: Oxford University Press, 1999).

How Not to Think About Medicare Reform†

T. R. Marmor*

I. Perspectives on Criticism

"Criticism is prejudice made plausible." H.L. Mencken
"A wise skepticism is the first attribute of a good critic." James Russell Lowell
"Prejudice, noun, a vagrant opinion without visible means of support." Ambrose Bierce

II. Introduction

Americans are fascinated by new things — new cars, fancier cell phones, hand-held computers that one can use to surf the Net and store family photos. For many, new is better and old is, well, old, out of date. As Medicare reaches the venerable age of 35, there is a lot of talk of "re-forming" it in the sense of changing the program substantially. The baby boomers's aging has fueled the sense that Medicare is — or soon will be — in crisis. Many believe this demographic shift demands a major re-casting of the program. Simply increasing funding (for Medicare), in the words of one of today's speakers, is like "putting more gas in an old car — it still runs like an old car and doesn't have any of the features of a new car."[1]

My aim today is not to prescribe how Medicare should or should not be changed. That role I have played elsewhere. Today, as someone who has spent a career studying Medicare (and medical care more generally), I want to raise some questions and question some assumptions. What, for instance, lies behind claims that America needs a "new" Medicare? Are those assumptions accurate? Such a critical examination is a precondition of sensible policy choice. Before deciding which new car to buy, we should first ask whether we need a new car at all.

I characterize and challenge four common assumptions that are employed to support the idea that Medicare requires transformative change. Again, my purpose is not to tell you what an ideal Medicare program would be. It is, rather, to suggest how not to think about Medicare reform.

Assumption 1. The aging of the baby boomers as fiscal tsunami.

The aging of the baby boomers, it is widely claimed, will bankrupt Medicare. This argument, popularized by Peter Peterson's Gray Dawn, has been reiterated by many journalists and politicians in recent years. This claim makes the mistake of confusing an incontrovertible fact — the population is aging — with an unwarranted conclusion — that aging will produce "unsustainable" expenditures for Medicare as currently structured.

The truth is that, despite the seemingly obvious causal connection, demography is not financial destiny. It is not the case that increasing numbers of elderly — even the "old old" (over 85 years of age) — requires unaffordable outlays. Other industrial democracies have already experienced the aging we anticipate. Their experience is relevant, and counterintuitive. There is no correlation between the aging of the population and spending on medical care. See Figure 1.

For those who have a hard time making sense of the scatter plot, take a look at Table 1 to see the same point.

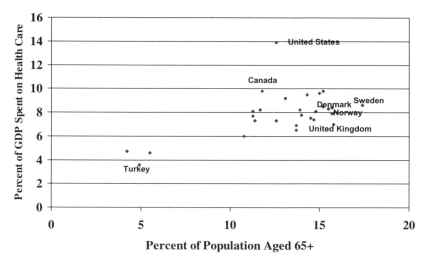

Figure 1. Relationship between age of population and health spending, OECD 1994. *Source:* OECD Health Data 2000.

Table 1. Relationship between age of population and health spending, OECD 1994.

OECD nations	% Population over 65	% GDP on health	Age rank	Health spending rank
Australia	11.6	8.5	17	9
Austria	15.0	9.7	9	3
Belgium	15.3	8.2	7	11
Canada	11.9	9.8	16	2
Denmark	15.4	6.6	6	18
Finland	14.0	8.3	12	10
France	14.7	9.7	10	3
Germany	16.0	8.6	3	7
Greece	15.2	3.6	8	20
Iceland	11.1	8.1	20	12
Ireland	11.5	7.3	19	15
Italy	14.6	8.6	11	7
Japan	14.0	7.3	12	15
Netherlands	13.3	8.8	14	6
New Zealand	11.6	7.7	17	13
Norway	16.2	5.5	2	19
Sweden	17.5	7.7	1	13
Switzerland	15.7	9.6	5	5
United Kingdom	15.8	6.9	4	17
United States	12.7	14.2	15	1

Age rank lists countries by percent of population above 65 years of age, with the oldest country having a rank of "1." Health rank lists countries by percent of GDP spent on health care, with the country with the highest expenditures having a rank of "1."
Source: OECD Health Data 1996 and OECD Labor Force Statistics 1974–1994.

Indeed, as health economist Thomas Getzen reports, "in those [OECD] countries where the fraction of population over age 65 has grown most rapidly, spending has not increased any more rapidly than in countries where the elderly population has grown most slowly."[2] It is true that the United States spends a higher percentage of its GDP on health care than does any other OECD nation. But that spending is not significantly "caused" by the growth of our elderly population. It is a reflection of inflationary forces in American medical care generally, not dominated by the age of our patients.

The assumption that an aging population will bankrupt Medicare ignores other factors. The affordability of any societal spending depends on the output of the workforce, and, of course, the size of the work force relative to those not working. When looking at demographics, therefore, one needs to look not at the ratio of elderly to workers, but of all non-workers to workers. As Figure 2 shows, the answer to this question — the so-called dependency ratio — does not conform to the conventional portraiture of a dire future.[3,4]

Note that although the ratio of non-workers to workers will rise from current levels, the dependency ratio projected for 2040 is still substantially lower than what was the case in the 1950s, 1960s, and 1970s. What we have as burdens depends, in short, on what else we are supporting. These projections, of course, are not infallible predictions. They do not assume, for example, that individuals over 64 will be gainfully employed. Improved health and extended life expectancy may well increase the number of workers over age 64 decades hence.

A final note on the implications of aging. If aging creates greater financial demands in certain sectors — say nursing homes — it does not mean those needs are unaffordable. Imagine a parallel argument about the defense department. At the time of the Gulf War, no one argued that US military involvement would cause the Department of Defense to go bankrupt. In a democracy we constantly make choices between competing demands.

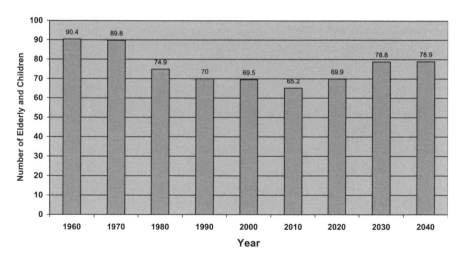

Figure 2. Number of dependents per 100 workers, age 20–64. *Source:*

A zero-base budgeting approach across decades and generations is unrealistic. No one would suggest that every school should be kept open and the total number of teachers kept at year 2000 levels if the school age population were to drop by one third. That a larger percentage of the population will receive Medicare in 30 years does not by itself demonstrate any one point. It does not prove that Medicare should be restructured. It does not show that the federal share of funding should be held constant. Rather, public choices about the allocation of government funds should be expected to change over time as successive generations address different social circumstances.

Assumption 2. Medicare must be reformed because it has been unable to control its costs.

Another asserted, but inaccurate assumption is Medicare's alleged inability to control its costs. Proponents of re-making Medicare in the image of private health insurance are quick to highlight seemingly decisive examples of profligate spending. So, for instance, critics point to Medicare's growing portion of the spending pie, up nearly 30 percent between 1980 and 1996 — from 15.2 percent to 19.6 percent. Another picture, using other years and/or other bases of comparison, is different. Indeed, over the last 25 years, Medicare has on average done as well as private health insurance in controlling its per capita costs, as Figure 3 illustrates.[5]

The more recent data (from 1993–1999) is, forgive the expression, manic depressive: a sharp increase in Medicare's relative spending from 1993–1995, followed in 1996–1999 by equally sharp relative decrease.

In assessing Medicare's performance, one must be certain to compare apples to apples — not oranges. For an accurate and meaningful per capita comparison, costs must be for services covered by both Medicare and private insurance. As everyone in this room knows all too well, many of the per capita savings in private insurance have been achieved by decreasing or denying coverage, by risk shifting and risk selecting. (In contrast, Medicare has reduced expected outlays largely by reducing payments to providers.) Figure 3 shows how Medicare's expenditure growth rate, through such instruments as DRGs in 1983 and RBRVS in 1989, fell below that of

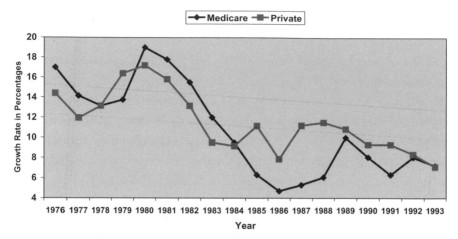

Figure 3. Per capita growth rates of services covered by both Medicare and private insurance, 1976–1993. *Source:*

private insurance. On careful examination, it turns out that the conventional image of a Medicare program ballooning wildly out of control is inaccurate: an example of how not to think about Medicare.

Assumption 3. That the forecasts of Medicare's future require that it be transformed.

Much of the debate over Medicare's future has been based on forecasts: forecasts of the program's likely aggregate cost, forecasts of the number of elderly beneficiaries, forecasts of the depletion of the Medicare Hospital Trust Fund, and so on. I am not here to say that forecasts are foolish. Forecasts can be useful in public policy making. They can alert one to potential troubles and in that way prompt reflection. But extended forecasts cannot and should not be the dominant justifications for reform.

Virtually everyone who has looked seriously at the Medicare program agrees about the perils of forecasting in this area. Henry Aaron's recent remarks are illustrative: "A fog of fundamental unknowability," he noted, "shrouds projections of Medicare costs beyond just a few years."[6]

Indeed, they do, as Figure 4 illustrates.[7] The CBO forecasts have varied dramatically over less than a decade. The longer the time-frame, the

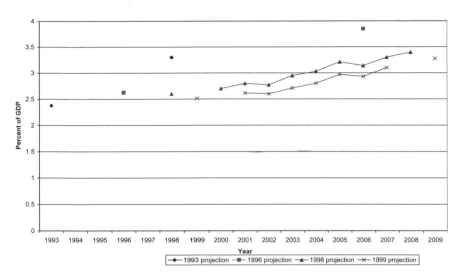

Figure 4. Medicare+Medicaid spending. CBO projections, selected years. *Source: Thinking About Aging: What we Know, What We Can't Know, and Why It Matters.*

less realistic is any forecast. Different rates of expected economic growth, for instance, dramatically change the projection of government revenues.

Consider the following illustration of forecasting variability in Figure 5.[8] Total government expenditures — federal, state, and local — are projected to rise from 34 percent of GDP in 1997 to a stunning 61 percent in 2030 if one assumes that the US economy grows 1 percent a year in real terms over the next 30 years. That crushing burden disappears if one changes a single variable. With real economic growth of 3 percent annually, government spending as a percentage of GDP is projected to decrease to 32 percent. Uncertain and debatable assumptions drive the forecasts, and there lies the peril of fatalistic futurology.

This variability is at least as great for Medicare projections, as the most recent CBO figures illustrate.[9] In 1993, the Congressional Budget Office projected that the Medicare Part A Trust Fund would run out of money by 1999. In 1999, the projection of so-called insolvency had moved to 2015. By March of this year, the projection had moved to 2023. Obviously, the booming economy explains the increasingly optimistic estimates. But economic growth is not the only important variable here. Projections

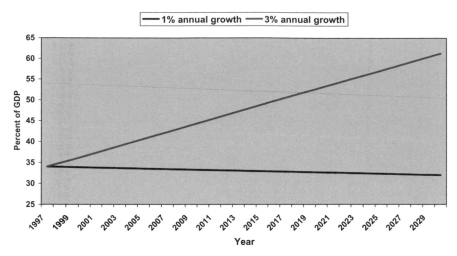

Figure 5. Total government expenditures as a percentage of GDP through 2030, using two assumptions of economic growth. *Source:*

of the number of elderly, their state of health, their preferences for medical care, and the types and cost of medical services in 30 years — all make it very difficult to predict Medicare expenditures with any degree of certainty. Technological advances may transform the care the elderly receive (and its costs) in ways that we cannot now begin to anticipate.[10]

This is not to claim, I repeat, that forecasting is fruitless. It is to say that one should be skeptical about long-range forecasts as the foundation for wholesale change now. As my colleague Jon Oberlander has documented, interest in "re-forming" Medicare peaks every time the Medicare trust fund is projected to become "insolvent" in seven or fewer years.[11] Although such crisis "trip-wires" are understandable, and prompt attention to costs, they do not justify transformative policy changes.[12]

Assumption 4. Medicare should be transformed to mirror current private health insurance plans.

One of the most striking assertions about Medicare's future is the claim that the program should mirror the now-prevailing structure of private health

146

insurance markets. To illustrate: During the Medicare debates of 1995, for example, Henry Aaron and Bob Reischauer asserted that "congressional reforms will — and should — bring Medicare more in line with the structure of health care financing and delivery that is evolving to serve the non-Medicare population."[13]

Human beings like parallels. That may help explain the appeal of calls for a public sector program to mirror the private sector pattern. But in the case of Medicare, the parallelism starts from a false analogy to Medicare's birth. At the time of Medicare's enactment in 1965, fee-for-service Blue Cross/Blue Shield plans were the norm for working Americans. The elderly sought, and with the passage of Medicare secured, a government program that mirrored what was viewed by the elderly themselves as desirable private insurance plans. The creation of separate Part A (hospital) and Part B (physician) coverage reflects Medicare's borrowing from private health insurance plans of the period.

Some point to this historical parallelism to suggest that today, when most American families are covered by "managed care," Medicare should be changed from its fee-for-service to a more "modern" managed care format. The argument is not that the elderly want such a change, or that they would be better off with such a change. No, the argument is that the elderly should not be allowed to have "gold-plated" fee-for-service coverage when the rest of Americans struggle along with increasingly restrictive HMOs, and prepaid group practices.

It is no surprise to those of you in this room that the public is far from enthusiastic about "managed care." In a 1998 Harris poll, managed care firms ranked second from the bottom in terms of the public's positive feelings about the industry. Whom did the public like less? Only tobacco companies.[14] If anything, those negative feelings have increased recently. Federal and state legislatures are deluged with constituent complaints about private, "managed care" plans. So, the argument for parallelism is particularly weak now.

Rather than using private sector comparisons to improve Medicare's coverage, as was done at Medicare's birth, the current proposals embrace more restrictive models. What explains these calls for "equal treatment?" The calls are not coming from the elderly. If one looks at what the elderly themselves want, one finds overwhelming support for Medicare in its present, largely fee-for-service form. Then why? Presumably to avoid resentment by those not in Medicare. If true, that resentment would indeed become a threat to Medicare's viability. Is there any basis for the assumption that Part B's less restrictive and arguably preferable medical coverage for the elderly has or will lead to resentment? Although younger age cohorts express concern for the long-term financial well-being of Medicare,[15] there is no evidence that they support changes to remake the program in the image of much-criticized managed care.

III. Conclusion

My topic today has been framed negatively: how not to think about Medicare reform. This was my choice, not the conference's promoters, who asked me to discuss what I regard as important for me to say to this audience. That I have done, emphasizing currently fashionable presumptions that are false, misleading, or inadequate as bases for adjusting Medicare to contemporary circumstances.

But I want to close with two qualifications, qualifications without which my message will not be understood. I, as well as others, recognize that Medicare could use adjustments. Any substantial program does after more than three decades of operation. As an advocate, I have ideas about prescription drugs, about changes in local offices handling Medicare questions, and so on. But I am not a policy advocate today, or in the book on Medicare's politics that I have recently published. As a scholar and a speaker today, I am concerned about how to understand Medicare and the discussion about change. And to do that, one must avoid common sources of distortion. They include conflating description with criticism, understanding with evaluating, unsure forecasts with accurate predictions, and the like.

I will have accomplished my task if my thoughts about how not to think about Medicare appear well-grounded, and not, as Mencken sardonically wrote, "prejudice made plausible."

Endnotes

†Originally published in the *Journal of Health Politics, Policy and Law*, Volume 26, Issue 1, Pages 107–117, © Duke University Press.

*Theodore R. Marmor, Professor of Public Policy & Management, Professor of Political Science, Yale School of Management, New Haven, Connecticut, USA.

[1] Senator John Breaux, "Opening Statement," National Bipartisan Commission on the Future of Medicare, Meeting (Mar. 16, 1999).

[2] Getzen, T. E., "Population Aging and the Growth of Health Expenditures," *Journal of Gerontology*, 47.3 (1994): S102.

[3] National Academy of Social Insurance, *Social Insurance Update*, 2.4 (Apr. 1997).

[4] National Academy on an Aging Society, *Demography is not Destiny* (1999) 12.

[5] Moon, M. and S. Zuckerman, *Are Private Insures Really controlling Spending Better Than Medicare?* (Menlo Park, CA: Henry J. Kaiser Family Foundation, 1995): Chart 2.

[6] Aaron, H. J., "Thinking About Aging: What We Know, What We Can't Know, and Why It Matters," Paper delivered at the conference on Policy Options for an Aging Society, Council on the Economic Impact of Health System Change, Leesburg, VA (Oct. 21–23, 1999). Also see recent piece by Paul Starr in *The American Prospect*.

[7] Aaron, H. J., "Thinking about Aging," *Policy Options for an Aging Society* (Oct. 21, 1999): 21.

[8] National Academy on an Aging Society, *supra* note 4 at 27.

[9] Pear, R., "Outlook Better for Social Security and Medicare," *New York Times*, (Mar. 31, 2000): A18.

[10] Marmor, T. R., "Forecasting America Health Care: How We Got Here and Where We Might be Going," *Journal of Health Politics, Policy and Law*, 23.3 (Jun. 1998): 551–571.

[11] See data supplied by Jon Oberlander, cited in Marmor, T. R., *The Politics of Medicare* (New York: Aldine de Gruyter, 2000): 130.

[12] For a more extensive discussion of the fallacy of speaking of "insolvency" of a public fund, see Marmor, *id.* at 135–137.

[13] Aaron, H. J., and R. D. Reischauer, "The Medicare Reform Debate: What Is the Next Step?" *Health Affairs*, 14.4 (1995): 8–30. See, also, the similar remarks of Stuart Butler of the Heritage Foundation in 1997: "Medicare should provide health insurance comparable to that received by others. Most workers have a choice among managed care plans with a defined contribution by employers," National Academy of Social Insurance, *supra* note 3.

[14] Blendon, R. J., *et al.*, "Understanding the Managed Care Backlash," *Health Affairs*, 17.4 (Jul./Aug. 1998): 80–94.

[15] *Id.*

Index

Aaron, H. 93, 94, 96, 97, 144, 147
Accidental Logics (Tuohy) 130
aging, of population
   elderly. *See* elderly
   health spending and 141f
Altenstetter, C. 129
AMCRA. *See* American Managed Care and
   Review Association
American Managed Care and Review
   Association (AMCRA) 29, 31
Anderson, O. 128

baby boomers 140–143
Barzelay, M. 15
basic care model
   Canada and 60
   cost control and v
   financial constraints on 58–59
   fundamental 57
   limits of 58–63
   OECD and 58
   Oregon plan. *See* Oregon Medicare plan
   rights and 57
   universal access to 56–58
Bell Curve, The (Murray) 24n7
Bennett, C. J. 118
Bernstein, J. 86
Beveridge Report 24n7, 134n7
Bjorkman, J. W. 129
Blair government 17, 18
Blendon, R. 24n9
Blendon, Robert 108n62
Blue Cross/Blue Shield system 147
Blumenthal, D. 85
bonding mechanisms 29
Bosanquet, N. 16
Bowman, K. 108n62
Boyum, D. 55–79

Breaux, J. 43
Breaux-Thomas Commission 90–91
Brown, L. 30, 89
Brown, Lawrence 30
Buchanan, Alan 57
Bull***Bingo game 4, 5, 5f

Canada
   Canada Health Act 78
   CMA and 60–62
   health expenditures 122f, 133n13
   health information and 18
   Lalonde Report of 1974 69
   Medicare and 114
   Mulroney and 116
   national health insurance 78
   rationing and 117
   socialized medicine 117
   United States and 117
Canadian Institute for Health Information
   (CIHI) 18
Canadian Medical Association (CMA) 60,
   61, 62
capitation 12, 32, 36
   defined 47n17
   fee-for-service and 39
   HMOs and 33–36, 49n29, 50n44
   managed care and 12, 31, 47n17
   PPOs and 49n29
   risk sharing 39
Cassel, C. 84
CIHI. *See* Canadian Institute for Health
   Information
Clinton administration 9, 27, 41, 96, 120,
   135n14
closed networks 40
Committee on Choices in Health Care
   (Netherlands) 59, 60–63

151

The CCP, the BDOS and the BIOS are installation-independent. That is, they are portable from one machine to another similar or upward-compatible machine without any change. These modules are normally written in assembly language to occupy less memory and to execute faster. Hence, a DOS implemented for an 8080-based machine can be used on any 8080- or Z80-based microcomputer, but not on a 6800 or 6502 machine.

Physical I/O drivers, on the other hand, are installation-dependent, and provision is made to customize them. 6800 and 6502 machines have standard I/O routines supplied in ROM by chip manufacturers (e.g., MIKBUG from Motorola for the 6800). There is no such standardization amount 8080 and Z80 machines. Even where a manufacturer supplies a monitor with his CPU board, there is no agreement on the registers used for parameter passing, nor on port number assignment. For this reason, most operating systems for 8080/Z80 machines include physical I/O drivers, but source code is supplied for these so that port assignments can be changed to suit the customer's system.

The CCP, BDOS and BIOS are supplied in a relocatable form to be put at the top of memory, a parameter for the user to enter when installing a system.

The Console Command Processor (CCP)

The CCP is the interface between the operator and the DOS, and therefore includes several basic functions. The number of these depends upon the architecture of the operating system as a whole. A minimum set includes these functions:

- Select a disk drive and bring the file directory from its diskette into memory.
- List or display the file directory from a diskette on one of the current drives.
- Create or destroy a file.
- List the contents of an ASCII file.
- Load an executable binary file from a diskette into memory and run it.
- Save a file, i.e., transfer the contents of a specified memory block to disk.

Some disk operating systems include monitor functions to:

- Transfer control (jump) directly to a specified memory location.
- Display the contents of a memory block.
- Alter one or more memory cells.

A debug/trace monitor, an assembler, a text editor and other utilities can usually be executed directly as other programs and brought in from disk when needed. The debug/trace monitor operates upon user programs in the standard transient program area of memory. It is usually loaded just below the operating system, so that it does not interfere with the user program under examination. In CP/M and its derivatives, this monitor (DDT) has its own interfaces to the console and DOS and overlays the normal CCP. The other utilities, however, are all loaded into the transient program area for execution.

The DOS

The main DOS component is the file management system. Microcomputer systems differ widely in their file management procedures. Some require that file size be declared at creation time; others allow dynamic allocation of space during sequential writing and reuse space released by deletions. We describe the file management system of CP/M*, a widely used microcomputer operating system.

The I/O System (IOS)

The I/O system normally resides above the DOS, and the first item in it is a jump vector containing jumps to each of the disk primitives and I/O drivers. This jump vector is always in the same location relative to the start of the CCP, regardless of where the operating system is located in memory. Thus, application programs can issue a subroutine call directly to a peripheral driver by referencing its location in the jump vector. A program can also issue calls to disk primitives (track seek, move in, move out, read sector, etc.). Utilities mainly concerned with nonstandard disk operations make use of this feature to speed execution. An application program customarily issues a call to the standard DOS entry point, passing the location of read/write buffers in one set of registers and a function code in another. A simple call thus avoids coding a routine which already exists for writing a string to the console, reading the next sector, opening or closing a file and other OS functions.

13.2 DISK ORGANIZATION

In this chapter, for the sake of simplicity, we consider only the standard distribution version of CP/M Version 1.4, issued on a single-density, soft-sectored, 8-inch diskette.

Main Divisions of Diskette Space

The standard soft-sectored, single-density, 8-inch diskette is divided into 77 tracks (numbered 0 through 76), with 26 sectors (numbered 1 through 26) per track. This conforms to the IBM 3740 diskette layout; such diskettes are called "IBM-compatible."

Each sector stores 128 bytes; the two cyclic redundancy check (CRC) bytes and other overhead bytes which follow the data are not included in this count. Thus, the total storage space is 77*26*128= 256,256 bytes, formatted. This, too, follows the IBM format, but again is a function of a BDOS table; it is possible to set the sector size to any multiple of 128 by changing the table entry, but files would not then be portable except to another system with the same blocking factor.

To run under CP/M, diskette storage space is divided into three areas:

- CP/M system area.
- File directory area.
- File data area.

CP/M System Area.   Tracks 0 and 1 are reserved for CP/M even though the system need not be present on every disk. The cold-start loader is contained in track 0, sector 1; the CCP and BDOS cccupy the rest of track 0 as well as 17 sectors on track 1; the remaining nine sectors (1,152 bytes) of track 1 are available for the customized I/O system (CBIOS). The number of sectors actually used by the CBIOS depends on what drivers and features are included by the disk controller manufacturer.

File Directory Area.   Sixteen sectors on track 2 are reserved for the file directory. Each entry is 32 bytes long; thus, there is room for (16 X 128)/32 = 64 entries in the standard system. Note, however, that sector allocation for the directory is controlled by a table in the BDOS; OEM's licensed by Digital Research, Inc., to reconfigure the system can expand the number of directory entries to 255 by changing this table.

File Storage Area.   The remaining 10 sectors on track 2 and all sectors on tracks 3 through 76 are available for files.

Files, Blocks, Records, Etc.

The application program is usually written in a POL such as BASIC. The programmer defines his file to contain a number of cohesive pieces of information called records. Most microcomputer POLs restrict us to fixed-size records—records that are all the same length. But that length can be set at creation time within wide limits—10, 100, even 1,000 bytes.

Now, let's concentrate only on BASIC. We can use our file, a collection of records, either sequentially, in the order in which they were created, or directly, by giving the ordinal position of the record relative to the beginning of the file.

Consider sequential retrieval first. When operating interpretively, the program makes a request for a record via the interpreter, which then makes its request of the file manager for the next record in the file. The file manager examines the file control block, a RAM buffer containing information about where the file is stored on the diskette. The file manager determines the next block number and converts it to an absolute block number. A block is the quantity of information delivered in one I/O action. Generally it is equivalent in quantity to one sector. Hence for the standard 8-inch diskette a block is 128 bytes.

From the above definitions we can say that there are

- Several small records in a block.
- Several blocks to a large record.

The file manager makes this all transparent to its users. As blocks are acquired, they are placed into memory areas called buffers as required by the program.

Skewing

You might expect sequentially numbered blocks to be kept in sequential sectors, but this is not expeditious. Each block ends with CRC bytes. On reading, these are checked by the controller using an algorithm which takes time to go through. Also, BDOS has housekeeping chores to perform. By the time we are ready to read the next sector, it has flown by; we have to wait for a full diskette revolution to get back to that next sector.

For this reason, consecutive blocks are mapped onto the disk one per sector, but with several sectors between those assigned to consecutive blocks. For example, in Figure 13.1, block 1 is assigned to sector 1, but block 2 is in sector 7, and block 3 is in sector 13. This is called skew. The standard IBM-compatible skew (sometimes called interlace) for CP/M is six sectors, shown in Figure 13.1; this mapping is identical for all tracks, whether for directory or file storage. Translation from block number to sector number is performed by a lookup table that is contained in BDOS. (Some OSs, including Version 2.2 of CP/M, put the table in the BIOS). Disk utilities that use disk primitives directly provide their own translation table. Thus, an application program using the disk primitives to gain access to blocks 19, 20 and 21 on a track would in fact access sectors 6, 12 and 18 on that track. After completing the housekeeping for sector 6, there is only a minimal wait before sector 12 (containing the next consecutive block) arrives under the read head.

Sector ID numbers formatted on disk	01	02	03	04	05	06	07	08	09	10	11	12	13	14	15	16	17	18	19	20	21	22	23	24	25	26
Logical sector #s																										
Read on pass 1	01						02						03						04						05	
Read on pass 2					06						07						08						09			
Read on pass 3			10						11						12						13					
Read on pass 4	14							15						16						17						18
Read on pass 5						19						20						21						22		
Read on pass 6				23						24						25						26				

Figure 13.1.   Skewing of sectors.

Modern diskette controllers are much faster than those for which this skew was designed. A system that uses a fast controller and version 2.2 of CP/M need not use any skew when creating files for its own use. However, distribution diskettes use the standard skew in the interests of general compatibility.

Direct Access

To obtain direct access (more often called random access in the microcomputer world) to a record by giving its record number, the file manager has to do some computation. For example, if records are 32 bytes long, each block contains four records. If the interpreter requests record 86, this number is divided by 4, the result of which is 21 with a remainder of 2. Thus, the required record will be found in relative block 21 of the file, which contains records 84 through 87. The file manager now consults the space allocation map in the file control block to find the absolute block number, converts this to the track and sector number and reads that sector into the disk buffer. The file manager reports completion of the read operation, and the interpreter then searches the disk buffer for record 86.

13.3 KEEPING TRACK OF DISK SPACE USAGE

Unlike some operating systems, CP/M does not require that file size be specified at the time of creation. Instead, space on the disk is allocated dynamically, as needed. Space that is released as the result of closing a file from which at least 1K has been deleted is available for reassignment to another file. The tools that permit this synamic space allocation are:

- The allocation bit map.
- The file control block (FCB).
- The directory.

Allocation Bit Map

For every drive configured in the system, the BDOS maintains a space allocation bit map for the diskette currently mounted there. This map (consisting of 243 individual bits for an 8-inch single-density disk under CP/M) is computed from the directory entries and placed in memory when the drive is first activated. It may be modified during write operations if any file's allocation changes. Typing Ctrl-C erases all bit maps in memory except those for drive A and for the currently logged-in disk. If the diskette on the currently logged-in drive is changed, the operator must type Ctrl-C or the application program must log in the drive again; if this is not done, the bit allocation will not correspond to the mapping of the new disk and data may be lost.

Each bit in the map represents a group (sometimes called a cluster) of eight consecutively numbered blocks on the diskette. The bit positions and their associated groups are numbered 00 through F2 hex (see Figure 13.2). The first two bits are associated with the first 16 on track 2; these two groups of blocks (00 and 01) contain the file directory. Bits 00 and 01 in the allocation map always contain 1s, even when no directory entries have been made, to ensure that the directory is never overwritten by a file.

When BDOS receives a request to create a file, it searches the allocation bit map to find a 0 bit; the number of this bit is the number of the first free group. BDOS then sets the map bit to 1 and places the 1-byte hexadecimal group number in the mapping area of the file control block (FCB) created for the new file.

Each time a write operation is requested for the file, BDOS examines the last group number in the FCB and also the next block

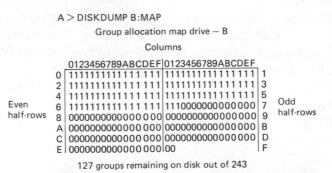

```
                     A > DISKDUMP B:MAP
                   Group allocation map drive — B
                              Columns

              0123456789ABCDEF 0123456789ABCDEF
            0 1111111111111111 1111111111111111  1
            2 1111111111111111 1111111111111111  3
            4 1111111111111111 1111111111111111  5
    Even    6 1111111111111111 1110000000000000  7  Odd
 half-rows  8 0000000000000000 0000000000000000  9  half-rows
            A 0000000000000000 0000000000000000  B
            C 0000000000000000 0000000000000000  D
            E 0000000000000000 00                F
```

127 groups remaining on disk out of 243

To find the hex group number of a bit in the map, take the first digit from the even or odd half-row and the second digit from the column in the same half. The first 0 represents 73.

Figure 13.2   Bit allocation map.

number, and from these computes the track and sector number where writing is to take place. When all eight blocks of a group have been filled, BDOS notes this and searches the allocation bit map again for the first 0 bit. When one is found, its group number is aded to the FCB and this map bit is set to 1. Thus, a file which has seven or fewer blocks is shown as occupying one group (1K); a file which has eight blocks is shown as occupying two groups, even though the second group is empty.

This action has several important results:

- The minimum space that can be occupied by any nonempty file is eight sectors (1K).
- Upon receiving a write request, BDOS searches the allocation bit map from its beginning and allocates the first free group it finds; hence, consecutive blocks of a file may be physically located anywhere on the disk, and are never in consecutive sectors.
- A write request is never denied until the disk is too full to hold the amount of data to be written. Denial of a write request is a fatal error unless the application program makes provision for mounting an alternate diskette. This rarely occurs if reasonable care is taken to gauge the size of the files in use and available space. Use the STAT utility to check available space before running application programs or utilities that create backup or temporary files.
- Disk space is efficiently used. In other systems that require file size to be specified, caution can result in considerable unused space allocated to files and hence not available to other files. Such space can be recovered by copying the data to a new file with the proper size specification. A similar procedure is followed to expand a file that has already used the space originally allocated to it: allocate new and larger file space and copy the existing file there.

The problem of file names becomes apparent, since two files may not have the same name. The copy in the larger allocation must have a different name during the copy operation. Thereafter, one should kill the old file and rename the new one.

File Control Block (FCB)

An FCB is a 33-byte block in RAM containing all the information needed by BDOS to find a file on the disk and to access any specified record of one extent, that is, an FCB describes just one extent. Whenever a new file is created, an FCB is created for it. The area from 005C to 007C hex is the default FCB area used by the CCP; it may also be used by application or utility programs. If a program requires more than one file to be open at the same time, it creates an FCB for each file that is to be accessed. These FCBs are in the TPA.

FCB Layout. The layout of a CP/M FCB is shown in Figure 13.3. When a file is first created, the BDOS clears all bytes of the FCB to zero and then initializes the first 13 bytes as follows.

Byte 0, 13 and 14 are not used and are initialized to 0 by the BDOS.

FN contains the file name left-justified. If the name has fewer than eight characters, the remaining bytes are padded with ASCII blanks (20 hex).

FT contains the three-character file type. Note that the period which separates file name and type in the command line is only a delimiter, so it is ignored. If the file type has fewer than three characters, the remaining bytes of the FT field are padded with ASCII blanks. For a temporary file, this field contains '$$$'.

EX, initialized to zero, indicates the file extent number. An FCB describes one extent, a file segment up to 16K in size, i.e., 128 blocks (sectors). When 128 sectors have been written, bytes 0 through 31 of the FCB are copied to the first free slot in the directory area, and the extent number in the FCB is incremented. Thus, we find a separate directory entry with a unique extent number for every 16K extent of a large file.

RC, initialized to 0, contains the current number of records in this extent. As new blocks are written to the diskette, this count is incre-

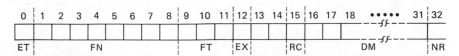

Figure 13.3. File control block.

mented by BDOS. Transition of this count from 7F to 80 is the signal for the end of an extent, and BDOS copies the FCB to the directory area of the disk and creates a new FCB with the EX updated.

DM. This disk map area is initialized to zeros. When a file is built, at the first write request BDOS inserts the number of the group now allocated for the file into byte 16. After all sectors of the group have been written, BDOS allocates another group and inserts its number into byte 17, and so on, until all 16 groups (128 sectors) have been written.

NR is initialized to 0 and updated by BDOS during sequential file operations to show the number of the next record to be read or written. For random access, the transient program places in this byte the number of the block to be accessed before issuing the function call to BDOS. Note that this byte is not copied to the directory entry; it is meaningful only when the file is in use.

Because the FCB is not written to the disk directory area until either 128 records have been written or the file is closed, a system crash (such as destruction of current memory contents by a temporary power failure) can cause the apparent loss of up to 128 records. The data is actually on the disk, but its location is not recorded in the directory; it is recoverable by a sophisticated user provided that the sectors are not overwritten in the meantime.

In applications that entail much data entry, it is good practice to close the file frequently and reopen it; this can avoid painful reconstruction of the directory and the possible destruction of vital data as the result of overwriting from other files after a crash.

FCB Location. Before we go on to discuss the directory, it is important to emphasize that there is no restriction on the location of an FCB. The CCP and DDT use the area from 005C to 007C hex; this is known as the default FCB area, and is usually given the symbolic label TFCB. When a large file has more than one 16K extent, sequential write operations build the data for each extent in the default FCB area. Sequential read operations cause each directory entry for the file to be fetched and placed in turn into TFCB. However, a user program may allocate enough memory to hold all the FCBs of a file simultaneously, passing the address of the appropriate FCB to BDOS as one argument of each access request. This is explained in more detail under file access operations. Much time and head movement can be saved during direct read operations if all the FCBs for a file are available in RAM, so that they do not have to be fetched from the disk each time a new extent is accessed.

File Directory

The BDOS maintains a directory on each diskette. Upon booting CP/M, the contents of groups 01 and 02 (16 sectors) are read sequentially from the addressed diskette, and the bit map for that drive is recalculated from the DM bytes of each entry. For a request to open a file, BDOS copies the corresponding entry into the FCB area. If the file is opened for writing, then when the program closes the file, BDOS copies the FCB back onto the directory area and rewrites all 16 sectors to the disk immediately.

Directory Layout. A directory entry consists of bytes 0 through 31 of the FCB created for the file, but not the next record bit in byte 32 of the FCB. The FCB layout is shown in Figure 13.3, and a set of typical directory entries is shown in Figure 13.4. These directory entries are for the same disk as the allocation map in Figure 13.2. Each entry occupies 32 bytes, or two lines of printout. The first line of each pair (third) address digit even) contains 00 in the first byte to indicate that the entry is for an active file. If the file has been erased, the first byte of the directory entry contains E5H; the rest of the entry and the file data remain on the disk (but are ignored by CP/M) until overwritten by new file allocations. This status byte is immediately followed by the file name and type. The extent number is in the twelfth byte and the record count in the sixteenth. The last 16 bytes (third address digit odd) of the entry contain 1-byte, two-hexdigit numbers naming each 8-sector group allocated to the file.

Directory Area. Directory entries on the disk remain intact, even though marked as deleted with E5H, until they are overwritten by new entries. When a file is closed, BDOS reads the entire directory from disk into memory and copies the FCB to the directory area into the first entry slot that contains E5 in its first byte. The modified direc-

```
A>DISKDUMP B:G 0-1

               DRIVE B - TRACK 2   SECTOR 1
0000   00 2D 57 4F 52 4B 20 20   20 30 30 32 00 00 00 01   .-WORK    002....
0010   45 00 00 00 00 00 00 00   00 00 00 00 00 00 00 00   E...............
0020   00 44 4F 57 48 49 4C 45   53 4C 49 42 00 74 00 07   .DOWHILE SLIB.t..
0030   26 00 00 00 00 00 00 00   00 00 00 00 00 00 00 00   &...............
0040   00 44 53 4B 44 55 4D 50   31 41 53 4D 00 00 00 80   .DSKDUMP 1ASM....
0050   29 2A 2B 2C 2D 2E 2F 30   31 32 33 34 35 36 37 38   )*+,-./0 12345678
0060   00 44 53 4B 44 55 4D 50   31 41 53 4D 01 00 00 13   .DSKDUMP 1ASM....
0070   39 3A 3B 00 00 00 00 00   00 00 00 00 00 00 00 00   9:;............. 

               DRIVE B - TRACK 2   SECTOR 7
0080   00 44 53 4B 44 55 4D 50   31 48 45 58 00 00 00 43   .DSKDUMP 1HEX...C
0090   56 57 58 59 5A 5B 62 65   6A 00 00 00 00 00 00 00   VWXYZ[be j......
00A0   00 44 53 4B 44 55 4D 50   31 50 52 4E 00 00 00 80   .DSKDUMP 1PRN....
00B0   50 51 52 53 54 55 5C 5D   5E 5F 60 61 63 64 66 67   PQRSTU\] ^`acdfg
00C0   00 44 53 4B 44 55 4D 50   31 50 52 4E 01 00 00 15   .DSKDUMP 1PRN....
00D0   68 69 6B 00 00 00 00 00   00 00 00 00 00 00 00 00   hik.............
00E0   00 44 53 4B 44 55 4D 50   31 53 59 4D 00 00 00 0A   .DSKDUMP 1SYM....
00F0   6C 6D 00 00 00 00 00 00   00 00 00 00 00 00 00 00   lm...... ........

               DRIVE B - TRACK 2   SECTOR 13
0100   00 4C 4F 41 44 20 20 20   20 43 4F 4D 00 00 00 0E   .LOAD    COM....
0110   6E 6F 00 00 00 00 00 00   00 00 00 00 00 00 00 00   no..............
0120   00 4D 41 43 20 20 20 20   20 43 4F 4D 00 00 00 5C   .MAC     COM...\
0130   02 03 04 05 06 07 08 09   0A 0B 0C 0D 00 00 00 00   ........ ........
0140   00 4D 41 43 52 4F 20 20   20 4C 49 42 00 00 00 80   .MACRO   LIB....
0150   3C 3D 3E 3F 40 41 42 46   47 48 49 4A 4B 4C 4D 4E   <=>?@ABF GHIJKLMN
0160   00 4D 41 43 52 4F 20 20   20 4C 49 42 01 00 00 08   .MACRO   LIB....
0170   4F 00 00 00 00 00 00 00   00 00 00 00 00 00 00 00   O............... 

               DRIVE B - TRACK 2   SECTOR 19
0180   00 4E 43 4F 4D 50 41 52   45 4C 49 42 00 12 00 0A   .NCOMPAR ELIB....
0190   18 19 00 00 00 00 00 00   00 00 00 00 00 00 00 00   ........ ........
01A0   00 50 49 50 20 20 20 20   20 43 4F 4D 00 00 00 37   .PIP     COM...7
01B0   0E 0F 10 11 12 13 14 00   00 00 00 00 00 00 00 00   ........ ........
01C0   00 53 41 50 20 20 20 20   20 43 4F 4D 00 00 00 04   .SAP     COM....
01D0   15 00 00 00 00 00 00 00   00 00 00 00 00 00 00 00   ................
01E0   00 53 45 4C 45 43 54 53   20 4C 49 42 00 69 00 0F   .SELECTS LIB.i..
01F0   27 28 00 00 00 00 00 00   00 00 00 00 00 00 00 00   '(...... ........

               DRIVE B - TRACK 2   SECTOR 25
0200   00 53 45 51 49 4F 20 20   20 4C 49 42 00 00 00 52   .SEQIO   LIB...R
0210   1A 1B 1C 1D 1E 1F 20 21   22 23 24 00 00 00 00 00   ...... ! "#$.....
0220   00 53 59 4D 53 54 41 43   4B 4C 49 42 00 44 00 05   .SYMSTAC KLIB.D..
0230   17 00 00 00 00 00 00 00   00 00 00 00 00 00 00 00   ................
0240   00 55 43 41 54 20 20 20   20 53 59 4D 00 00 00 0B   .UCAT    SYM....
0250   43 44 00 00 00 00 00 00   00 00 00 00 00 00 00 00   CD..............
0260   00 57 44 49 52 20 20 20   20 43 4F 4D 00 00 00 02   .WDIR    COM....
0270   70 00 00 00 00 00 00 00   00 00 00 00 00 00 00 00   p............... 

               DRIVE B - TRACK 2   SECTOR 5
0280   00 57 48 45 4E 53 20 20   20 4C 49 42 00 3B 00 06   .WHENS   LIB.;..
0290   25 00 00 00 00 00 00 00   00 00 00 00 00 00 00 00   %...............
02A0   00 44 53 4B 44 55 4D 50   31 43 4F 4D 00 00 00 18   .DSKDUMP 1COM....
02B0   16 71 72 00 00 00 00 00   00 00 00 00 00 00 00 00   .qr............ 
02C0   E5 E5 E5 E5 E5 E5 E5 E5   E5 E5 E5 E5 E5 E5 E5 E5   eeeeeeee eeeeeeee
02D0   E5 E5 E5 E5 E5 E5 E5 E5   E5 E5 E5 E5 E5 E5 E5 E5   eeeeeeee eeeeeeee
02E0   E5 E5 E5 E5 E5 E5 E5 E5   E5 E5 E5 E5 E5 E5 E5 E5   eeeeeeee eeeeeeee
02F0   E5 E5 E5 E5 E5 E5 E5 E5   E5 E5 E5 E5 E5 E5 E5 E5   eeeeeeee eeeeeeee
```

Figure 13.4. Part of directory.

tory is then written back to the disk. As a result, entries for several extents of the same file are not necessarily adjacent, nor even in numerical order, on the directory track of the disk.

User Program File Access Procedures

CP/M provides 27 different functions, all of which are available to user programs.

- Functions 1 through 11 relate to peripheral I/O.
- Functions 12 through 27 are disk I/O functions.

A BDOS function call (that is, a request to BDOS to perform some function) always consists of three operations:

1. Load register C with the function number of the desired operation.
2. Load register pair DE with a parameter, usually the address of the FCB for the file to be accessed.
3. Call BDOS (entry point is 0005H).

Some, though not all, functions return a result. Single-byte results are returned in the A register. Double-byte results are returned with the low byte in the A register and the high byte in the B register. It is the responsibility of the user program to interpret and use any results returned by BDOS.

Note: BDOS uses all the registers. If any register values have to be preserved, save them before the BDOS function call and restore them when the function is complete.

14
Telecommunications

Telecommunications is concerned with the transmission of data over a long distance. The transmission media might include microwave radio links overland or via orbiting satellites, or long-distance fiber optics links or all of these. But the first link in any such chain is a telephone line, and it is the connection of a computer or terminal to a telephone line that is our primary concern here.

The information transmitted may consist of images, speech or computer-generated digital data. We discuss here only the equipment required for digital data transmission and reception.

14.1 THE PHYSICAL CONNECTION

Short Links (up to 50 feet)

In Chapter 1 we discussed how data in parallel format is transferred from register to register and how it is processed in the ALU, where a separate conductor is provided for each bit. The data may also be converted to a serial bit stream that can be sent over two wires to a serial device such as a cassette or floppy disk. For a short, bidirectional connection, a separate signal wire is provided in each direction. The two circuits share a common return (or ground) so that only three conductors are required (Figure 14.1).

Keyboards, printers and CRT displays are parallel devices. However, when these devices are located more than six feet from the host computer, serial transmission is preferred because:

- Long multiconductor cables are expensive.
- High-frequency signals at TTL levels suffer attenuation and distortion on lines more than a few feet long.

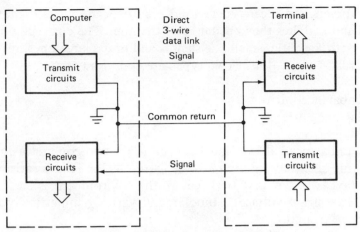

Transmission in both directions simultaneously

Figure 14.1.   Local connection; full-duplex mode.

The latter objection can be overcome by conversion to larger bipolar signals at levels conforming to Electronic Industries Association (EIA) standards. If this is done, an EIA interface driver and receiver is required for each conductor, thus adding to the expense.

A serial data link is economical; only two signal conductors and a common return are needed for two-way communication. An EIA interface driver at the sending end converts TTL (transistor/transistor logic) signal levels to 12-volt bipolar signals, and an EIA interface receiver at the other end reconverts bipolar signals to TTL levels (Figure 14.2). One chip may contain four drivers or four receivers. Serialization circuits for transmission and deserialization circuits for reception are contained within a single LSI universal asychronous receiver/transmitter (UART); one UART is needed at each end. EIA drivers and receivers that conform to the RS232 standard allow equipment separations of up to 50 feet. Drivers and receivers that conform to the newer RS449 standard allow separations of up to 200 feet.

Intermediate Distances

In a private installation, where the owner takes responsibility for the installation and maintenance of all cables and equipment, reliable communication on direct data links up to several miles long is possible if line drivers and receivers are used. A driver amplifies digital TTL signals and matches the impedance of the line. The corresponding receiver both amplifies small line signals and limits large ones, restoring TTL levels at the output. Two types are commonly used:

- Unbalanced drivers.
- Balanced drivers.

The unbalanced driver and receiver use a two-conductor link, of which one side may be grounded (Figure 14.2). This is satisfactory for distances of up to 5,000 feet if the environment is electrically quiet. The signal voltage is bipolar and varies symmetrically above and below ground.

For longer distances, or where the environment is electrically noisy, a balanced line is preferable (Figure 14.3). Here the two signal con-

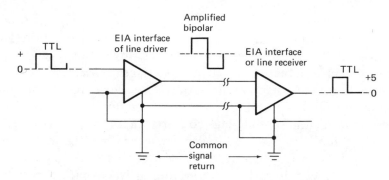

Figure 14.2.   EIA interface of unbalanced line driver.

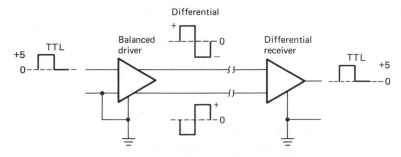

Figure 14.3.   Balanced line interface.

ductors are driven to equal and opposite voltages with respect to ground. The differential receiver responds mainly to the difference between the voltages at the two input terminals. Electrical noise from the environment induces "common mode" voltages of the same magnitude and polarity on both signal lines; these voltages cancel each other out in the receiver. The degree of cancellation is frequency-dependent and is seldom complete, but common mode noise is less than that in the unbalanced line by a factor of 10,000 or more. Additional noise reduction results if two twisted pairs are used, each pair consisting of a signal line and a ground line.

Long Links

Communication over long distances normally entails connection to public telephone lines. *Repeaters* (audio amplifiers) in the lines every few miles maintain signal strength; dial-up lines pass through switching equipment also. Bipolar dc signals generated by EIA interface equipment are not acceptable to telephone lines; they are converted to audio signals in the range of 300 to 3300 hertz, the passband of telephone lines and equipment. If a dial-up line is used, the passband is further restricted, because the band from 2,400 to 3,300 hertz is reserved for telephone company signaling tones and may not be used by the data communications equipment. A *modem* (*mo*dulator-*dem*odulator) converts between bipolar and audio signals, as described later.

14.2 HALF-DUPLEX, FULL-DUPLEX AND ECHOPLEX MODES

Although the computer hardware and software treats the keyboard and the display device of a terminal as two separate and independent devices, some terminals (such as the IBM I/O Selectric) have a built-in mechanical or electrical connection between the keyboard and the printer. When a key is struck, the character is printed, regardless of whether or not it is sent to the computer.

A terminal of this kind, using a two-wire data link, can send to the computer or receive from it, but cannot do both at the same time. The interface at each end switches the line between the transmit circuits and the receive circuits (Figure 14.4). Switching is governed by

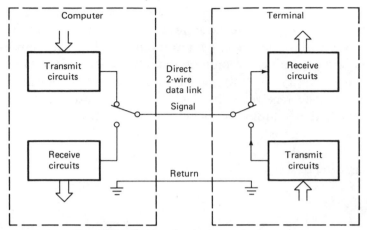

Transmission in either direction but not both at once

Figure 14.4. Local connection; half-duplex mode.

a *line protocol,* described later. This mode, *half-duplex,* must be used whenever equipment in the link is incapable of passing data in both directions simultaneously. It is sometimes employed when these restrictions do not prevail.

Full-Duplex

Full-duplex mode is used primarily for communication between two computers when the data being transferred need not immediately be displayed. The protocol usually calls for the receiving computer to acknowledge each error-free block; the ability to do this without switching the line from receive to transmit and vice versa can appreciably reduce transmission time for large messages.

Echoplex

Echoplex mode is used more often between a terminal and a computer. In dumb terminals, the keyboard and display device are independent. As a key is struck, the corresponding code is sent to the computer but not to the display device. Instead, the computer echoes to the terminal each character it receives. Hence, the operator knows not only what he types but also what the computer receives. Echoplex mode does not compromise the ability to send in both directions simultaneously. For example, when the computer is sending text to the terminal, the operator can abort the operation by pressing the break key or sending a control character. This signal is transmitted to the computer and is acted on, but not echoed.

14.3 SYNCHRONOUS AND ASYNCHRONOUS TRANSMISSION

At speeds up to 9,600 bits per second (direction connection, or 1,200 bits per second over a telephone line) each character is sent as a separate entity and consists of:

- A start bit (space signal, equivalent to logic 0, for one bit time).
- Seven data bits (least significant first).
- A parity check bit.
- One stop bit for 300 to 1,200 bits per second, or two stop bits below 300 bits per second. Each stop bit consists of a mark signal (equivalent to logic 1) for one bit time.

During an idle condition where no characters are sent, a continuous mark signal is transmitted. Since each character contains a built-in indication of the start and end of the character, the interval between any pair of characters may vary considerably. This is the case when the sending device is a manually operated keyboard. Transmission in which the individual bits of a character are strictly timed (synchronized), but there is variable time between characters, is synchronous by bit, asynchronous by character, or simply *asynchronous*.

When large quantities of data are regularly transmitted, a higher transmission rate reduces connect time charges. Connect time is saved and more stringent error detection and correction methods are available when blocks of 256 or more characters are transmitted in *synchronous* mode. No start or stop bits are transmitted. In the idle condition, the transmitter sends a continuous series of synchronizing characters (ASCII SYN). When initially establishing the link, and after each block, or when multiple errors make it evident that synchronization has been lost, the receiving logic searches the bit stream for this unique SYN bit pattern. When two successive SYN characters have been found, the receiver logic resets the receiver clock and bit counter to match the state at the transmitting end. Thereafter, even though there may be minor differences between the clocks at each end, the start and end of each 8-bit character is positively identified by the state of a modulo-8 counter, without the need for start and stop bits. This reduces the number of bits transmitted by about 20 percent.

14.4 LINE PROTOCOLS

A dumb terminal merely sends character codes as keys are struck and displays characters for all printable codes it receives. A direct connection exists between one terminal and a computer or other terminal, so no selection process is needed to sort out messages. A data link serves only one terminal (Figure 14.5).

This configuration is satisfactory to service a few remote terminals at short distances. It is uneconomic, because of line costs, when the host talks with several terminals that are miles away but located in the same general direction (Figure 14.6). In that situation, it is desirable to provide a single *multidrop* line to which this group of terminals is connected. The routing of the line should be designed for minimum mileage, the basis of the telephone company's charge.

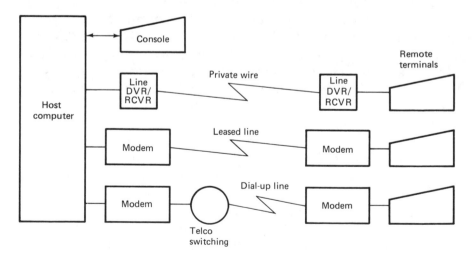

Figure 14.5. Data links to dumb terminals.

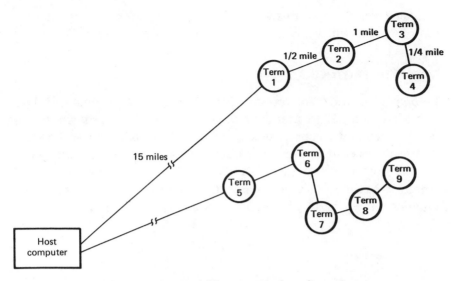

Figure 14.6. Multidrop terminal configuration.

However, to avoid interference, with consequent loss of data, a procedure called a *line protocol* is needed for regulating the flow of data.

The four principal protocols are:

- IBM's bisync, or BSC (for binary synchronous communications protocol).
- Its successor SDLC (synchronous data link control).
- ANSI (American National Standards Institute) data link control.
- The international packet switching standard, X.15.

Perhaps the most important for the microcomputer user is bisync, so its details are described below. All three protocols require remote equipment capable of:

- Identifying a station address.
- Checking incoming blocks for errors.
- Acknowledging good reception.
- Sending stored blocks of data on request.
- Retransmitting any incorrect block.

A *smart terminal* performs all these functions; so, of course, does a dumb terminal when it is part of a microcomputer system.

14.5 BISYNC PROTOCOL

The *bisync* protocol for transmission of one or more blocks of data from the computer to a terminal on a multidrop line is shown in Figure 14.7. When two computers are involved, one is known as the *host*, because it has control over transmission procedures. When the line is idle, the host sends a continuous series of SYN characters. When the computer has data to send to a particular terminal, it transmits the sequence shown at the top left. This consists of a number of non-

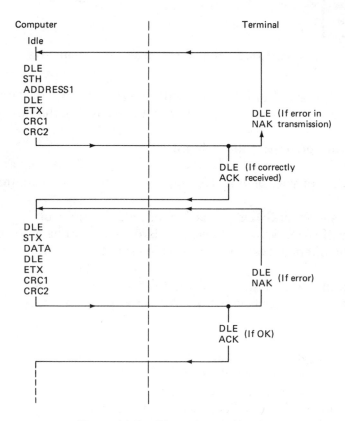

Figure 14.7. Bisync line protocol.

printing codes assigned specifically to telecommunications. Each 1-byte code is shown as several capital letters (e.g., DLE below), where:

- The DLE (data link escape) indicates that the code following is a control code.
- The STH (start of header) indicates that this block contains a terminal address, and the address character(s) follow immediately.
- The DLE-ETX (end of text) indicates completion of the address; it is followed by two CRC (cyclic redundancy check) bytes.

The computer now awaits a response from the terminal it addressed, attending to other things, perhaps, in the meanwhile. If the check bytes computed during reception agree with the two check bytes received, the terminal sends the response DLE-ACK (acknowledge); if not, it responds DLE-NAK (negative acknowledge) to request retransmission.

Upon receiving an ACK, the computer sends the second sequence. After DLE, find STX (start of text), indicating that the block contains data. After the last data character the sequence ends with DLE-ETX-CRC1-CRC2. The maximum block length is normally 255 characters including control characters but not check bytes. The bisync protocol requires that each block sent be acknowledged before the next block is sent. For half-duplex transmission, acknowledgement is time-consuming; each line turnaround takes 20 to 30 milliseconds. The X.25 protocol avoids delay by allowing up to eight blocks to be sent before acknowledgement of the first block is received. Blocks are identified, and ACK indicates which block is acknowledged. Each block contains addressing and control information, which can be followed by data. Blocks for different addresses may be interspersed in one transmission.

Error Detection and Correction

Error detection and correction may be done by hardware or by software or by a mixture of both. The methods used depend upon the importance attached to data integrity and the budget allotted to ensuring it. Where the data originates at a manual keyboard, transmission errors are usually fewer than typing errors.

For terminals used as remote consoles, a simple parity check may be adequate, although certain kinds of errors will not be detected.

Where numeric data (particularly if it is financial data) forms the largest part of the traffic between two computers, the detection of transmission errors is vital. In many such networks, correction is accomplished by retransmitting any data block in which an error was detected until it is received error-free. Detection is usually by means of check bytes computed for each data block sent. The check bytes themselves are transmitted at the end of the block. The receiving station computes check bytes as characters arrive; if the final result agrees with the transmitted check bytes, the block is considered error-free.

Where the highest importance is placed on data integrity, special codes may be used to represent the data. There is a whole family of codes which not only detect errors but correct them as well. As always, there is a tradeoff, which in this case involves the transmission of more bits for each character and more complex hardware and/or software. These codes are worthwhile when very large quantities of sensitive data are transmitted. On most networks, however, a good error-detecting algorithm and retransmission of flawed blocks is considered adequate.

14.6 MODEM PRINCIPLES

FSK Encoding

Digital data transmission over the public telephone network must meet two restrictions:

1. Only two conductors are provided.
2. Bipolar dc signals are prohibited.

To comply with the latter restriction, a modem changes the bipolar digital bit stream into audio signals within the telephone passband.

A modem might turn on a single tone to indicate a logic 1 and turn the tone off to indicate a logic 0. However, telephone lines are vulnerable to noise from such sources as motors, welding or radiotherapy equipment, power transmission lines and other telephone lines running in the same conduit. This one-tone scheme is error-prone during the off (or 0) operation.

Instead, two tones are used. The frequencies chosen are just far enough apart to allow sharp filters to separate them at the receiving end without difficulty; they are close enough to each other that many pairs of tones can be transmitted over the same pair of wires without natural interference. In any pair of tones, the upper frequency is the mark frequency, in telecommunications jargon, which indicates a logic 1; the lower frequency is the space frequency, which indicates a logic 0. This is shown in Figure 14.8, where the higher tone appears as more waves per unit horizontal length. This method, called frequency shift keying (FSK), is used by modems operating at rates of up to 1,200 bits per second.

Some 1,200-bit-per-second modems (such as the Bell 202 Series) work only in half-duplex mode and contain within them the send/ receive switching. However, most modems used with microcomputers normally operate at 300 bits per second in full-duplex mode; they can be switched to half-duplex operation. For full-duplex operation using only two wires, four different tones are required. One pair is assigned to the "sender," who is in *originate* mode; the other pair is for the "receiver," who is in *answer* mode. However, once the mode of each participant is established, each may send or receive when his turn arrives, as we now discuss.

Answer/Originate Modes

For 300-bit-per-second transmission, the two mark/space frequency pairs are standard throughout the United States. One modem oper-

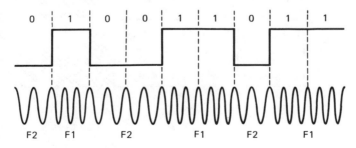

Figure 14.8. Bit stream converted to two frequencies.

ates in originate mode, transmitting 1,270 hertz for mark and 1,070 hertz for space, and receiving 2,225 hertz for mark and 2,025 hertz for space. The other modem operates in answer mode, transmitting 2,225 and 2,025 hertz and receiving 1,270 and 1,070 hertz. Modems designed specifically for use with remote terminals (including most acoustic couplers) operate only in originate mode. Some modems, designed for use only at the computer end, operate in answer mode only. Some modems can be switched to either originate or answer mode; when there is a computer at both ends of the link, the master station uses originate mode and may operate automatic dialing equipment to establish communication with a satellite station that is switched to the answer mode.

A modem is specified as originate only, answer only, or originate/answer, depending upon the frequencies it uses for transmission and reception. However, an answer modem for use with a computer has features not included in originate modems. One of these is the ability to detect a 17-hertz telephone ringing signal and generate an associated digital output signal. Other options may also be available.

Restrictions on FSK Data Rates

The frequency spectrum of telephone links is shown in Figure 14.9, with the two bands used at 300 bits per second for originate and answer tones. Data transmission at 1,200 bits per second requires a greater bandwidth. To obtain satisfactory separation, the mark fre-

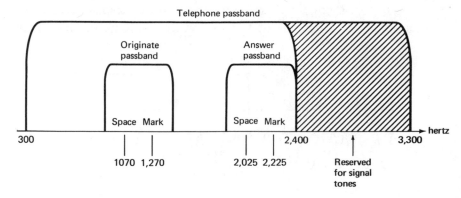

Figure 14.9. Frequency spectrum for 300-bits-per-second operation.

quency is 2,200 hertz and the space frequency is 1,200 hertz. Because there is considerable attenuation of frequencies lower than 1,000 hertz, and because the region above 2,400 hertz is reserved for signaling tones, a second pair of tones cannot be accommodated. Thus, on a two-wire circuit, such as a dial-up line, 1,200-bits-per-second FSK transmissions are restricted to half-duplex operation. When leased lines are used, full-duplex operation is possible by using a second line to form a four-wire circuit.

Other Encoding Methods

There is often confusion about the terminology used to specify data transmission rates. Up to now, we have spoken of bits per second, which is unambiguous; however, modem speeds are normally specified in bauds. The baud is defined as the reciprocal of the length of the shortest signaling element in the code. Morse code, for instance, has two elements—a dash is three times as long as a dot. For digital data transmission the unit is the bit, and the only signal element is of one bit time. When using FSK a speed of 1,200 baud is exactly equal to a data transmission rate of 1,200 bits per second.

At higher speeds, this equivalence no longer holds true. The bandwidth of the telephone lines and equipment restricts us to 1,200 bits per second in half-duplex; we cannot use full-duplex at that speed on a two-wire circuit. How, then can we achieve data rates of 2,400, 4,800, or even 9,600 bits per second?

As with magnetic tape or disk recording, one way to increase the data density while remaining within the restrictions imposed by the medium is to use more efficient coding methods. Then a signaling element no longer conveys exactly one bit; each element conveys more. Two such coding methods are phase modulation (PM) or Quadrature amplitude modulation (QAM).

PM represents the four possible values of a 2-bit pattern (*dibit*) by transmitting a fixed-frequency, fixed-amplitude carrier tone and shifting its phase angle by 90, 180 or 270 degrees with respect to a reference (Figure 14.10). Each phase angle represents one two-bit pattern. A data rate of 2,400 bits per second requires transmission of only 1,200 phase angles per second. Thus, a two-wire circuit can use full-duplex mode at 1,200 bits per second (600 baud) or half-duplex mode

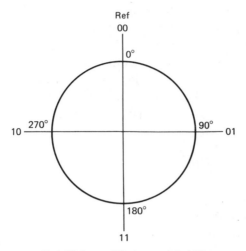

Each 90 degree shift changes only 1 bit

Figure 14.10. Phase-modulation representation of a dibit.

at 2,400 bits per second (1,200 baud) within the bandwidth restrictions.

QAM transmits a continuous sine wave and a continuous cosine wave of the same frequency. The amplitude of each wave can be varied in discrete steps representing multiples of its idle-state amplitude. If each wave has two amplitude values (apart from the idle value), their combined states can represent 4 bit patterns. If each wave has five amplitude values of 0.25, 0.5, 1 (the idle state), 2 and 4, then their combined states can represent 16 bit patterns, as shown in Figure 14.11. In this case, a simultaneous change of sine amplitude from 0.25 to 4 and of cosine amplitude from 4 to 0.25 might represent a change from binary 1000 to binary 1100, but it is still only one signal element. If more than four amplitude steps can be distinguished, 5-bit or 6-bit digital numbers can be conveyed by the relative amplitudes of the sine and cosine waves.

There is no standard for carrier frequencies or for the manner in which bit patterns are assigned to relative amplitudes. But all the modems on a network must use the same system and frequencies, and the computers must follow the same protocol. The pattern shown in Figure 14.11 represents the European CCITT standard V.29

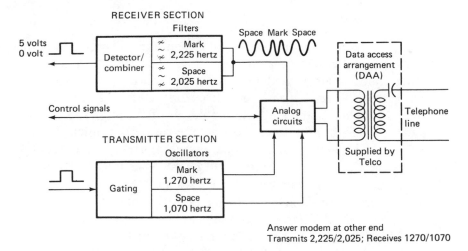

Figure 14.11. Quadrature amplitude representation of a 16-bit pattern.

for 9,600-bits per second transmissions, and is compatible with neither ATT's series 209 modem nor Vadic-Racal modems.

Timing Considerations

A low-speed interface (bit rates up to 1,200 bits per second) accepts serial data clocked locally into the deserializer. Synchronism is derived from the computer master clock, or from a separate crystal-controlled oscillator.

At 2,400 to 9,600 bits per second, however, the margin for error is small. At the transmitting end, clock pulses generated in the modem are passed to the interface circuitry on a separate conductor. They shift data out of the serializer; the modem also combines them with the data. The analog signal placed on the telephone line is a composite of data and clock signals.

At the receiving end, clock pulses recovered by the modem from the analog signal are passed on a separate line to the interface circuitry. They time the shifting of data bits into the deserializer. Thus, the same clock is used at both ends of the link. The expense of including an accurate clock generator and combining circuits in the modem is offset by the ability to maintain synchronism at high transmission rates and by obviating a clock generator on the interface board.

Data Access Arrangements

Figure 14.12 shows a data access arrangement (DAA) connecting the modem analog circuits to the telephone line. The DAA consists of an isolating transformer and surge limiters (not shown) to isolate the modem from the line. The DAA passes only audio signals between 300 and 3,000 hertz, and limits the amplitude of outgoing audio. This protects the telephone equipment from any surges that might be generated by a malfunction of the modem or computer. It likewise protects the modem and computer equipment against the 40-volt dc always present on the telephone line, surges induced on the telephone line and overload or damage from the 17-hertz ringing signal (which can sometimes reach 60 to 100 volts).

It is illegal to connect a modem directly to the telephone line; the connection must be made either through a DAA supplied by the telephone company or through an equivalent device of FCC-approved type supplied by the modem manufacturer.

Acoustic Couplers

The acoustic coupler indirectly couples the modem to the line. As shown in Figure 14.13, it consists of a microphone and speaker

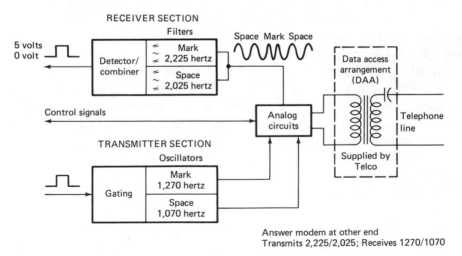

Answer modem at other end
Transmits 2,225/2,025; Receives 1270/1070

Figure 14.12. Originate modem; simplified block diagram.

Figure 14.13.   Typical acoustic coupler.

equipped with rubber cups and mounted at an angle to the upper surface of the coupler casing. The handset of a standard telephone is
placed into the coupler so that the earpiece is over the coupler microphone and the microphone is over the speaker. The rubber cups hold
it in place and exclude room noise. The acoustic coupler deals only
with sound and hence provides complete electric isolation.

At transmission rates up to 450 bits per second, using FSK modulation, the acoustic coupler works well. It obviates the expense
of DAA installation and the need for a special switch on the telephone
to silence it during data transmission. There is no compatibility problem at 300 bits per second or less; all modems with built-in or external
acoustic couplers for rates up to 300 bits per second are completely
compatible with the Bell series 103 modems and with each other. A
few 103-compatible couplers operate up to 450 bits per second.

If an acoustic coupler is used at 1,200 bits per second, the modem
at the computer should be compatible. Some commercial 1,200-bits-
per-second modems have a built-in acoustic coupler or can be used

with an external one; these modems are *not* compatible with Bell modems in the 212 series, and 1200-bits-per-second modems of different makes are not necessarily compatible with each other.

Interfacing

A modem or acoustic coupler can be connected to any serial interface equipped to handle RS-232C bipolar signals. For transmissions up to 1,200 bits per second, nine connections are made to the modem, though not all of these need be used by the interface circuitry and software. A standard 25-pin D-type connector is used on all telecommunications equipment. Pin numbers in the descriptions below refer to this connector. A terminal or computer which connects to the modem is called a *data terminal* (in telecommunications jargon) and is normally equipped with a male connector. The modem or acoustic coupler is called the *data set*, and is equipped with a female connector. This is shown in Figure 14.14. Wiring connections are shown in Figure 14.15.

Grounds. Two ground connections are provided: the protective ground, AA/1 (the letters are the circuit designation and the number

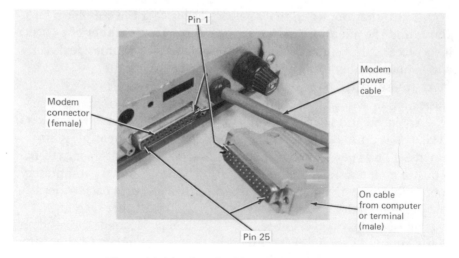

Figure 14.14.   Standard 25-pin D connectors.

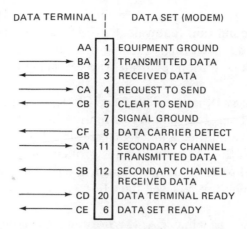

Figure 14.15. RS-232 connector, pin connections of most commonly used lines.

is the pin number), connects the frame of the data set to the frame of the data terminal; signal ground, AB/7, is the common return for data and control signals.

Data Lines. Transmitted data, BA/2, carries serial data from the data terminal to the data set and thence to the line. Received data, BB/3, carries serial data received over the line from the data set to the data terminal. These lines are held in the mark condition (negative) during intervals between data words and at all times when no data are being transmitted.

Ready Lines. The data set ready line, CC/6, is on (positive) when the data set is ready to send and receive data. This does *not* mean that a communications link has been established, but does indicate:

- Data set power on.
- Off hook condition.
- Automatic dialing completed.
- Data set has sent any answering tone that is under its sole control.

The data terminal raises the data terminal ready line to the on (positive) state to prepare the data set to establish and maintain communication. If the data set has ring detection and automatic answer features, turning the data terminal ready line on puts the data set into the off hook condition (equivalent to lifting the telephone handset) to answer the detected ring. Turning this line off returns the data set to the on hook condition (equivalent to replacing the handset).

Received Line Signal Detector. This line, CF/8, is sometimes called the carrier detect line. The data set turns this line on when a communication link is established and a signal suitable for demodulation is being received. If the line connection is broken, or if the received signal is too distorted to allow demodulation, the data set turns this line off, thereby clamping the received data line (BB) to the mark condition.

Request to Send. This line, CA/4, is normally used only on half-duplex circuits to switch the data link from receive to send. On full-duplex circuits the data terminal holds this line on to maintain the send condition.

Clear to Send. This line, CB/5, is turned on by the data set to indicate that serial data presented on the BA line will be transmitted. On half-duplex circuits this line remains on for as long as the data terminal holds the request to send line (CA) on.

When the telephone link is dialed up manually and monitored by the operator, control lines are seldom used. However, when the computer system automatically answers incoming calls, or dials to remote stations, all the control and status lines are used by the (software) modem driver.

14.7 TELECOMMUNICATIONS HARDWARE AND SOFTWARE FOR PERSONAL COMPUTERS

The addition of telecommunications facilities to a microcomputer system opens up a whole new world, giving individuals access both to large commercial databases and to other private microcomputer owners.

Almost any microcomputer which has a serial I/O port can be connected to a modem or acoustic coupler compatible with the Bell 103A modem. The microcomputer can then communicate over the switched telephone network with a commercial time-sharing network or with another microcomputer similarly equipped. Many computer clubs and individuals have established Computer Bulletin Board Systems (CBBS) for the exchange of messages and software, without charge. The de facto standard is 103A-compatible, asynchronous, full-duplex link, capable of transmission speeds of up to 600 baud over a good telephone connection. A few systems can also communicate over a 202A-compatible link at 1,200 baud half-duplex.

Telecommunications software for microcomputers is available both through commercial means and through computer clubs. The programs range from simple routines to turn the microcomputer into a dumb terminal to sophisticated programs that can transfer files of any type in either direction, block by block, with retransmission of a block if a transmission error occurs.

Hardware

A number of inexpensive acoustic couplers and modems have recently been produced specifically for the individual microcomputer owner. Among the couplers, the Novation Cat is one of the most popular. It provides reliable communication at 300 baud at a price of about $150. Unlike the majority of industrial couplers, which can be driven at up to 450 baud but are limited to the originate mode, the Cat can be switched to either originate or answer mode; thus, two microcomputers using the Cat can talk to each other, one of them selecting originate and the other answer mode.

Modems that plug directly into an Apple or S-100 microcomputer bus are available from D.C. Hayes, Inc., International Data Systems (IDS), or Potomac Micro-Magic, Inc. (PMMI).

Of these, the PMMI Model MM-103 is the most versatile. The circuit board and the FCC-approved coupler that connects it to the telephone line are shown in Figure 14.16, and a simplified block diagram is shown in Figure 14.17. The comparable Hayes and IDS boards have most (but not all) of the main features found in the MM-103, and lack some of the subsidiary features that make the MM-103 outstanding in its class.

The computer interface consists of four contiguously numbered parallel I/O ports:

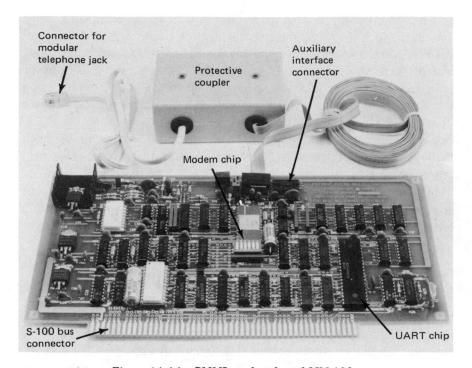

Figure 14.16.   PMMI modem board MM-103.

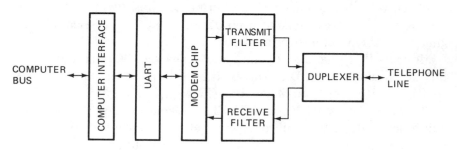

Figure 14.17.   PMMI modem; simplified block diagram.

- Data port.
- UART control port.
- Modem control port.
- Timing control port for baud rate and dialing pulse control.

The UART is the serializer/deserializer for converting parallel bytes from the computer to a serial digital bit stream, and vice versa. Status and command registers, accessed via the UART control port, allow the CPU to set word length, parity generation and checking and the number of stop bits.

The modem chip is a Motorola 6860, which has separate send and receive sections. The send section converts the digital bit stream from the UART to the two standard audio tones of either answer (high pair) or originate (low pair) mode. The receive section converts incoming audio tones to a digital bit stream for input to the UART.

Timing signals throughout the board are derived from a 10-megahertz crystal oscillator. The CPU can set the division ratio of the data rate counter via the timing control port; a wide varity of data rates can thus be set. The user is not restricted to the industry standard rates when communicating with another computer equipped with the PMMI MM-103; the rate can be as high as the telephone line will support. In practice, reliable communication is usually possible at 600 baud, while on a very good line, 710 baud is sometimes possible with an error rate that requires retransmission of one block in five or six. The timing signals also provide dialing pulses of the correct 60-40 duty cycle; the dialing rate can be set to 10 or 20 pulses per second under program control. Dialing pulses operate a relay and supporting circuitry in the coupler.

The MM-103 not only allows computer-controlled dialing of numbers contained in a software library but also provides automatic answering of incoming calls under program control. Full, monitoring of the data link is provided so that the software can check for dial tone, perform the dialing, place carrier on the line, initiate data transmission and disconnect the line if carrier is lost either by accident or when the remote equipment disconnects.

In addition to controlling the data link, the MM-103 has an auxiliary interface accessible to the program. There are two buffered output lines and two input lines that can be sensed by the computer. These can be used in a variety of ways—for example, to activate an audio tape recorder or other devices. If the coupler unit is powered from a source that is independent of the computer, so that ring signals can be detected, the auxiliary interface can activate external equipment that will turn on the computer and establish a voice or data link.

Software

A wide variety of telecommunications software is available both by commercial means or through computer clubs; a large proportion of the programs are for S-100 systems running the CP/M operating system, but similar programs are available for the Apple, Radio Shack TRS-80, North Star Horizon, Atari and other personal computers.

A typical program is MODEM, available from the CP/M Users' Group. This originated in 1976, and has been frequently revised and upgraded. The latest version, MODEM7, is currently for the PMMI MM-103 only but, like previous versions, it will soon accommodate the Hayes and IDS boards, and acoustic couplers. It has two main modes, terminal and file. The terminal mode allows keyboarded conversation between two microcomputers. One must be in originate mode and the other in answer mode; usually the system in answer mode also echoes data received from the modem to be echoed back to the originator. Options allow manual or automatic dialing, change the baud rate or dialing rate and log all received data in a buffer in memory, which can later be written to disk.

The file mode allows files of any kind to be transmitted in either direction, in blocks of 128 bytes. A header precedes the data, and check bytes follow the data. If the check bytes computed by the receiving system do not agree with the transmitted check bytes, the receiver sends a NAK code and the sender retransmits the block. If the check bytes agree, the receiver sends an ACK code and the sender proceeds to the next block. A 2K memory buffer is used at each end of the link, the sender filling it from disk and the receiver writing the contents to disk before sending an ACK. A batch option allows any number of files to be sent with a single command.

The latest version has a greatly improved user interface, with easily remembered commands and a command menu that may be displayed or suppressed by one of the commands.

IV
SYSTEM INTEGRATION

15
Operation of a Typical
Operating System

Computer hardware alone does not make a system; the hardware is of little value without an operating system and utilities. Application programs make extensive use of the facilities provided by the operating system, and especially of the file management facilities.

The choice of an operating system (OS) is crucial to the ease and availability of the system features. Some form of operating system is always supplied by the manufacturer of the disk controller and/or of the complete computer. But software available on the open market, which varies greatly with the computer, may provide advantages worth the added expense of purchasing a different OS than that which was supplied. The choice depends upon whether the user intends to create his own application programs or to purchase them, and upon the programming languages he uses or needs for the packages.

This chapter is concerned with what is done after the hardware is unpacked and interconnected. The system chosen for examination is the most general and most widely used. It is called CP/M*—which stands for Control Program/Microcomputer. Versions of it are available for many hardware configurations, and a large percentage of the software currently on the market is designed to run under it.

---

*CP/M is a registered trademark of Digital Research.

15.1 GENERAL DESCRIPTION OF CP/M

CP/M was designed by Digital Research to support 8080, 8085 and Z80 computers equipped with single or dual 8-inch, single-sided, single-density, soft-sectored IBM 3740-compatible diskettes. However, it became so popular that computer and disk controller manufacturers were licensed to adapt it for other formats, including dual-density and double-sided 8-inch and 5-1/4-inch diskettes, both hard- and soft-sectored. Until hard disks became available for small systems, Version 1.4 of CP/M could support up to four disk drives and file sizes up to 256K. Version 2.2 accommodates up to 16 disk devices in a mixture of minifloppy, floppy and hard disk drives. It supports files up to 8 megabytes in length; the total space on the maximum configuration is 128 megabytes.

CP/M is only for single-user systems. Digital Research also sells MP/M, a multiuser system that is compatible with CP/M and supports a computer with up to 512K of memory in switched banks of 64K each. Rivals are beginning to appear on the market, some of which take advantage of technology developed since CP/M became firmly established. They include:

- ONYX, which has many similarities to the UNIX operating system for PDP/11 systems.
- MARC, a UNIX-like operating system that is partially compatible with CP/M.
- OASIS, containing many features not otherwise available on microcomputers.

These are sophisticated development systems for larger configurations.

15.2 MEMORY REQUIREMENTS FOR CP/M

CP/M Version 1.4 requires a contiguous memory block of at least 16K, which normally starts at location 0000. Versions for systems which have a BASIC interpreter in low memory ROM start on the first page above the ROM. The memory map for the standard 16K version is shown in Figure 15.1; page 0 is reserved for the following items:

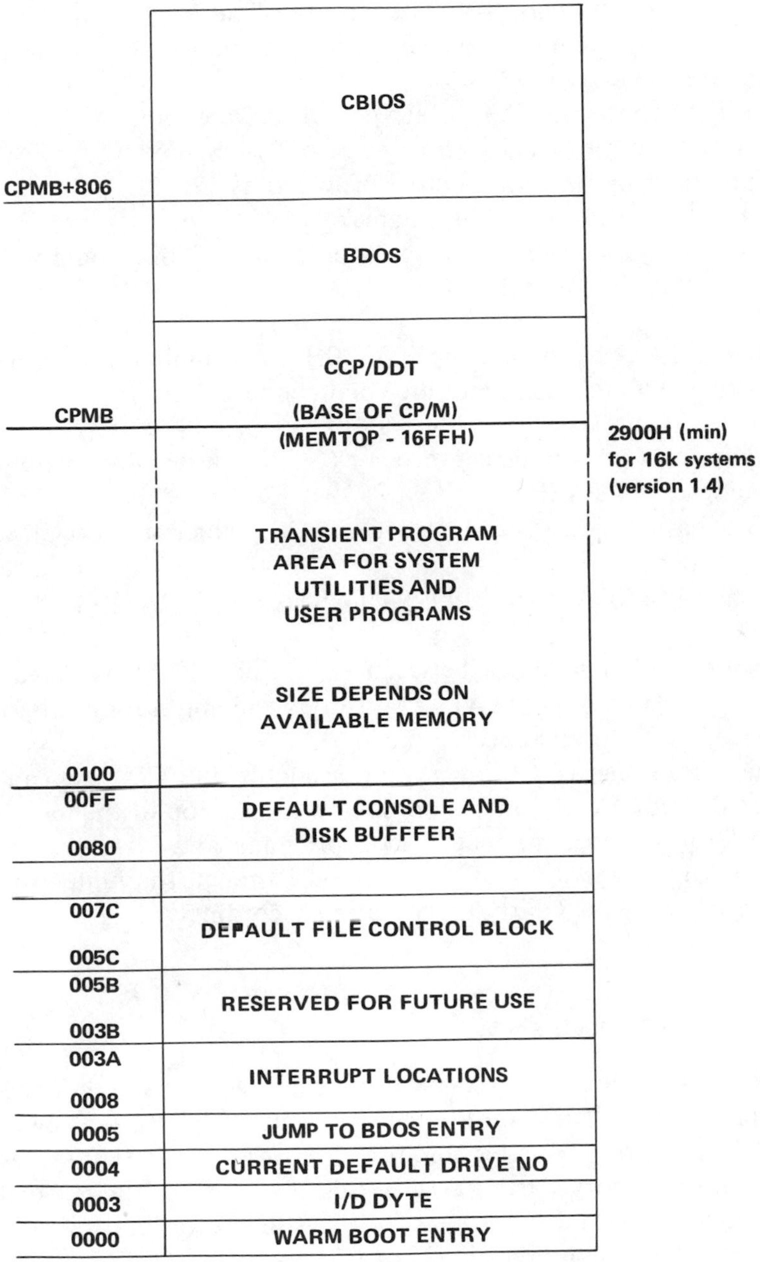

	CBIOS
CPMB+806	
	BDOS
	CCP/DDT
CPMB	(BASE OF CP/M)
	(MEMTOP - 16FFH)
	TRANSIENT PROGRAM AREA FOR SYSTEM UTILITIES AND USER PROGRAMS
	SIZE DEPENDS ON AVAILABLE MEMORY
0100	
00FF	DEFAULT CONSOLE AND DISK BUFFFER
0080	
007C	DEFAULT FILE CONTROL BLOCK
005C	
005B	RESERVED FOR FUTURE USE
003B	
003A	INTERRUPT LOCATIONS
0008	
0005	JUMP TO BDOS ENTRY
0004	CURRENT DEFAULT DRIVE NO
0003	I/D DYTE
0000	WARM BOOT ENTRY

2900H (min)
for 16k systems
(version 1.4)

Figure 15.1.   CP/M memory map.

- A jump to the warm start entry point of CP/M.
- An I/O byte containing a code that determines the current peripheral device configuration.
- A byte containing the current default drive number.
- A jump to the primary entry point of BDOS, used by application programs in invoking facilities provided by CP/M.
- A 33-byte file control block area.
- A 128-byte buffer used both for console input and for one-sector disk reads and writes.

The top 5,887 bytes, starting at 2900H in the minimum system, are occupied by CP/M. There are three main components:

- The console command processor (CCP), whose starting point is designated CBASE.
- The basic disk operating system (BDOS), which starts at CBASE+1500H.
- The basic I/O system (BIOS), which starts at CBASE+1500H.

The remainder of memory between 100H and CBASE is called the transient program area (TPA). All utilities and application programs are loaded at 100H and execute there.

When more than 16K of memory is available, the TPA is expanded so that the CP/M components are located at the top of the memory. Hence, the TPA accommodates larger programs and data areas. Page 0 is the same, regardless of memory size, though the jumps to the warm start and BDOS entry are modified accordingly.

15.3 INITIAL LOADING

The computer and/or the disk controller manufacturer supplies a bootstrap program in PROM on the controller board. Turn on power or press RESET and it executes, and for CP/M it reads the first sector of the disk into memory starting at 00H; this first sector contains a loader. The controller PROM has a jump to 00, which gives control to this loader. It reads in the remainder of CP/M starting 16FF hex (5887 decimal) bytes below the top of memory. That address was put into the loader when this version of the operating system was assembled. When loading is complete, the loader transfers control to the start of CP/M.

Tables within CP/M are adjusted by the computer or disk controller manufacturer to suit the disk system in use. The CP/M BIOS (basic I/O system) contains device drivers that match the standard port assignments for the system (e.g., North Star Horizon, Exidy Sorcerer, Radio Shack TRS-80, etc.). On any standardized system, installing CP/M for the first time requires only insertion of the CP/M system disk in drive A (some systems call this drive 0) and execution of the bootstrap.

However, in a system with components from several different manufacturers, the console port assignments of the distribution disk may not correspond with those of the user's configuration; in this case CP/M hangs up when loading is complete, because it is waiting for a console command from an I/O port not supported by the hardware. In a nonstandard system it is essential to have some means of modifying CP/M in memory to make it display console output and accept keyboard input. CP/M modification is done with the aid of one of these:

- A debug and trace utility (DDT) provided as part of the CP/M package.
- A monitor in PROM, if available.
- The front panel switches, if any.

Once the CP/M system in memory is operative, its utilities can be brought to bear to construct a new version of CP/M containing suitable device drivers. The stages of the process are:

1. Modify the loader and BIOS device drivers with the CP/M editor to suit the user's system. Assembly language source code for these is always included on the distribution disk as part of the CP/M package.
2. Assemble the new loader and BIOS with the CP/M assembler.
3. Read the current loader and CP/M system into a special area (starting at 900H) of the TPA with the SYSGEN utility or DDT.

4. Read the newly assembled loader and BIOS into memory with the CP/M debug and trace utility (DDT) to overwrite the distribution versions in the TPA.
5. Write the modified CP/M from the TPA in memory to tracks 0 and 1 of the new system diskette, mounted on drive B, with the SYSGEN utility.
6. Copy all files from the distribution diskette to the new system diskette, with PIP (peripheral interchange program utility).

When this procedure has been completed, remove the distribution diskette, transfer the new diskette from drive B to drive A and boot up the new, modified CP/M. This is still a 16K system. If a larger system is required, the procedure for constructing it is similar. The MOVCPM utility constructs the system according to the amount of memory you specify and places it in memory in the TPA; if the BIOS has already been modified, the editing and assembly steps are not required.

Changing the BIOS to suit the hardware configuration is not difficult, but is tedious and error-prone. Some software distributors provide CP/M diskettes configurable for several common types of console device. Configuration routines request details of terminal type (Hazeltine, Soroc, memory-mapped VDM, etc) and modify the BIOS accordingly before writing the new system out to a fresh disk.

15.4 BUILT-IN COMMANDS

CP/M obeys six built-in commands, keyed in at the console in either upper- or lowercase, calling internal subroutines to provide the services:

- DIR displays the file directory of the currently logged-in drive or of a specified drive.
- SAVE N D:FILENAME.TYP saves N pages (of 256 bytes each) starting at 100H onto drive D, calling it FILENAME. The file type (TYP) is specified as .COM for an executable program or .ASM for an assembly language source file to be assembled by the CP/M assembler. Other files may have an arbitrary file type or none. Some utilities assume .TXT for a text file to be formatted and printed, and .LIB for a library file to be called in by a macro assembler.

- TYPE D:FILENAME.TYP reads and displays on the console:
  - From drive D,
  - the file called FILENAME, consisting of printable text,
  - of type .TYP—Note that this command produces meaningless results if the named file contains object code.
- ERA D:FILENAME.TYP makes the specified file unavailable hereafter by placing hex E5 in the first byte of the directory entry. The file is still on the disk and its mapping is still in the directory entry. Recovery of the file is possible by changing the E5 back to 00 with a disk editor, provided that neither the directory entry nor the file have since been overwritten by creation of a new file.
- REN NEWFILE.TYP=OLDFILE.TYP renames OLDFILE.TYP as NEWFILE.TYP. A new file type may be specified, as well as a new file name.
- FILENAME loads and executes the program stored on the currently logged-in disk under the name FILENAME.COM. If the file is absent or of the wrong type, CP/M displays the error message: ?FILENAME

This is a restricted list of commands. However, the last command, which loads and executes a named program, gives CP/M its power and versatility. All utilities (such as SYSGEN) and all language processors (such as MBASIC) are called thus into the TPA of memory and executed. Thus, if the diskette containing MBASIC is mounted on drive B, to execute MBASIC first key in the drive name:

A>B: (where A is the current drive and ">" is the system prompt, an indicator to the operator to enter a reply). The system responds:
B>

Now simply key in "MBASIC" after the prompt. The system loads MBASIC and executes it.

15.5 UTILITIES

The CP/M distribution disk, in addition to the standard operating system on tracks 0 and 1, contains a set of utilities described below.

ED is a context-oriented text editor for building ASCII files of any kind, including descriptive material and assembly language program source files. All insertion, deletion, replacement, search and append operations are performed with reference to a character pointer—a marker that points to the text character at which commands for insertion, deletion, replacement, etc., take effect. Since the marker is invisible —does not appear on the screen—many people find ED difficult to use; however, ED has very powerful macro facilities. A user at a typewriter terminal can perform complex editing with few keystrokes.

Some users with memory-mapped video or CRT terminal consoles prefer Wordmaster*, a superset of ED purchased as a separate item, in which the cursor is the character pointer and which has facilities suited to video consoles:

- One keystroke can move the cursor one character or one word in either direction, or directly to line ends.
- Deletion of a character, a word or all words to the line end, at the left or right of the cursor.
- Direct replacement of text by typing over it—no replace command necessary.
- Scrolling up or down by line or by full screen.
- Insert mode allows insertion of material; characters at and to the right of the cursor are pushed to the right to make room.

DDT

This dynamic debug and trace utility has all the more common monitor functions: display, examine and substitute, fill, move, etc., described in Chapter 2. It can also list an object program with mnemonics or insert code directly into the ML program in memory from assembly language mnemonics furnished at the console. The trace function controls execution of a program under test. After execution of one or a specified number of ML program instructions, as directed by the DDT command, the CPU state is displayed.

---

*Wordmaster is a registered trademark of Micropro International Corporation.

MOVCPM (or RELOC)

This utility brings a copy of CP/M into the TPA starting at 900H; branch instruction destination addresses are changed to suit the specified system size. The BIOS of this relocated version can also be changed, either by the use of DDT or by overlaying a previously assembled BIOS containing the new routines. The new system can be SAVEd, or can be written out to another disk by the use of the SYSGEN utility.

FORMAT (Or INTLIZE)

This utility formats a blank diskette by writing track and sector addresses onto the diskette and filling the data area of every sector with hex E5. It is required for both soft-sectored systems and hard-sectored disks.

DUMP

This displays an object code file. The standard version prints an address, 16 bytes of code in hexadecimal format and the 16 corresponding ASCII characters. Codes corresponding to nonprintable characters are shown as a period.

ASM

The standard CP/M assembler reads a disk file (call it X.ASM) containing assembly language statements in standard Intel format. It generates object code in Intel hex (X.HEX) format, and an assembly listing (X.PRN) containing the original source statements preceded by the addresses and code generated by the assembler. X.HEX and X.PRN can be directed to any disk drive in the system, or can be suppressed if the assembly is done merely to find syntax errors in the source code. ASM has no macro facilities and can operate only on one source file. A macroinstruction (or just MACRO) is a sequence of instructions that is defined once and given a name; thereafter, invoking just the macro name causes the complete sequence to be inserted into the program at that point. For large assemblies, the CP/M users' group has a modification called LINKASM which can link any number of source files. LINKASM optionally generates a third file (X.SYM) containing the accumulated symbol table, which can subsequently be formatted and printed.

Macro assemblers for CP/M are available from several sources. MAC from Digital Research, Inc., supports Intel 8080 mnemonics only. MACRO-80, from Microsoft, Inc., and PASM from Phoenix Software Associates support both Intel 8080 and Zilog Z80 mnemonics, and produce relocatable, linkable output. Other macroassemblers are available through the CP/M User's Group.

LOAD

This utility creates and saves the executable X.COM file from the X.HEX file, which contains code generated by the assembler. This is convenient for programs which execute in the TPA at 100H. However, LOAD cannot be used for programs which do not execute at 100H; these must be loaded into memory by the DDT utility.

PIP (peripheral interchange program)

This utility, modeled on a similar one found in DEC systems, can concatenate files, transfer files from one device to another, (e.g., from disk to printer, to print a PRN file) and perform fairly complex manipulation of files and I/O devices. It can be used for backup by logging in (entering Control-C) a formatted diskette mounted on drive B (to create a bit allocation map for the blank disk) and then giving the command:

A>PIP B:=A:*.*

This copies all files (*) of all types (*) from drive A to drive B, reporting completion of each file copy action to the console. If a file on drive A already exists on drive B, a second copy is made on drive B; the previously existing copy is erased only when PIP has verified error-free completion of the new copy.

STAT

This utility provides file and I/O device reports. When used without a file name, it reports the amount of free space on the current drive. If a file name and type are specified, it reports the number of records in the file and its size. It may also be used to report the current I/O assignments, or change them.

15.6 LANGUAGE PROCESSORS

Two language processors are supplied with CP/M: ASM (discussed above) and EBASIC. EBASIC is a semicompiler in the public domain which accepts BASIC source code and converts it to a highly compressed intermediate code. The intermediate code is subsequently interpreted by RUN. EBASIC reports compile-time syntax and other errors; RUN reports run-time errors. EBASIC is not interactive, and a text editor is used to correct errors or make program changes in the source code file, after which the program is recompiled.

When supplied, EBASIC should be considered as an introductory processor. Other BASICs are more convenient and have many features not present in EBASIC.

16
Some Real Systems

In this chapter we examine three complete systems to satisfy three kinds of user:

- The home user who wants a portable machine and requires enough computing power to run graphics, computer music, and data management programs (Apple).
- The small business user with a limited budget (Radio Shack TRS-80 Model II).
- The small business or scientific user with a moderate budget and the need for sophisticated color graphics and equipment that can accommodate a wide variety of programming languages and peripheral devices (Cromemco System III).

16.1 THE APPLE II AND APPLE II PLUS

The Apple systems are among the most popular on the market. They provide a great deal of computing power at very moderate cost: $1,330 for the basic computer with a ROM-resident BASIC interpreter and 32K of RAM; A double-density minifloppy and interface to hold 140K per drive costs $645. The interface can handle two drives.

Memory is expandable to 48K of RAM in addition to the resident BASIC interpreter. An additional Language System is available, consisting of a card with an extra 16K of RAM, and BASIC, UCSD Pascal and utilities on disk. The Language system (which costs $495) includes an operating system, an editor for Pascal source language programs, a compiler and linker for Pascal P-code and an assembler for machine language routines.

The keyboard is built into the computer housing. Console output is composite video, brought out on a cable to be connected to a TV monitor, or via an RF modulator to a black-and-white or color television set. The display is 24 lines of 40 characters. In spite of this limited display area, quite good word-processing software is available —but neither the display nor the software are particularly convenient for large documents or sophisticated print layouts. People have been known to write books with an Apple, but other computers with more sophisticated word-processing software are far easier to use.

The real strength of the Apple is in the excellent graphics and the power of UCSD Pascal as a programming language. There are two graphics modes:

- Color graphics mode, with a resolution of 40 (horizontal) by 48 (vertical) pixels and 15 colors.
- High-resolution graphics mode, with a resolution of 280 (horizontal) by 192 (vertical) pixels in black and white, or 140 × 192 pixels with six colors.

These two graphics modes are supported by Apple Plot, a $70 package with routines for creating bar graphs and plotting mathematical curves, and by Turtlegraphics, a set of routines included in the Pascal package. The Applestuff code unit, also included in the Pascal package, provides randomizing functions, interfaces to the paddles that are part of the standard Apple hardware package, and routines to generate sounds on the built-in speaker. Other routines supporting the graphics capabilities are included in the $75 DOS Tool Kit (which contains an editor/assembler and various utilities to help the assembly language programmer).

Peripherals and interfaces available from Apple include a dot matrix printer with parallel interface, a high-speed serial interface, a graphics tablet and a clock/calendar card. For letter-quality printing, Apple offers the Qume Sprint 5/45 daisy-wheel printer and an interface card for it.

Other manufacturers also offer peripherals and interfaces for the Apple computer. Notable among these are the D.C. Hayes modem card and the Alpha Syntauri music synthesizer. The modem card, which is compatible with the Bell 103A, plugs into the computer and allows computer-controlled dialing, answering and monitoring of a 300-baud, full-duplex communications link. The Alpha Syntauri Synthesizer is a sophisticated unit designed for use with the Apple and for control by Pascal programs.

Users who wish to run CP/M on their Apple can obtain a special CP/M circuit board which plugs into one of the Apple slots. This board, which costs about $400, contains a Z80 microprocessor and supporting circuitry, together with CP/M in ROM. The Apple's 6502 microprocessor is disabled, and all processing is done by the Z80. This allows Apple users access to all the CP/M software on the market and available in the public domain.

16.2 RADIO SHACK TRS-80 MODEL II

The Radio Shack TRS-80 Model II is a general-purpose Z80-based computer. The basic machine is contained in one desk-top cabinet which houses a 12-inch black-and-white monitor and one 8-inch floppy disk drive with a single- and double-density controller. Storage capacity at double density is 416 kilobytes. The keyboard is detachable, and has a number of function keys, as well as the four basic cursor movement keys and an 11-key numeric pad for convenient entry of numeric data. This basic machine costs $3,450 with 32K or RAM or $3,800 with 65K. The TRSDOS disk operating system and Radio Shack TRS-80 Model II disk BASIC are supplied on disks.

The TRS-80 Model II is designed as a small-business computer, and is available in a number of different configurations. The disk controller can handle up to four drives; a cabinet to hold the extra three drives can stand on a desk top or be housed in a compartment of a specially designed computer desk available from Radio Shack. Prices of these systems range from $4,727 for a single-drive system with 64K of RAM and a 9-1/2-inch-wide dot matrix printer, through $6,197 for a word processor with a single disk drive, 64K RAM, 43-characters per second daisy-wheel printer, and the SCRIPSIT word-processing software, up to $8,666 for the Business Management System with 64K RAM, four disk drives, and a 14-inch dot matrix printer that runs at 160 characters per second.

TRSDOS occupies the first 10K of memory, as far as 27FF hex, and may extend to 2FFF when some utilities are called; however, the area from 2800 to 2FFF is also available to the user, who has complete control of memory from 3000 hex to the top of memory. Files are specified by name (up to 8 characters) and type (up to 3 characters), and may be password-protected against unauthorized use. In addition, files may be given attributes that permit full access (including erasure), read/write only, read only or execute only (for program files).

Many of the routines used by TRSDOS itself are also accessible to application programs by means of function calls similar to those described for CP/M in Chapter 15. In addition to standard file management facilities, application programs can use a command parser, a sort, arithmetic add, subtract, multiply, and divide routines, a table-lookup routine, binary/hex/decimal conversion and input or output routines, system date/time (which is initialized from the keyboard at power-up) and a delay routine.

The utilities include copying disks for backup, a memory test, a spool utility that saves program output in a disk file for later printing and also allows printing to take place while other operations are in progress, and a comprehensive communications program that allows remote use of the computer via a communications link and computer/computer file transfers.

Languages for the TRS-80 Model II, supplied by Radio Shack, include TRS-80 Model II COBOL, an implementation of the ANSI 74 subset priced at $299 for the Development System and $40 for the Run-Time Package; and TRS-80 Model II FORTRAN, based on the ANSI-66 version of the language ($299). A compiler BASIC is also available from Radio Shack. Since the 8-inch disks can handle either the Radio Shack double-density format or single-density IBM-compatible format, the CP/M operating system and all the languages, utilities and applications designed for CP/M can also run on the TRS-80 Model II.

Radio Shack software to support the Model II includes an Inventory Management System ($199), a statistical analysis package ($99) consisting of programs for descriptive statistics, graphic histogram, one- and two-way analysis of variance, one-way analysis of covariance, chi-squared analysis, time series analysis, multiple regression, etc; a payroll system that calculates and prints checks, computes various taxes, and prints W-2 forms at the end of the year; a general ledger system handling up to 504 accounts, up to 3,072 documents per month, and up to 11,420 entries per month; accounts payable and accounts receivable systems; and a mailing list system. Other business packages are available both from Radio Shack and from other software vendors.

16.3 CROMEMCO SYSTEM III

The Cromemco System III is an S-100, multiuser system for professional work in almost any field. The basic computer consists of a rugged metal case housing a 21-slot motherboard, a dual 8-inch disk drive, with room for another dual drive and a 30-ampere power supply. The CPU is a Z80A running at 4 megahertz, and the system is supplied with 64K dynamic RAM, controller for four disks, and printer interface card for both dot matrix and daisy-wheel printers. A serial interface with programmable baud rates up to 76,800, and 24 bits of bidirectional parallel I/O, are provided on the CPU board. Prices range from a two-user system at $11,575 up to a six-user system at $18,145. These prices do not include user CRT terminals, printers or other peripherals, but do include additional memory (which is expandable to 512K) and necessary interface boards.

The operating system for the multiuser system is CROMIX, which is based on the Unix operating system developed at Bell Laboratories. It provides both multiuser and multitasking capability, hierarchical directories, completely compatible file and device I/O and other features not found in other microcomputer operating systems. The compatibility of file and device I/O means that input and output may be directed to or from any source or destination interchangeably; no reformatting is required. Separate directories can be maintained for different users, with no chance of conflict, and each file is individually protected by four separate access privileges in each of three categories of user. Thus, one user's files can be protected against unauthorized success by other users.

The software support provided by Cromemco for use with either CROMIX or the single-user operating system CDOS includes COBOL, with all the features of level 1 of the ANSI-1974 standard, as well as useful features from level 2 ($595); ANSI-Standard FORTRAN IV ($295); the RATFOR structured FORTRAN preprocessor ($395); a

Z80 Relocatable Macro Assembler ($295); 16K BASIC ($195); an enhanced version of the LISP language ($395); a 'C' language compiler ($595); and a wide variety of payroll, accounts payable, accounts receivable, general ledger and other business packages.

Of particular importance to sophisticated graphics users is the SDI Graphics software package ($595), which provides fast line generation, fast generation of circles, rectangles, polygons, and other shapes, and color-fill of these shapes; text generation and rotation; the ability to simulate motion (for animation); and the ability to scale the display area of the work page. This software is designed to work with Cromemco's two-port memory boards or the high-resolution graphics interface board. A Cromemco graphics system is by no means inexpensive ($795 for the graphics interface board, $2,995 for the high-resolution color monitor), but the 754 X 482 pixel resolution and the wide color range (selection of 16 out of 4096 colors) makes it suitable for scientific and industrial requirements.

The Cromemco System III can also be configured as a single-user system, with the CDOS operating system. CDOS resembles CP/M and can run all software that adheres strictly to CP/M conventions. CP/M software that overlays the CCP may encounter difficulties, since CDOS is slightly larger than CP/M and so a little less memory is available to the user. However, most commercial CP/M software can be run under CDOS. Software written for CDOS may not run under CP/M, because CDOS has functions not present in CP/M. The CROMIX language packages mentioned above are also available to run under CDOS, at the same prices.

Glossary

acoustic coupler. A device for coupling the computer to your telephone. You place your telephone headset into the cradle. The computer produces sounds which are gathered by the telephone microphone. It receives sounds from the telephone loudspeaker and submits them to your computer.

ACK. The *acknowledge* code is usually transmitted from the receiving station to indicate that it has apparently received the transmission correctly.

address bus. See *bus, address*

allocation bit map. A map containing a bit for each group of eight sectors on the medium. A bit is set to 1 for a group which is allocated and 0 otherwise. The map is computed from the directory entries constructed in memory the first time that the disk is activated. A separate map is kept in memory for each drive known to the operating system.

alpha lock. See *lock, alpha*.

alphabet. The set of symbols, especially those used for a code set, for which a code exists.

alphanumeric. Referring to all the letters, numbers and special symbols of the alphabet in use.

analog recording. A technique used for magnetic tape recording where a tone is recorded on the tape in such a way as to convey a set of bits.

answer mode. When two stations are communicating in full duplex by means of modems, one of them is in the answer mode which establishes the choice of a pair of tones used with frequency shift keying. Standard *answer* mode uses 2225 hertz for mark and 2025 hertz for space.

application program. See *program, application*.

ASCII. Acronym for American Standard Code for Information Interchange. See Appendix 2 for a table of the code set values.

assembly language. See *language, assembly*.

asynchronous recording (and transmission). Asynchronous recording does not depend on internal timing generated within the equipment. Instead, each byte recorded or transmitted begins *and* ends with a timing bit. The time between recorded or transmitted bytes is unimportant since the initial bit begins the character.

backup. A second copy of a file preserved, preferably on a separate disk, in case the first copy is damaged.

BASIC. A POL which is simple to learn and use and is popular for programming microcomputer systems.

bidirectional. Capable of conveying data in either direction, such as reading or writing and sending or receiving.

Binary Synchronous Communication Protocol (BSC or BISYNC). A communication protocol in common use for microcomputers.

bit. An electric signal or a piece of data, or a number which is viewed as having exactly two states which might be: on or off, one or zero, yes or no.

bit map allocation. See *allocation bit map*.

blank. A character which, if we are writing with black on white, is entirely white.

blanking. Characters are written on the display along a line from left to right. When the beam returns from the right-hand side of the screen to the left, it should produce no spots. The action of turning off the beam during this period is called blanking.

block. The amount of information read from an input device, or written to an output device, with a single computer command. For the disk, a block and a sector are the same size. Blocks are numbered consecutively, but the sectors that contain them may be interleaved on the disk under the prevailing skewing discipline.

board, CPU. See *microprocessor board*.

boot. The action of bringing in the operating system and making the system and the computer available to the user. Generally this happens automatically when the system is turned on. If difficulty arises, the system may be rebooted by pressing the reset button on the computer.

bootstrap. The means by which the operating system is brought in and the system is made usable.

bounce. See *key bounce.*

break. Applies to a key on most keyboards and the 200-millisecond spacing signal produced by the keyboard when that key is touched. The break signal tells the computer that the current telecommunication operation is to be aborted.

breakpoint. A command entered in a compiler or assembly language program so that the computer stops and makes available to the user the contents of various registers to check the operation of his program.

buffer. A temporary storage area which holds data.

buffer, hardware. A buffer which is in the form of hardware registers. For example, the printer has built into it a buffer which holds one or even several lines of data to be printed and control commands to which the printer responds.

buffer, printer. The hardware memory within the printer.

buffer, software. A data storage area in memory, accessible to I/O devices and also to the user program.

burst. To separate a continuous printed output by tearing it along the horizontal perforations.

bus. A collection of wires common to many circuits. The computer bus generally consists of three types of wires: data, control and power.

bus, address. Wires in the bus which carry the address.

bus, data. Wires in the bus which carry data.

byte. A collection of 8 bits.

cable. A set of wires used to connect a device to the main computer chassis.

carriage (printer). A platform which holds the ribbon cartridge, the print element and the striking mechanism, and which may be horizontally positioned so that the print element will strike the paper at the proper position to produce a letter.

carriage advance. Movement of the carriage across the paper to the right.

carriage advance increment. The smallest unit by which the carriage may be advanced. For daisy-wheel printers this is generally 1/120 of an inch. By varying the number of units by which the carriage is advanced, different typefaces and proportional spacing can be accommodated.

carriage return. A key on the keyboard and a corresponding code which conveys to the computer the end of a line or a paragraph, and returns the carriage (or cursor) to the left margin.

carrier. A fixed frequency caused to vary in some prescribed manner to transmit intelligence between two stations.

carrier return. See *carriage return.*

case. Refers to the form in which a letter is printed. A capital letter is referred to as uppercase; a small letter is called lowercase.

cassette. A plastic container with two hubs properly separated. A length of tape is originally wound about one of the hubs. During reading or writing on a cassette recorder, tape is wound off the feed hub, moved past a read/write head and wound onto the takeup hub. The tape may be rewound or advanced at much higher speeds than that used for recording or playback. Most recorder cassettes are reversible—that is, they may be flipped over and put back in the machine. They can then be read or recorded on another track of the tape. Computer recording records only a single track and does not usually use the second side.

cassette drive. A drive mechanism for recording and reading from a cassette.

cassette drive, audio. A standard audio cassette machine attached through the remote outlet so that the computer can turn the drive capstan on and off and thus start or stop tape motion.

cassette drive, digital. A cassette drive mechanism in which the computer can determine whether or not the cassette is in record or play mode and can govern all tape motion and speed.

cassette drive, incremental. A cassette drive used for digital recording only, where a stepping motor (controlled by the computer) moves the tape past the read/write head by one character at a time.

cathode ray tube (CRT). A tube which provides a display screen for presenting alphanumeric information and graphics.

character generator. An electronic device with a memory, usually ROM, which contains an encoded form of one dot matrix for each character of the screen display alphabet.

chassis. A metal frame onto which the hardware components are placed. It supports the connectors, the printed circuit boards and all the components.

chip. A number of electronic circuits which perform a few to a large number of functions. Can be manufactured and put onto a tiny chip of silicon about the size of a head of a pin. This is mounted onto a socket with a number of pins projecting. These pins fit into a receptacle on a printed circuit board.

chip, microprocessor. See *microprocessor chip.*

clock. An oscillator which produces pulses continuously and at a constant rate.

clock rate. A frequency generated by an electronic clock and the rate at which operations happen within the computer. The popular Z80 and 8080 computer operate at rates of 2 megahertz to 4 megahertz.

close. When a file is no longer needed, an application program issues a *close* command to the file manager, which then writes the FCB to the file directory.

cluster. A group of eight consecutively numbered blocks on the disk.

cluster. A small computer facility with multiple terminals which collects data to be sent to or received from a remote computing facility.

COBOL. A business language primarily used on large computers.

code. A collection of bits which represents a letter, numeral or symbol.

code key. The same as *control key* (see *key, control*).

code set. A set of codes, one for each letter, numeral or symbol in the alphabet which is to be represented in this data system.

comparator. An electronic device which determines when the value held in a register is less than, equal to or greater than the value held in another register.

compressed printing. By reducing the distance between verticals in a dot matrix printer, characters can be made to print narrower, although of the same height, so that there are more characters per inch and thus a compressed format.

computer. A problem-solving device instructed in how to solve the problem by a program, which is contained in memory.

computer system. A computer, a number of devices for bringing data into and removing data from the computer, an operating system and a number of programs which makes it possible to solve a number of problems.

console. A device which provides a keyboard and a display usually for direct entry into a microcomputer system.

console command processor (CCP). The CP/M component which receives a character string from the keyboard, identifies it, validates it and executes it as a command.

continuous form. Paper in the form of a roll or a fanfold with holes punched on either side so that pins may pull the paper through the print mechanism evenly and positively. The paper is perforated horizontally at page length intervals so that it can be torn apart into separate sheets.

control key. See *key, control.*

controller. Hardware, usually contained on a printed circuit board within the microcomputer cabinet, which controls one or more devices of a particular kind. It mediates control signals from both the computer and the device and regulates the flow of data between computer memory and the device accordingly.

controller disk. See *disk controller.*

copy, hard. See *hard copy.*

counter. An electronic device which stores a count that can be advanced by entering a pulse at the proper input. Some counters can also have their count decreased by one in a similar fashion; others allow a value to be loaded before counting up or down from that value.

counter, scan line. Records the number of the line now being scanned from a CRT display.

counter, column. Records the column of the character presented on the screen.

counter, cursor. A counter which maintains a count indicating the current position of the cursor on the screen with reference to the upper left hand corner.

counter, display. A counter which keeps track of the character position for which the character display is currently being created.

coupler, acoustic. See *acoustic coupler.*

CP/M. Control Program for Microcomputers, a widely used operating system manufactured and sold by Digital Research, Inc.

CP/M system area. The disk area allocated to a disk resident copy of the operating system.

CPU. The central processing unit which is the portion of the computer that interprets the program and does arithmetic and logical operations to solve a problem. For the microcomputer system, the CPU is contained in a single miniprocessor chip on the CPU board.

crosspoint switch. A switch, usually mechanical, which connects one of many input wires to one of many output wires. It is often used in older telephone exchanges to link one caller to the party that he is calling. To service many subscribers, a large number of cross-point switches are connected together in tandom automatically.

CRT. See *cathode ray tube.*

cursor. A marker which appears on the video screen to inform the user where he is keying in information or which function he might select. The marker might be an underline which is stable or blinks, or a rectangle which contains a letter in reverse video, either static or blinking.

cursor key. A key, which, when pressed causes the cursor to move in a designated direction. Arrows engraved on the keys indicate direction of cursor movement: up, down, right, left, or home (top left corner of screen).

cyclic redundancy check (CRC). The cyclic redundancy check is an algorithm or set of operations performed upon a bit stream as it is recorded on, or read from a sector of the disk. This set of operations is performed on the 0s and 1s which constitute the bit stream to come up with two bytes which are the *check bytes.* For recording, these bytes are added on at the end of a sector and recorded there. When the sector is read back, the identical set of operations is later performed on the bit stream. The result should be the same bytes which are written at the end of the sector. If the two check strings do not agree, the data is said to be *invalid*.

daisy chain. The practice of hooking up devices so that one is attached to the next in a chain. Information or commands going to an intermediate device pass through all the earlier devices in the chain.

daisy wheel. A print element for several popular printers, consisting of a plastic or metal disk with spokes radiating from the center portion. At the end of each spoke is a circular area with a type impression on it. This little disk is like the petal of a flower—hence the name daisy wheel.

data access arrangement (DAA). Hardware to isolate a modem from the telephone lines to prevent damage by the user of telephone equipment.

data bus. See *bus, data.*

data set. The modem or acoustic coupler used to connect a data terminal to a communication line.

data terminal. The name for a remote terminal or a computer when it is used as part of a communication system.

debug. The action of taking a program without syntax errors which does not solve the user problem properly and making it work. The bugs or defects are removed from the program.

decoder. A device which accepts a code consisting of 0s and 1s and activates exactly one of a number of output lines. Thus, a 3-bit decoder accepts a set of three 0s and/or 1s and activates one out of eight output lines.

demodulation. The extraction of intelligence from a modulated carrier.

density. The closeness with which information is packed on a medium. It is measured linearly in terms of bits per inch. It is measured radially on the disk in terms of tracks per inch.

descender. The portion of a letter which lies below the line on which a letter normally sits, such as the tail of the letters j, g, p, etc.

deserializer. A device which accepts 8 serial bits as input and converts them into a parallel byte as output.

device, logical. See *logical device*.

dibit. A pair of bits to which a pattern is assigned under phase modulation.

digital recording. A magnetic recording scheme whereby the information content is independent of the amplitude of the signal. In fact, saturation recording is usually used.

digitizer. An input device for entering in machine readable form the coordinates of a sequence of points that make up various line segments which constitute a line drawing or a multiple-line display.

direct access (random access). A device which can position from one data area on the medium to another without passing through all the intervening areas.

directory, file. See *file directory*.

disk controller. Circuitry for controlling one or more disk drives. Usually the controller circuitry is on its own printed circuit board which plugs into a bus; it can control eight or more disk drives, although few systems use more than four drives and two is the usual number. Control signals from the CPU select and direct one of the disk drives. Status signals from the controller tell the CPU the progress of the activity. Data are reorganized by the controller as they pass between the drive and memory.

disk controller logic. The controller circuitry includes: a number of registers to keep track of all variables concerned with the drives in question; a serializer and deserializer to convert from a bit stream to byte-oriented information, and vice versa; and an arithmetic logic unit to perform incrementing, decrementing and comparison, and to check the CRC to determine if the sector read is valid.

disk operating system (DOS or OS). The microcomputer operating system that mostly runs the computer for the user. It includes drivers for all the peripheral devices in the system. It keeps track of files and manages space on each of the disks. It provides communication with the operator and accepts and inteprets commands.

disk primitive. Disk driver routines which perform primitive actions such as *track seek, read sector, home.*

diskette. A single removable plastic disk in its own paper envelope which is flexible—hence the term floppy disk.

DLE. Data link escape, which indicates that the code which follows is a control code.

dot matrix. A rectangular grid defining the relative placement of visible dots on a display or printout. One matrix is provided for each symbol of the alphabet. Each pattern follows the shape of the printed letter, numeral or symbol. Matrix size is defined by two numbers which are the width and height in dots, respectively. For a given physical character size, increasing matrix size (say, from 5 × 7 to × 9 or 9 × 13) both increases the total number of visible dots in the character and decreases the space between dots, so that the character can contain finer detail.

double density diskette. The magnetic medium of the first floppy disk allowed recording and reading at a maximum density of about 4,000 flux changes per inch. The encoding methods required at least one flux change for each 0 and two flux changes for each 1. Improvements have been made in the media to allow a maximum of 6,400 flux changes per inch. A diskette recorded with the new techniques can hold twice as much data as can one recorded at the standard single density.

double-sided diskette. A double-sided diskette provides two surfaces on which data may be written by the computer. This doubles the amount of storage that each diskette provides. It requires that the drive have two heads selectable by the computer.

drive selection. When multiple disk drives are attached to a computer only one can transfer data with memory at any given time. The computer *selects* this drive.

driver. A program which receives simple I/O commands from the user or system. It converts them into a series of machine-language commands to operate an input or output device.

driver (hardware). Circuitry for amplifying and shaping signals.

driver, I/O. See *I/O driver.*

dual-tone phase encoding. Two tones, the first actually twice the frequency of the second, are used to encode, respectively, a 1 and a 0. The tones are chosen to be multiples of the clock rate, so that the system is self-timing.

dumb terminal. A terminal which is not smart. See *smart terminal*.

duplex. A communication line which permits transmission in both directions simultaneously.

EBCDIC. A code set originally devised by IBM called the Extended Binary Coded Decimal Interchange Code. See Appendix 2 for a table of this code.

echoplex. A transmission mode where codes from the keyboard are sent to the computer and echoed over the return line to be presented on the screen. Thus there is no direct connection between the keyboard and the screen; all characters appearing on the screen are those which were received by the computer, thus verifying the transmission.

editor. A program by which text can be entered into the computer memory, and displayed on the screen and manipulated as the user choses. An editor is an aid for writing a program. It is also the central component of a word processor.

editor, context-oriented. An editor which helps you find portions of the text for editing by means of the strings of letters which constitute the text you are searching for.

editor, line-oriented. Some programming languages such as BASIC require that each statement have a number. An editor designed to call forth text by line numbers is called line-oriented.

encoder. A device which has input lines, only one of which carries a signal. The device has a number of output lines. For a signal on one of the input lines the encoder produces a signal on 0, 1 or several output lines. This bit pattern of signals is the code for the input and identifies the input. An encoder is used in the keyboard to take a signal from a key closure and produce an output code for that letter.

encoder, scanning. An encoder which works by scanning the entire keyboard many times per second, looking for a key that is depressed and producing the corresponding code.

ETX. The end of text code indicates that a block of transmission has ended.

expanded printing. Increasing the spacing between verticals for a dot matrix printer so that the characters print wider and there are fewer characters per inch, but of the same height.

external storage. A combination of a medium and a device which is not part of the CPU and which can store information in large quantities to supplement the CPU memory. The storage is nonvolatile, remaining safe when the power goes off.

FCB.   See *file control block.*

file area.   The area on the disk available for storage of files containing data or programs.

file control block (FCB).   A control block is fabricated by the file manager from the entry in the file directory when an existing file is opened, or is created from scratch for a new file. One such block is prepared for each file, which becomes active under the user program. The FCB identifies the disk sectors allocated to the file.

file directory.   The disk area allocated to hold a directory which names and indicates the area occupied by each file and the available space on the disk.

file manager (BDOS).   The file manager keeps track of all files and records and reusable space on all of the disks. It is the basic disk operating system (BDOS) for CP/M.

file, source.   The file of statements which constitutes your program as written in assembly language or a compiler language.

floppy.   A diskette, usually 8 inches in diameter.

form, continuous.   See *continuous form.*

formatting.   The action whereby a virgin disk is checked out and written with whatever information is needed by the system. For a hard sectored disk, this usually means: (1) writing all data tracks with track identifiers and filling data fields with a fixed character to show that the track is empty. Soft sectoring requires writing track and sector identification at the beginning of each sector of every track. Some formatting programs attempt to verify the ability to write and read successfully on every sector.

FORTRAN.   A POL particularly useful for mathematical programs and associated with large computers.

frame.   A complete scan of the screen from top to bottom which writes on the screen the contents of refresh memory.

frequency modulation recording (FM).   FM recording is based on signal transitions from one polarity to the opposite polarity. For FM, a transition *always* occurs at the clock pulse at the beginning of the pulse time. Another transition occurs at the middle of the bit period for a 1; no transition occurs in the middle of this period for a 0.

frequency shift keying (FSK).   A transmission or recording scheme where one tone indicates a 1 and another tone indicates a 0.

generator, graphics. See *graphics generator.*

graphic. A symbol not usually part of the writing or printing alphabet but one that has a special purpose for designating information on the display. It may also be used to compose designs and other graphic presentations in a graphic display terminal.

graphics generator. A read-only memory module used in a graphics display terminal to produce various symbols for making up a proper display pattern.

group-coded recording (GCR). A method that uses an information theory technique for encoding or representing each sequence of 0s and 1s in terms of a code. It provides the same recording density as MMFM. It requires greater hardware complexity for decoding and encoding information. It provides more reliability because of a larger timing margin than MMFM.

half duplex. A communication line which permits transmission in either direction but not both simultaneously.

hard copy. A printed output document.

hard sectored. Sector pulses for the hard-sectored diskette determine the beginning and end of each sector.

hard-sectored disk. A disk which contains sector holes for marking each sector of any track.

head load. Heads are kept away from the disks while they are positioning. When they have reached the right position they are then either pressed against the disk or allowed to ride on the air surface created by the rotation of the disk. This is called head loading.

hexadecimal. A means for representing sets of 4 bits, called nibbles. Nibbles with binary values between 0 and 9 are represented by the numerals 0 through 9, respectively. Nibbles with binary values between 10 and 15 are represented by the capital letters A through F, respectively.

higher-level language. See *language, higher-level.*

highlight. To make one or more characters displayed on the screen stand out with relation to the others, usually by showing them brighter or dimmer than the others, but sometimes with reverse video or underlining or blinking.

hole, index. See *index hole.*

home. A known position on the CRT screen. Generally, the upper left-hand corner. Sometimes other home positions are provided, such as the left-hand side of the line or the bottom left-hand corner of the screen.

home (disk). The position where the head is over the outermost track (track 0).

home command (disk). A request for the heads of a particular disk drive to return to track 0, or for a CRT cursor to be moved to the home position on the screen.

I/O addressing. The way in which a computer command designates I/O device.

I/O driver. A routine called by a program or by the operating system which gives directives to the device to perform the desired operations. The routine interprets the parameters sent by the program and makes conversions so that physical input or output is properly directed.

I/O, memory mapped. An I/O device is designated by addressing it as though it were a memory cell. This cell does not exist in real memory. Memory read and write commands reach only the I/O device.

I/O, interrupt driven. Device action takes place simultaneously with execution by the CPU of some program. When the device is finished it causes an interrupt which gives control to the operating system, temporarily taking it away from the currently executing program.

I/O, port. The I/O command contains a number which designates a port and not a memory address.

I/O, program driver. When an I/O device completes its activity, it does not interfere with the currently executing program. Instead that program must check for completion.

idle. When no transmission is taking place, an idle condition exists whereby a mark signal is continuously presented.

index hole. A hole in the disk and in the envelope containing it, both at the same radius so that the two become aligned as the disk rotates. That event can be detected optically to produce an index pulse.

index pulse. A pulse produced when the index hole in the disk and in the envelope are aligned.

input. The process of bringing data into the memory of the computer from the keyboard, a medium or an external source.

interface. The circuitry which comes between two devices. In the computer system the interface generally goes between the CPU and an I/O device.

interface. Circuitry which goes between two devices, the computer and a device or two portions of the computer.

interrupt. A hardware-initiated activity whereby the existence of some condition in the hardware or a device causes control to be taken from the currently executing program and given to another program, generally the operating system. This action takes place in such a way that the interrupted program can regain control at some later point as though it had not been interrupted.

interrupt driven I/O. See *I/O, interrupt driven.*

interrupt mask. A hardware register which can be set by the program or operating system to prevent temporarily the occurence of one or more interrupts.

interrupt, nested. The occurence of an interrupt during the processing of a preceding interrupt.

interrupt, nonmaskable. An interrupt which cannot be prevented from occurring.

interrupt, vectored. An interrupt such that control goes to one of several routines according to the hardware cause which initiated the interrupt.

I/O device. A device which performs input or output or both.

jump vector table. A table in the operating system area of memory which contains a jump command for each major component of the operating system. One component can thus give control to a desired component by jumping to the vector table plus a standard offset for that desired component. This table allows different systems to use different-sized components and place them at different positions in memory. Thus, regardless of the extensiveness of the system and the number of devices that it contains, the table is the means for standardizing the entry points.

key. A square button such as is found on a typewriter. The top is labeled with one, two and sometimes four symbols. When the key is struck, the keyboard generates a set of signals, the code for the character of the code set. Unless some other key is also pressed, the code generated generally corresponds to the bottom letter inscribed on the key.

key bounce. On some keyboards when you press a key, the key switch makes an initial contact, releases and then makes a second and even a third contact because the moving element bounces back and forth on the fixed element. Dirt or oxidation can also cause multiple makes and breaks. This will cause the production of repeated letters in the text or command and hence should be avoided.

key, code. See *control key.*

key, control. If the control key is held down and some other key on the keyboard is then struck, a special code, usually nonprinting, is produced. The computer usually interprets this as a request to perform a specific action (such as halting a listing or rebooting the operating system).

key, cursor. See *cursor key.*

key, programmable. A key, usually unmarked, which operates a keyswitch when pressed. This activates an encoder to produce a code. However, by changing jumper wires on the encoder, the code can be set to whatever the user desires.

key, shift. The key that when held down while some other key is pressed allows the code corresponding to the upper symbol engraved on the key to be produced by the keyboard.

key, special purpose. A key, which when touched causes the keyboard to create a special code, usually nonprinting and conveying a special function such as *backspace, linefeed* or *clear* (the CRT screen).

keyboard. A set of keys, generally laid out on a rectangular pattern, consisting of 4 or 5 rows and perhaps 15 or 20 columns. The layout usually corresponds to the standard typewriter keyboard. Additional keys correspond to extra functions required with the computer.

keypad. See *numeric key pad.*

keyswitch. When a key on the keyboard is pressed, it causes a contact to be made on the keyswitch. Thus, the keyswitch produces a signal each time a key is pressed.

kilobyte (kb). A collection of a little more than a thousand bytes—to be precise 1,024 bytes.

language, assembly. A low-level language by which a programmer can enter commands which resemble machine language commands in their function, but which are easier to use since they are in symbolic form.

language, higher-level. A language which performs special functions not usually found in POLS. Such languages often incorporate a compiler language as a subset.

language, machine. The 1s and 0s found in memory which constitute a command as interpreted by the computer hardware.

language, procedure-oriented (POL). A language for programming whereby procedures for performing logical actions are easily written. Sometimes called a compiler language. Examples of such languages are BASIC, COBOL and FORTRAN.

large-scale integration (LSI). Placing a large number of circuits, perhaps a hundred or more, on a single chip (the size of a pinhead).

latency. The time it takes, once the head is positioned at the proper track, to find the desired sector. Latency generally means average latency, the average length of time to reach the desired sector.

leader. An additional piece of tape at the beginning and/or end of a cassette or reel of magnetic tape. The leader is made of clear plastic or conductive metal, and cannot be recorded upon. The clear plastic provides for optical recognition of the end of tape; the metallic leader provides for electrical detection of tape end.

light pen. An input device whereby the console operator can choose among alternatives. When a menu is presented on the screen, for instance, a number of choices are given the operator, each with a box next to it. He positions the light pen to a box representing his choice and then presses the entry button on the pen. The pen contains a light sensor which returns a signal. The time of return of the signal indicates to the computer which choice he has made.

line feed. The action of advancing the paper or the cursor so that it is aligned to print the next line below the previous one.

line printer. A printer that has a print mechanism which is rotating constantly at a high speed. The mechanism might be a drum, a chain, a train, a band or a belt. Printing occurs whenever some print slug arrives at the position at which it should be printed and then a hammer strikes it to make an impression on the paper. Hence, different character positions of the line are printed almost randomly. Only when all the characters for the line have been printed does the paper advance.

line, scan. See *scan line.*

link. A program, sometimes called the linkage editor, that takes an object module produced by the compiler and any additional modules required to make a running program and *links* them together.

load module. A module of machine language code which is executable if it is loaded into memory starting at the position incorporated into the module.

loader (linking loader). A program which takes one or more relocatable object modules and combines them into a load module which is now executable if loaded into memory starting at a specific location.

local network. A special transmission line and the devices and computers hooked on to it. Such a line can support devices separated from each other by thousands of feet.

lock key. A key which when pressed causes the shift to be maintained as though held down through the striking of subsequent letters. See also *lock, alpha* and *lock, shift.*

lock, alpha. A keyboard lock that when pressed results in letter keys producing uppercase character codes. Numeric keys still produce codes for the numerals.

lock, shift. A keyboard lock which when set causes the keyboard to produce the code for the upper symbol on the key when a key is pressed. That is, for an alphabetic key, a capital letter is produced. For a numeric key, a symbol above the numeral is produced, and so forth.

lockout. A condition of the keyboard such that, after a key is pressed, the keyboard does not respond to pressing other keys until the computer releases the lockout.

logical device. A symbolic name which refers to a device of a particular class. This allows the user to apply this name to address the device rather than the physical port address by which the device is attached.

logical I/O system (BIOS). A component that relates standard names to the physical addresses of various components such as the console, the reader, the listing printer and so forth. If it contains all the device drivers for CP/M, it is called the basic input output system (BIOS).

LSI. See *large-scale integration.*

machine language. See *language, machine.*

magnetic tape. Thin mylar or plastic tape on which is coated a magnetizable medium. Information can be recorded and read from the tape as it passes beneath a read/write head on the disk drive.

manager, file. See *file manager.*

mark. In telegraphy, a 1.

matrix printer. An impact printing mechanism with a number of small, thin, flexible rods which make the impression on the paper as a series of vertical dots or undots. A character is formed by combining a number of such verticals.

medium. A material which may be altered or deformed to store information.

megahertz. A repetition rate of one million times per second.

memory. That portion of the computer which holds the program and data which the computer needs to solve a problem.

memory mapped I/O. See *I/O, memory mapped.*

memory, random access. A memory which can be altered by the computer in a fraction of a microsecond.

memory, read only (ROM). A memory from which the computer can read information at will but cannot alter or change the information stored there.

memory, read only, programmable electrically alterable (EAPROM). A memory which, after programming by the user, is normally read only. However, the computer can modify individual locations by writing to them repeatedly a large number of times.

memory, read only, programmable (PROM). A read only memory into which data can be written by an external programming device.

memory, read only, programmable, erasible (EPROM). A read only memory which the user can take out and erase by a special process, usually involving ultraviolet light. Then, by a computer-assisted procedure he can enter new data which is now stored in a read only fashion.

memory, refresh. A memory in the video display terminal which stores the codes for all the characters currently being displayed on the screen.

MHz. megahertz.

microcomputer system. A computer system which features a microprocessor at the center of the computer system.

microfloppy. A very small floppy which is 3 1/2 inches in diameter.

microprocessor board (CPU board). A printed circuit board for which the main component is the microprocessor chip. It contains other components such as those to generate the timing signals and to shape the pulses which are necessary to run the microprocessor.

microprocessor chip. The microprocessor chip contains all the circuitry of the CPU—the portion of the computer which does the calculating and executes the program. It is mounted in one socket of the CPU board.

microsecond. One millionth of a second.

millisecond. One thousandth of a second.

minifloppy. A small diskette 5-1/4 inches in diameter.

mnemonic. A set of letters which represents the activity performed by a command. It suggests these actions so that the programmer can easily recall the letters which represent the command (e.g. LDA = Load the A register).

mode, answer. See *answer mode.*

modem. A device capable of both modulating and demodulating a fixed carrier for transmission generally over telephone lines.

modified frequency modulation recording (MFM).   MFM provides a considerable improvement over frequency modulation recording because the same information is recorded with fewer transitions. This means that more information can be packed into the same area. The technique is described in the text.

modified MFM recording (MMFM).   A modification of MFM and hence a second modification of frequency modulation. It provides further improvement in pulse packing and hence increased information content for a given frequency of recording. The text elucidates.

modulation.   A means of applying a variable signal to a carrier so that intelligence may be transmitted over a considerable distance.

monitor.   A portion of the resident operating system which gets control when a program fails or when an interrupt occurs.

monitor, TV.   A display unit containing a CRT, Video amplifiers, horizontal and vertical scanning and synchronization circuits, and power supply. Usually capable of better resolution than a standard TV set.

motherboard.   A printed circuit board onto which other printed circuit boards connect or attach, or from which a bus eminates.

NAK.   The *negative acknowledge* code transmitted when a station has received a block but has detected the occurrence of an error and wishes to indicate that to the transmitting station.

nanosecond.   One billionth of a second (one thousandth of a microsecond).

nested interrupt.   See *interrupt, nested.*

nibble.   Four bits or half a byte. Usually the first four bits or the last four bits of a byte.

nonreturn to zero recording (NRZI).   A 1 records as a pulse which does not return to the base line. A 0 records as no pulse. A series of 1s records as a long positive pulse; a series of 0s records as a long negative signal.

notch, write protect.   See *write protect.*

numeric key pad.   On a keyboard, an extra set of keys for the purpose of entering numeric data, including some control keys. The keys are arranged as on an adding machine so that numerical entry is facilitated.

object module.   A file containing machine language code produced by a compiler, assembler or other translator, which may or may not be in executable form.

open. A request in an application program that a file be made available. The file manager creates an FCB from scratch for a new file or from information in the file directory for an existing file.

operating system, disk. See *disk operating system.*

originate mode. When two stations are communicating in full duplex by mans or modems, the mode which establishes the choice of tones between which it shifts when frequency shift keying is used. Standard *originate* mode uses 1,270 hertz for mark and 1,070 hertz for space.

output. The action of taking data from the computer memory and putting it onto an external medium or printing it.

paper bail. A horizontal rod on the printer pivoted so that two paper bail rollers press the paper against the platen and the paper is moved up evenly and positioned properly beneath the print element.

parallel. A set of wires that carries a number of bits simultaneously. Usually *parallel by character* is implied, meaning that the 8 bits of 1 byte are transmitted at once.

parity. A reference to the fact that the code for each character contains an odd (even) number of 1s. This provides for checking data transmission. A character is *valid* only if the number of 1s in its code is odd (even).

parity, bit. An additional bit appended to a character code so that the number of 1s in the code is odd (even). Thus, for instance, any 6-bit code set can be made into a 7-bit code set with the addition of a parity bit for checking data transmission.

Pascal. A rigorous programming language, a POL, which tends to provide its own documentation.

peripheral device. Devices which perform input or output or both, such as the printer, terminal, keyboard and disk.

phase modulation. A transmission encoding scheme where each alternative pair of bits is represented by one of four possible phase relationships between two carriers of the same frequency.

pin feed mechanism. A set of projecting pins on both sides of the platen. The pins fit into holes in continuous form stock of the proper width and advance it automatically without friction feed.

pixel. Contraction for picture element. One of a number of elements used to compose graphs, charts and other graphic nonalphabetic displays.

platen. A rubber cylinder or one made with a rubberlike surface so as to provide a high coefficient of friction between it and the paper, which it moves up by friction. It also holds the paper against the impact made by the print slug.

plotter. An output device driven by the computer which moves a pen across a sheet of paper, lifting it away from the paper in some areas and putting it down in others so as to create a multiple-line pattern.

POL. See *language, procedure-oriented.*

polled I/O. An activity whereby the main program interogates each device attached to it to see which, if any, requires service.

port. A line or set of lines to an input or output device or to a controller. These lines carry data or control signals or both. A port is selected or addressed by a computer command.

print band. A flexible metallic band which rotates at a high speed along the printing line of a line printer.

print belt. A polyurethane belt on which embossed metalic slugs are imbedded. Used in the medium-speed printer.

print element. A mechanical device, part of the printer, which is used for making the inked impression on the paper. For example, the spherical golf-ball element or the wire matrix.

print wheel. A generic term for print elements such as the daisy wheel and the thimble.

printed circuit board. A laminated thin plastic board, about a sixteenth of an inch thick on to which wiring is electroplated. This wiring connects components and sockets which are fastened to the board. The sockets receive chips. A printed circuit board constitutes a complete functional unit, such as a memory or a processor. One of the edges of the board is set up so that all the wires which leave or enter the board appear here as thin printed lines. This edge fits into a receptacle which connects it to other components of the computer.

printer. A device for entering characters, numerals and symbols onto paper.

printer, dot matrix. Here a set of nine or so vertically aligned thin wires is the print element. Individual hammers, one for each wire, hit these wires to form a character out of little dots, as for the CRT.

printer, impact. A printer where the character is formed on the paper by the impact of a hammer hitting a typed slug against an inked ribbon to impart an inked impression upon the paper.

Printer, ink jet. A nonimpact printer which uses multiple jets of ink which are turned on or off to form a character as a matrix of dots.

printer, nonimpact. A printer which does not use impact to form a character on the paper, but rather uses heat, light or electric current or a jet of ink.

printer, read only. A printer without a keyboard.

printer, read/write. A printer with an attached keyboard so that the printer may be used directly like a typewriter where characters are keyed in and printed.

printing, bidirectional. The ability of a printer to print onto the paper when the carriage is moving either to the right or to the left. This speeds printing because it eliminates carriage returns during which no printing can take place.

printing, multipass. The actions of certain higher-priced matrix printers to scan a line more than once. The second pass of the print mechanism is displaced vertically so that now each vertical which makes up a character is printed twice and perhaps slightly differently. This produces a much greater definition and higher-quality printing.

priority. The importance generally of an activity relative to another activity.

procedure-oriented language (POL). See *language, procedure-oriented.*

processor. The portion of the microcomputer which does the arithmatic and logical operations.

program driven I/O. See *I/O, program driven.*

program, application. A program primarily written to solve a user's problem.

program, utility. Programs written by a supplier to provide standard services for the user. They do not usually perform an application function.

programmable key. See *key, programmable.*

prompt. A symbol presented on the CRT screen to tell you that the operating system is ready to accept a new command or line of text.

protocol. A set of codes which must be transmitted and received in the proper sequence to guarantee that the desired terminals are hooked together and can talk as desired.

pulse ratio recording. An analog recording method where a tone burst lasts for a different length of time according to whether it represents a 0 or a 1.

pulse, index. See *index pulse.*

quad diskette. A name sometimes used for a diskette which is double-sided and records in double density.

quadrature amplitude modulation (QAM). A transmission encoding scheme.

RAM. See *memory, random access.*

random access memory. See *memory, random access.*

raster. A sequence of horizontal lines swept out one below the other by the beam of a cathode ray tube in creating a display. If the beam is turned on, the line is visible. If the beam is turned off, no visible line appears.

read only memory. See *memory, read only.*

recording, analog. See *analog, recording.*

recording, group-coded. See *group-coded recording.*

refresh cycle. A VDT cycle which presents a frame of information on the screen.

refresh rate. The number of frames or refresh cycles which are performed each second to make a steady and constant display. A common refresh rate is 60 cycles per second.

register. A small and very fast hardware device for holding information temporarily. The computer, memory and external devices all contain registers to hold both data and status information.

relocatable module. Machine language code which does not have specific addresses associated with it and hence must have these assigned by the loader before it can be executed.

remote terminal. A terminal (display and keyboard) which does not have computing power near at hand and communicates with the computing power by means of communication lines such as telephone lines.

retrace. The time during which the beam returns from the right-hand side of the screen to the left, or from the bottom of the screen to the top, during which time it is blanked.

retransmission. When two remote stations communicate, it is important that data sent is received correctly. To ensure this, various precautions are taken as provided by parity and cyclic redundancy checks. Should the receiving station detect invalid data, it returns the NAK code to the transmitting station. The transmitting station then retransmits this block of information according to the protocol.

return. An abbreviation for carriage return, or carrier return, which see.

return to zero recording (RZI). A 1 is recorded as a positive signal (pulse) which returns to 0; a 0 is recorded as a base signal. A series of 1s records as a series of on and off signals; a series of 0s records as a stable 0 signal.

reverse video. To cause one or more characters on the screen to display in opposite video terms so that dots which were white now appear black and vice versa.

ribbon cartridge. A plastic case containing an inked ribbon on one spool and an empty spool on the other side. The cartridge may be installed onto the printer carriage without the operator getting dirty hands.

ribbon, fabric. An inked fabric ribbon which is moved back and forth in both directions, being reused many times until the impression gets too hard to read.

ribbon, multistrike. A coated plastic ribbon on which successive characters strike at overlapping points, moving in one direction until it has been used up and then must be discarded. It cannot be reversed.

rollover. When two or more keyboard keys are pressed, the first one released produces a proper code. One or more of the other keys may also produce correct codes.

rollover, *n-key*. When several keys are pressed simultaneously, the first one released produces a correct code and then the second, and third, and so forth, up to *n*.

rollover, two key. When two keys are pressed simultaneously, proper codes are produced in the order in which the keys are released.

ROM. See *read only memory*.

row. When referring to the CRT display, a row is the set of scan lines which are required to make up one line of text which might be presented. The row includes spacing lines where nothing appears, which separates characters on one row from those on the next.

saturation. When a magnetic medium is magnetized to saturation, a stronger magnetic field cannot induce further magnetism.

scan line. One line swept out by the CRT beam as it forms letters and graphics on the screen.

scanning, encoder. See *encoder, scanning*.

sector. A portion of a track lying between two sector holes or as defined by the formatting process.

sector hole. A hole in a hard-sectored disk. There are a fixed number of such holes around the circumference of a circle of fixed radius. There is a single hole in the envelope. Each time a sector hole passes underneath this hole in the envelope, a sector pulse is generated optically.

sector pulse. A pulse generated by the sector hole as it passes beneath a similar hole in the envelope to mark the sector.

seek. The action of the disk drive to position a head to one of a number of discrete positions (over a desired track).

seek command. A request to move the heads in or out to a specified track.

seek time. The time it takes to move the heads from one track to another. This is usually rated in two ways: the time to seek to an adjacent track and the time to seek from the inside to the outside of the disk. Seek time is rated in milliseconds (ms).

sequential access. A requirement of the file that accessing a record requires scanning through all the intermediate records from the starting position. Sequential access is an inherent feature of a medium such as magnetic tape or punch cards where the medium must be reviewed in a fixed order.

serial. Signals represent data by transmitting the bits which represent them over a single pair of wires. Bits appear sequentially in time.

serializer. A device which takes the eight parallel bits of a byte delivered in parallel and converts them into eight serial bits.

set, code. See *code set*.

set, data. See *data set*.

shift key. See *key, shift*.

shift lock. See *lock, shift*.

single-density disk. Diskettes, as originally developed, that could read and write at 3,200 bits per inch, a density known as single density.

single-tone keying. An analog recording method whereby a tone is turned on for a 1 and off for a 0.

skew. With skewing, the next consecutive block is not placed in the next consecutive sector. Time is required for operating system functions between reading one block and the next. Hence, one or more sectors are skipped to provide this time and the next block is assigned to a later numbered sector.

smart terminal. A terminal which has capability to do editing and store data for transmission as a unit. It usually contains a microprocessor chip.

soft sectored. For the soft-sectored floppy diskette, an initialization formatting program writes track and sector information at the beginning of each sector of each track. A sector is identified by the file manager from the sector information it reads.

solenoid. An electromechanical device which, when energized, causes a linear motion of a plunger, much like a piston in a steam engine. It is often used in a printer to provide the impact to hit the print element against the paper.

source file. See *file, source.*

source statement. See *statement, source.*

space. In telegraphy, a 0.

spacebar. A key, usually a long thin horizontal bar, which produces a code for a blank when pressed.

split screen. Dividing the screen into different portions, where each portion shows a different display document or kind of information.

start bit. Sent to initiate the asynchronous transmission of a single character; always a space.

statement source. One of the statements of an assembly or compiler language.

status. Information about the activity and processing taking place in a device or within the computer.

stepping motor. A motor which moves discretely. Each time it is energized with a pulse, it makes an angular rotation of a fixed size.

STH. The start of header code indicates that this block contains a terminal address which follows.

stop bit. Indicates the end of transmission for one character during asynchronous transmission. It is always a mark, and at transmission speeds below 300 bits per second. 2 stop bits are used.

storage, external. See *external storage.*

stroke written display. A display for graphics whereby your program indicates the initial and terminal point on the screen for a line which is then written by the display electronics. The image is made up of a number of such lines.

STX. The start of text character, indicating that the text follows immediately hereafter within the communication.

surface. Each disk, whether large or small, has two physical surfaces. Sometimes only one surface is usable for recording. The technical term applies to a physical surface on which recording can take place.

sync character. A unique code which is continuously retransmitted for synchronous transmission. It is so called because it coordinates the clock used at the receiving with that at transmitting end.

Synchronous Data Link Control (SDLC). A recently developed communication protocol, mainly in use for communication with large computers.

synchronous recording (or transmission). Characters are recorded or transmitted at a continuous timed rate. The activity is preceded by a set of timing pulses which serves to synchronize the reception.

system, computer. See *computer system.*

telecommunication. The transmission of intelligence over a distance. In this case we are talking about transmitting data, probably over telephone lines.

terminal. A receiving and transmitting device for use by a human operator. The input is almost always a keyboard; the output to the human may be either a printer or a video display. A terminal communicates with an adjacent host computer or a remote computer via telephone lines.

terminal, dumb. A terminal incapable of processing data but sends one character at a time to a central computer. The central computer returns the character for verification either on the printer or on the video display.

terminal, data. See *data terminal.*

terminal, intelligent. A single terminal with a microcomputer built in for complete editing facilities and processing capability, including conformance to complex line protocols.

terminal, printing. A terminal which includes a printer instead of a video display.

terminal, remote. A terminal which communicates with a computer that is at a considerable distance and usually uses telephone lines or hard wires for communication.

terminal, smart. A terminal with built-in editing facilities and a program which allows a full screen of data to collect to be sent to the computer or to be collected for display from the computer.

text formatter. A program which reads a file of data and puts it in the proper form so that it may be printed as desired by the human user.

thimble. A print element much like the daisy wheel, but with all the spokes bent upward so that the effect is like a thimble.

trace program. A program that operates with an application program to help the programmer find its defects and cure them.

track. The circular area swept out by the head when it occupies (seeks to) one of the fixed standard positions. Tracks are numbered from outside in, starting from 0 and going to a maximum applicable to that disk.

tractor feed. A mechanism with a train of feed pins on each side which fit into the pinholes of continuous paper stock. Line advance commands from the computer then cause the paper to advance. Each pin tractor is movable so that the tractor can accommodate continuous forms of various widths.

transfer rate. For a disk or other peripheral device, the rate at which information is transferred from the device to memory, or vice versa. The customary unit is kilobits per second (kbs). This should not be confused with kilobytes per second. A transfer rate for single-density diskettes is 250 kilobits per second and that for double density is 500 kilobits per second.

transient program. A program which is loaded and executed by a command to the operating system. Once the operating system is running and you receive a prompt at the console, you enter the name of the desired program in its standard form. The operating system finds the program on the disk, brings it into the transient program area and gives control to it. When the program has finished executing, it returns control to the operating system, which then gives you a prompt.

transient program area (TPA). An area in main memory into which transient programs are loaded, and in which they execute.

transmission, asynchronous. See *asynchronous recording.*

universal asynchronous receiver/transmitter (UART). An LSI chip which performs all activity required for interfacing the computer with one or more asynchronous devices. It converts the form of the data with a serializer and a deserializer. It adds start and stop bits, generates parity bits and clocks the data at the required rate for transmission. To receive, it recognizes and deletes the start and stop bits, checks the parity and counts down an external clock to the data rate. It provides control signals to the computer and receives control signals from the computer. An external clock is internally divided by 16 to clock the data at the proper rate.

universal synchronous and asynchronous receiver/transmitter (USART). May be used for synchronous transmission and reception. Either mode may be specified by the computer. In asynchronous mode, it operates exactly like the UART. In synchronous mode, it has the capability of examining the incoming data stream until it identifies a sync character; thereafter, the bit stream is divided into groups of 8 bits which are passed as parallel to the computer. An external clock at 16 times the data rate is required for both transmission and reception.

video display terminal (VDT). A terminal with a CRT display screen for showing letters, textual information and graphic displays.

volatile. A memory in which information storage continues as long as the power is maintained. When the proper is turned off, the information in memory is lost.

volume. The amount of information mounted upon and available from the device. For example, a diskette is a volume for a disk drive; a cassette is the volume for a cassette drive.

window. A portion of a display characterized differently from the rest of the screen. A window may show letters of magnified size or from a different area of memory.

write protect. Each diskette has a notch in one of its corners which is scanned optically to inhibit writing on those disks for which protection is desired. For the floppy (8-inch disk), this notch must be covered to write upon the disk; if the notch is not covered, the disk is protected. The opposite holds for the minifloppy, where a covered notch prevents writing.

Index